In 1985, three other guys and I—in Kentucky, of all places—formed a band, hitched our sled to the rock and roll dream, and screamed mush from the pits of our souls. We had nothing going for us save a vehement, greasy, turbo-psychotic vision of how things might turn out, and we went for it. It is good to pursue an outlandish dream. Latch on to the wild dogs. Grab that whip and yee-the-hell-hah! Eventually the sled comes out from under you, and from that point on, you either run like hell or you get your face dragged all over God's creation, scraping on rocks and bouncing off the sides of trees. There will be great incidence of contusions, highway motel dog breath and bottle-ringed cocktail napkin blitherscribble. Things move faster and faster. Everything you packed for the trip—relationships, standards, your future—gets tossed or bounced off somewhere, and all the while, you know you can stop at any time, just by letting go of the dream. Under no circumstances whatsoever do you let go of the dream.

# cheese chronicles

*The True Story
of a Rock and Roll Band
You've Never Heard Of*

by Tommy Womack

EGGMAN PUBLISHING

Edited by:
  Richard Courtney, Maryglenn McCombs, Craig Owensby
  and the Author

Cover illustration and Jacket design by:
  Brad Talbott

Photography:
  Page 272, Robbie Hatcher
  Back Cover, Bill Thorup

Design, typography, and text production:
  TypeByte Graphix

ISBN:   1-886371-02-4

Library of Congress: 94-61722

Eggman Publishing
2909 Poston Avenue
Suite 203
Nashville, Tennessee 37203
1-800-396-4626

*This book is for my parents,
the Reverend J. C. and Lorene Womack
of Madisonville, Kentucky, who will have
the same amount of trouble wading through
the profanity that I did whittling it down
to the amount that remains.*

Thanks to Richard Courtney for his initial interest in this project, and for all his effort and care since then. Thanks to Maryglenn McCombs for the long hours with her take-no-prisoners editing pen. Thanks to Brad Talbott for his cover illustration. Thanks to Donnie Bott for loaning me his computer to write on, and to Chris Heric for loaning me another when Donnie needed his back. Thanks to Craig Owensby for his attention to detail. Thanks to Ken McMahan for reading it all and making sure I remembered everything the way it should be. Thanks to Trip Aldredge for the legal help. Thanks to Beth for many things, among them decoding my scribble and sharing the ride.

# contents

## part three: the road home

# introduction:

## in the beginning
## there was revelation

It was July of 1976. I was thirteen years old when Gene Simmons puked blood and changed my life. It was a beautiful Sunday afternoon, and we were fresh home from church. I was still in my good leisure suit, back in my sister's room watching the somewhat portable Magnavox black-and-white television, lying across her bed on my stomach, digging my Sunday shoes into her pillows and waiting on dinner.

I don't remember what program I was watching. *Hogan's Heroes*, I believe, but I'm not sure. All I remember for certain is the commercial.

*KISS* is coming! Friday! July whatever! Typical 30-second ad probably. 60 seconds, maybe. I can still see how it started. Four long-haired geezers from New York in pancake makeup vomiting blood and spewing flame from their mouths, smashing guitars and standing between great gouts of fire that shot out of the ground with fifteen thousand blown-out teenage minds on their feet with spotlights feeling them up. Oh God! Oh God! Yes! Yes!

I remember it all like it was ten minutes ago, and in vivid color now too, for some odd reason. From then on, nothing mattered but rock and roll. It just looked *so cool!*

It got in my glands. My obsessive streak was torqued. My sister bought *Kiss Alive!* and I pretty much took it away from her. I got their first three albums. Until then, rock and roll had been boring guys who needed shaves, but a bass-player who could *breathe fire?* That was something else, entirely.

Mom and Dad's reaction could best be summed up as all-consuming and total horror. The Reverend J.C. and Lorene Womack, Cumberland Presbyterians, born under Woodrow Wilson and Warren Harding. Good people who *really did* pick cotton as children. People who worked three jobs with three kids to feed. A father who studied nights to become a real ordained minister. Did they bring the last flesh-of-their-flesh into this world to feed, dress, teach the Lord's Prayer, wipe his bottom, take his temperature and what-all else just to have him fall in with *THIS SHIT? UH, UH!*

The grudge-match began. For the next three years, I daily went toe-to-toe with Mom on the merits of such culturally weighty matters as Ace Frehley's guitar playing, and how it justified papering my whole bedroom in Kiss posters. I had my flared-and-faded, Frampton-loving elder sibs in hopeless squabbles—about whether Peter Criss was a *great drummer*, or how ''Calling Dr. Love'' was a *great song!*

For the record, Peter Criss was a decent drummer, and ''Calling Dr. Love'' remains an awesome song.

I spent the next fall down the street, in the front seat of Terry Cates' AMC Gremlin, a truly great car of the '70s. The Gremlin was a Doonesbury eye with wheels on the bottom. We would sit in that thing after school and listen to 8-tracks. We very rarely went anywhere. We would just sit in the car, rock out, and run the battery down.

Terry had *Destroyer, Kiss Alive!*, all the Aerosmith, Brownsville Station, Edgar Winter. You name it. Oh, to once again hear those songs on 8-track in an AMC Gremlin tape deck. That exact same sound. The tape noise. The rumble. The way some songs would fade out. Silence. Ka-chunk! The tape would change channel. The song would fade back in. Cheap Trick's ''Clock Strikes Ten'' did that. So did Zeppelin's ''Ramble On'', right before the '' . . . but Gollum, in huh *EEE*vul wheyhey . . . crept up and slipped away with herher . . . herher . . . *huhhhhyeh!*''

Terry ruled. He had a CB we'd jabber on and at least three different porno mags under his front seat. One particular spread-eagled redhead filled my ninth-grade reverie. I know I don't look much like that ninth-grader any more. And that spread-eagled redhead with the part-it-down-the-middle-layer-it-back do probably doesn't look much like that picture any more, either. But to this day, whenever I hear ''King of the Nighttime World'' she still comes in view for me, still supple, aging not a day, her eyes begging a ninth-grade boy to do things he couldn't quite picture exactly how to do yet.

I was born November 20, 1962, in Sturgis, Kentucky, in the western part of the state, where my father was preaching at the time. I was the last of four kids. My oldest brother, who played touch football with Elvis at Graceland once, was already out of the house by then. So, from my perspective, I had an older brother and an older sister and that was it. I don't remember much of Sturgis. When I was two, we moved to Paducah, which I remember more of. We moved to Madisonville, in the western coal belt, two days past my sixth birthday, the same day the Beatles released the *White Album*. I was in Madisonville the rest of my wholesome enough childhood, and entire godforsaken toilet of an adolescence.

I had a very staid and moral preacher's family upbringing. We watched a lot of television, went to the grandparents' place in Arkansas once a year, had no drinking or cussing, and ate fried potatoes every night. Dad did double mortgage payments to get the house paid off before he started falling apart, and he timed it pretty well, too. I drew pictures from the moment I could hold a crayon, and because of that everyone thought I was going to be an artist. As soon as I could write with a fair bit of juvenile flourish, though—about the age of twelve—I took that up. Then, everyone thought I was going to be an artist and writer. Those media were way too static for my tastes, however. Nothing jumped around or exploded. Then I saw that Kiss commercial when I was thirteen, and nothing else ever mattered from then on.

In my early teens, I began a slow slide into a moderate long-term depression that would go untreated for years, like it does with most people. I went from being the semi-gifted kid with a great future in sixth grade to being the bespectacled moper in eleventh grade who wasn't going anywhere. It would get worse before it got better, and I'd have a few suicidal periods here and there.

For a while I was on Elavil, which is a little pill that wipes out depressive thoughts, along with most others. I don't remember much of the Elavil period except nodding out in class and sitting in front of the television all the time very placidly, until something sudden would happen, like the phone ringing or a car-horn blaring, at which point I'd shit myself momentarily and then slip back into my little fog again.

It was also discovered that my tendency to blink and jerk my head

was a condition known as Tourette Syndrome, and that I had an excuse when Mom told me to stop it and I told her I couldn't.

I was never a prize-winning convulsive Tourette like they drag
out on *Donahue* once a year for sweeps. I have a thankfully mild case,
but it was just evident enough in high school to make everyone, especially girls, assume I was slightly crazy from halfway down the hall
before I ever got near them. In a way, that was liberating. When
everyone assumes you're crazy, you may as well let your inner self
go, and most all of us are more than a little unbalanced on the inside.
We just hide it to get laid, employed or elected. If you can turn a
nickel being your own real crazy self, they call you a genius. Until
then you're a freak looking to get his ass kicked.

1977. Jeans were still flared, but *cuffed*, in some weird fashion
pupal stage. Every girl in school had the Dorothy Hamill haircut, the
short wedge thing. You'd call a girl by name from behind, she'd turn
around and be the wrong girl. Steve Martin was the funniest man on
the planet. Star Wars, Travolta Fever, Sex Pistols on the evening
news, *If ah kaint have yew, ah don'y wawnt nobody bay-beh! If ah
kaint have yew, ah, ah, ah! Oh!* The kid in high school who should
have been reading books but was doodling band logos in his note-
book? That was me.

In May '78, I got my first guitar, a Stella acoustic for seventeen
dollars. I didn't know which end was which. I wish now I'd asked
someone earlier, but I didn't. I just sat there at home and tried to figure it out all on my own. After a year, all I'd learned was that those
sounds they were getting on those records sure as hell couldn't be
pulled out of any seventeen-dollar Stella.

So I got an electric guitar, a Kalamazoo SG copy with white
enamel and two pickups. She was a beauty. Sixty-five dollars from
Don's House of Music. No amp; didn't need one. I found that if I
plugged the guitar into the 'mic' jack on the back of my stereo, and
moved the 'mode' switch halfway between 'phono' and '8-track',
then I got the record in the left speaker and fairly bitchen destructo-
blast guitar in the right speaker. Okay, I thought, *this* is fun. Now
we're getting somewhere.

Day after day I would come home from school and practice, although "practice" might be too constructive a term for what I was
mainly doing, cradling the guitar in my hands while I watched television. I watched ungodly amounts of television. While a large percent-
age of my classmates were doing drugs at a grand '70s pace—turning

their brains into cute little Cornish game hens—I was getting cathode-ray burn on my retinas. The effect is that, to this day, I have about a twelve-minute attention span, followed by the need for a brief commercial message of some sort.

The bedroom, the tube, my records. That was life. I'd have my own private Playboy After Dark parties and wear this old tux I'd come across. Nobody there but me, in my tux, playing my guitar. My mom was at her wit's end with a husband in the coronary care unit hooked up to machines, and there I was in my bedroom, in a tux, serving drinks and playing my guitar for people who weren't there.

My six-string shred-tone was making short work of my speakers. They lost a bit of treble and definition every day. *Double Live Gonzo* at peak volume didn't help them much, either.

I'd sit in front of college-prep English class and doodle guitars and band logos, openly picking my nose in front of Becky, whose last name I swear I can't remember. Yeah bitch, like I care. Like you'd ever whiz down my throat if my guts were aflame. Umm, that's a good one. Wanna bite?

I was a smartass, and narrowly averted getting my smart ass kicked once or twice, but I was basically a pleasant kid, maybe way too convinced I was fun to be around, but essentially nice, in a gross and twitching way, or at least innocuous enough. Your basic, blond-headed, seventies, wire-framed übernerd. I was the second or third-string court jester to the beautiful kids. You know, you tell a few jokes at their lunch table and then you're expected to leave.

October of 1979. I bought the Clash's first album—the American version with extra cuts—and took it home. I jacked those Soundesign faders way up, and "Clash City Rockers" tore through the house like a howitzer shell. I'd set a glass of heavily sugared iced tea on a throbbing speaker, and it had begun to shake and shimmy. It tumbled off the side and onto the spinning record, sending spidery limbs of tea all over. Tea on the needle. Tea on every groove. Tea making that blue Epic label bubble up. I don't know what polymer I'd stumbled upon, but you couldn't make that Clash record skip after that. I felt like the guy who discovered Lucite. That record doesn't skip to this day. Sounds like eight kinds of shit, but doesn't skip.

Gee, I thought at the time, maybe the Clash will come play *my* hometown. Sure, and perhaps I'll flap my arms and fly to the moon, too. Counting myself, maybe fifteen other people in Madisonville even knew who the Clash was.

Madisonville, Kentucky. One flatland piece of Hopkins County coal country with 18,000 people living there. If you weren't one of the coal miners, then you sold groceries to them, or doctored them, or preached to them like my dad did. There was no legally-sanctioned public drinking and no rock scene at all. Rock scenes were something you read about in *Rock Scene*. You stayed up Friday night for *The Midnight Special*, caught *Don Kirchner's Rock Concert* whenever it came on, and saw whoever played *Saturday Night Live*. That's all the rock and roll you got to see, except for the mainstream dinosaurs who'd come to Roberts Stadium in Evansville. Evansville was an hour up the road, in Indiana, Hoosierland.

Kentuckians hate Hoosiers, and they hate us right back. It's a good thing. It keeps the people busy. A Kentuckian who goes to Indiana for anything swallows a side of beef's worth of pride. Kentuckians hate Hoosiers because they're uptight, humorless descendents of the French who more honk than speak and think bowling 280 consistently is just about as good as life's ever going to get. They hate us because we're barefoot, psychotic cousinfuckers who drink bourbon and carry guns. Why is there a bridge over the Ohio River? So the Hoosiers can swim across in the shade. Heh. I got a million of 'em.

Evansville got only the big bands with wide redneck appeal, though, and not even all of that lot. Zeppelin? Floyd? The Stones? Give it up. You'd drive half a day if you wanted to see *them* anywhere.

Roberts Stadium was the venue for whoever did come, a big, smoky '70s barn full of wasted young heartland Americans of few words. PA systems in that place neatly captured the sound of that Clash record after it took the Nestea plunge. The effect to this day is that I still get in moods where I like bad sound. I still harken to those '70s shows and those records. Hashy high-mid frequencies. Raspy surface noise on cheap vinyl left outside the jacket on the unused twin bed. Late nights with the Koss headphones at death volume. Those headphones are what get your ears. All that high-end aimed at your cochlea with no runoff drain. Not good. Ask Pete Townshend how bad it is. Ask me if you can't get Pete on the phone. Go ahead. Ask me. Speak up.

By the time I was seventeen, I wanted to be in a band so bad I could taste it. That's all there was to life any more. Bands. You got together with friends, you talked about bands. You debated who was better. You bought the records and talked about the bands. You bought *CREEM* magazine at Robards Drugs and read about the bands. Bands, bands, bands. And all the bands lived and breathed in some world very far from mine. Big cities with seamy underbellies. Tough street corners where the kids wore safety pins in their noses. Dark bars at four in the morning. I could read about it all, but it was damned hard to attach any reality to it. There was nothing in my world like it. Nothing at all.

Actually, there *were* two bands my senior year. The first was Archive, named after a Rush album. They did a pretty mean Bachman-Turner Overdrive, and Tim Beeny had a boss, foam-padded, blue-glitter Kustom amp. They did "You Really Got Me" and the required boatload of Skynyrd.

Then there was XBJ, Madisonville's power trio, led by Jeff Calhoun, a great guitarist. He caused a riot on Senior Class Day by continuing to play after Mr. Henry turned the lights on and made it abundantly clear that playtime was over. Hey, can't stop "Stairway to Heaven" midway through, pardner. It sorta builds, takes a while. Last I heard, Jeff was in a Christian rock band with some Hebrew-sounding name I can't remember.

I went to high school football games by myself and pretended the lights and the cheering crowd were all there for me, giving me some sense of adulation I felt I wasn't getting anywhere else. I would stand by the marching band and get off on the big noise they put out, when I wasn't staring at this clarinet girl I had a crush on. I loved our band. They sucked about as much as any high school band sucks, but I loved them. I thought the guy banging the bass drum was eighty times cooler than any Neanderthal out on the field could ever be. Go figure.

I learned to live on the dreams in my head, munching on them like a desperate veal through the bars of a cage. I dreamed rock and roll dreams. Big, ridiculous rock and roll dreams.

May 1980. I graduated from high school. That same month, a band from Athens, Georgia named R.E.M. played their first gig, a keg party in an abandoned church. A hog farmer's son in southern Illinois named Jason Ringenberg was getting ready to move to Nashville and play his music. Big, ridiculous rock and roll dreams.

Off to Western Kentucky University for me. WKU. The Hilltoppers. Bowling Green, in the wavy hills of central Kentucky cave country, where I-65 crosses 31-W. A state school in a tobacco town, where everybody went home for the weekend after classes. No band for Tommy yet, nor likely ever. I stayed in my dorm room and played my Kalamazoo SG copy through those poor old Soundesign speakers. I still didn't know the first thing about tuning it, or even what barre chords were, or how to keep an attention span for a whole piece of music. Ken McGhee down the hall offered me a dollar if I could play a whole song all the way through. Couldn't do it. Didn't know any. What was the point of learning a whole song if I didn't know any other musicians to learn whole songs with? Didn't meet any. Didn't leave the room.

The music. It had gone from Kiss to Cheap Trick to the Kinks and the Stones and the Sex Pistols, Eddy Arnold and B.B. King. It was more than the bands or the sound any more. It was a fountain. A place to dunk my head and live in a better world. It was Van Halen at Roberts Stadium, John Prine in Diddle Arena, Springsteen in Municipal Auditorium. It was a reason to live. I used to drive around in my '74 Ford Maverick aimlessly, with nowhere to go, all alone with my music. *The River*, Nick Lowe's *Labour of Lust* on a weird Canadian label, The Ramones' *Road To Ruin* on the 8-track. If I turned the stereo all the way up, it sounded like Roberts Stadium.

I'd sit in my dorm room with *The Kinks Are The Village Green Preservation Society*, the single greatest album of all time. Buy it today. It's the only album I've gone through four copies of. Come to the end of a side, flip it over, play that side, flip it over, play the other side again, flip it over, the sun comes up, play the other side, flip it over.

I was trying to write a song that sounded like ''Just Like Starting Over''—with a similar intro, one strum per bar—the minute John Lennon was shot in New York. Years later, on tour, I'd stand in the very spot where he was gunned down. You're not supposed to be able to do that.

If a seventies kid wants to cling to a special date that unites us all, John Lennon's death is all we have, and we have to share even that with the baby-boomers who have always been lording over us as long as we can remember. We place value on significant dates everyone is supposed to commonly relate to somehow. Where were you when Kennedy was shot? Me, I don't know. I guess I was fouling my diaper. For that matter, the only time I remember seeing the Beatles on *Ed Sullivan* was the last time they did the show, when they were stoned and looked like trolls. I'm not a baby-boomer. I barely remember Woodstock. I'm too old to be a Generation X-er. I hated Woodstock '94. All I am is a seventies kid, some poor, dumb sonofabitch who got to *grow up with disco* in Middle America sometime after the great peak of everybody and everything.

And if you grew up in the seventies, you wanted to be a rock star. Oh yes, you did too. Don't give me that. You might not have entertained the fantasy for too long, but it *did* occur to you, at least once or twice, and it was because no one else touched rock stars. Politicians were crooks. Television was lame. Sports figures lacked sass in comparison. Rock stars were the pasty, skinny, stupid and surly sponge idols for every licentious, decadent notion we could come up with. It's a tribute to the power of the music itself, that rock stars could cavort (and still do) with all the panache of the town drunk: slobbering profane acceptance speeches on live awards shows, casually dumping grand pianos out seventh floor hotel room windows, savagely flogging wide-eyed groupies with motorcycle chains and partially thawed fish . . . and wind up half-deified in the process.

There were no rock stars a century ago (save perhaps Paganini and Oscar Wilde), so who filled the need then? Or was there one? Which came first: The need? The role? The market? The song? All I know is this. To stand on a stage with a roomful of like-minded animals, playing a guitar loud enough to kill something, shouting how you feel things oughta be and if you were in charge you bet some shit would get done, and drums are exploding with people screaming and spotlights feeling everybody up and amps are surging this juice . . . Oh God! It looked damn fun. And wouldn't it be fun if you got to do it too?

But you get over that feeling, right? One year, you're twenty, still going to shows and playing air guitar with Angus or Carlos or B.B. Next year, you're some sober-sided tie-rack with legs, buying *Time-Life* compilation CDs market-tested to reach your soul and bring back all those wonderful memories, as if by the time you're twenty-one, all you're supposed to have is memories, and the rest of your life is folderol. The slowest-moving movie-credits ever. The rest of your life, baby. What would you like to do with THE REST OF YOUR LIFE?? Insurance, babies, payments, sour love affairs, fear of death, graduate school, premature baldness—what is it you're going to do with THE REST OF YOUR LIFE???

1984. How did I get here? Still in Bowling Green. I was 21 years old, still playing my guitar on the corner of my bed. No band yet, and I was no less obsessed with it than I'd been all those years before.

It was this monstrous unfulfilled thing in me, this monkey on my back I didn't tell people about. They wouldn't understand. For some reason, life was going to be a mid-tempo waste of time until I'd found me a band to play in. Somehow, that was going to solve everything to me. I just figured that if I was in a band, then that would wipe away every adolescent hang-up and grudge I'd ever nursed. All those pangs of inadequacy would just splinter and sparkle away in the wake of some phoenix-like glittering New Day. If I was in a band . . .

Back and forth I walked to class, wrapping up a broadcasting degree I'd wound up getting without realizing it. Sometimes a broadcasting major is just a theater major with a button-down, a conservative means of letting loose some yearning to perform. It got more ridiculous every day I sat with my guitar on the edge of my bed in a shitty apartment on the corner of 12th and Park. I still didn't know how to tune the damn thing. And singing, well, singing wasn't even worth thinking about.

And so I waltzed in silly exchange. On one hand, I wanted my band! It was out there somewhere, and it was *mine to grab.* On the other hand, I'd somehow become this preppy, myopic dweeb with neither the personality, the musical acumen, nor the cool-school credentials to find *any* band, much less *my* band.

January, 1985. Somehow, I'd graduated. I didn't mean to; it just happened. The check cleared, so they shit me out. Now I was a preppy, myopic dweeb with a BA. An adult. I had a couple of laughable job interviews and nipped all further ones in the bud right away. My diploma went in the sock drawer. I had a Fender Telecaster now, a nice one with a fast neck, and I sat on my bed, playing along with records.

I got a job at Lee's Famous Recipe Fried Chicken. I knew by now that Gene Simmons wasn't the answer, but maybe Paul Westerberg was. And I learned how to fry chicken both regular and extra crispy, and how not to waste flour 'cause everybody's raise is in the bottom of that sack, and I learned how to catch the drippings out of the bottom of the deep-fryer because that's tomorrow's biscuit gravy. I wondered why the hell I was ever born if feeling this way all the time was all there was to living. I wondered where desires come from. I cursed that Kiss commercial as hard as I cursed the life that came before and made that commercial stand out so attractively. I cursed a society that puts a premium on glitz and makes you think it's somehow worthwhile to be famous and adored from afar. I cursed myself for knowing that fame was bullshit and still wanting to be famous in the face of that knowledge. I cursed WKU for not sending me my diploma after ten phone calls while my on-campus traffic tickets found my mailbox no problem and sometime in January of '85 I helped form a band called Government Cheese and this is that story. Got it? Good. Here we go.

* * * *

# part one

## home

# 1

# hot nuns
# in the
# summertime

I first saw Skot Willis[1] in the Kentucky Derby infield, May 1982. For those who watch it at home on television, all those tightly-massed bodies you see inside the track aren't paid extras, those are authentic drunk hillbillies. It's Ancient Rome for a day in there. The screws confiscate only the stupidest and most obvious of smuggled-in substances, so for every dumb twit who tries to sneak in a case of Bud, there'll be ten plastic bottles of violated 7-Up. Or maybe what's swishing around the ice in the bottom of the cooler is Everclear as much as it is water. Liquor-filled binoculars, hollow prosthetic limbs, all sorts of tricks. By noon, things are pretty ugly. Hulking, bovine women losing their bikini tops. Bubbas gulping hooch with bright red lips and madness in their eyes. Bic-pen tattoo dropouts. Crazed masses, untethered pets and wriggling, putrified vulvatude at its best.

There I was, crosslegged on my blanket corner, the typical geek 19-year-old college sophomore, gulping pink sludgy hooch and surveying the Derbyness. It was early May, and the sun was intensely

---

1. Skot's name is, in case you care, actually spelled the normal way on all legal documents. That's how I spelled it for years. For some reason, when we formed the band, we started spelling his name differently. I don't remember why. Anyway, it doesn't look like Skot's name to me now unless I spell it this way; and if I don't start writing it that way from the beginning, I know I'll do it later without thinking about it. So that's that. Sorry, Skobbie.

flat washout bright. I had no sunglasses, and looking over the throng was like watching a TV with the brightness jacked all the way up. I felt my face all squinted and scrunched like a hardbitten fisherman's. It was twice as hot as it was bright. I was getting that crosslegged tan, where you wind up blistered and wild with pain on your inner thighs and shins while the other side of your gams retain their milky-white sharkbait quality. When what to my melting eyes should appear, picking their way through the crowd, but three nuns.

A few steps closer scratched any notion they might be true novice novena types. Yes, three blokes more or less my own age were tooling their way through thousands of blind-drunk rednecks, and they were doing it dressed as Holy Sisters. They had on the authentic get-up from head to toe, and had to be absolutely boiling underneath it all. Their toe-length robes blew back as they walked. The three triangular penguins made their way through a crowd alternately bemused with and none-too-approving of this trashing of the sacred image. I watched as they passed me by and disappeared, taunting all with their bearing.

I decided I liked these guys, whoever they were. They were Mike, Ken and Skot. I didn't know them yet, but a year later we'd be sharing a house in Bowling Green. And in several years I'd tour the countryside with one of them, playing rock and roll, breaking every vow the nunnery might come up with.

1983. Latent New Wave was showing its age in Kentucky. We got every trend two years late. Only now had skinny ties been put on mark-down racks. I watched it all from the sidelines, absently strumming my black Fender Musicmaster, which is the guitar I'd traded the old white SG for.

Bowling Green. We called it Boring Green back then. A beautiful place. My Dear Old College Town. Modest two-story houses on tree-lined streets. Placid. Very Mayberry. But when you're twenty, the last thing thing you're looking for is Mayberry. I wanted rock and roll. I wanted West Hollywood. I wanted those mean Lou Reed streets. I wanted scenes out of *CREEM* magazine. Johnny Thunders falling off a stool at Max's Kansas City, or Iggy kicking the front row senseless.

If anybody told me they'd been to New York City, I'd reach out and touch them, as if they'd been sanctified by all that urban sin and vitality. And I'd get really drunk and depressed a lot, because I figured I'd never go there myself. That sort of thing happened to cooler people. I had no idea what constituted ''cool'' though I was pretty sure I wasn't it. The best I could manage was a fifty-cent blazer, a Squeeze button in the extra-thin lapel, a half-price skinny tie, standing on the keg-party porches with my spiky short hair, playing that first Clash album while the crickets chirped.

For two weeks in spring '83, campus grades dropped like a mallet thrown down a well. That's when MTV came to town.

It was an amazing thing. It captivated me as much as anyone. For the first time ever, you could actually *see* bands all the time. Of course, its own nature wrecked itself immediately—all those bogus video-friendly acts. But for a fortnight, even *they* were riveting. Who IS this Duran Duran? Boy George? Kaja-what?

For two weeks MTV dominated everything. The channel was different back then. They just played videos and nothing else. It was wonderful in that respect. We used to stupidly discuss which *veejay* (new word) played the best videos, as if they had any choice *what* they played. Who your favorite veejay was spoke volumes about you. (I'm a Martha Quinn man to this day.) We assessed all these new hot acts no one remembers now, like Heaven 17, the Members (remember "Hey! Hey! I'm in love with a working girl!" They all fall in a swimming pool at the end), Nena ("99 Luftballons"), Kim Wilde, Planet P, Missing Persons, Berlin and dozens more. Who could it BE now? (Da da DAHH da da.) Who could it *BE* now? (Da da DAHH da da.)

Then it was over. Two weeks got the shine off *that* pumpkin. You realized you saw the same videos more than you cared to. You realized that to watch MTV more than an hour was to call into question where your life was headed.

There was also a darker portent in that, from the moment Storer Cable picked up this little network, no longer could Bowling Green lag behind New York and L.A. We could no more hold onto New Wave two years past its demise than we could keep our raccoon coats and rumble seats. From now on, the hippest in all things came straight off a satellite to Bowling Green, Tulsa, and Saipan. Finally, *everyone could be hip at the same time!* No more regionalism. No factions. At last, all those music and fashion decisions are made for you. Sit back, relax. Have a Coke. It was a slicked-up, crass, astonishingly cynical thing, and a crass nation of cynics ate it up. I sat on my ratty college couch, and wondered where to send the congratulations card. Big Brother doesn't have an address.

When I met them, Skot Willis and Ken Flaherty lived in something between a dorm room and a pop culture storage facility. On about the tenth floor of Pearce-Ford Tower, they crammed their precious few cubic feet with enough records, clothes, posters, musical instruments, curios, and anything you might imagine, to qualify the place as a national landmark. A safe haven for collegiate trinkets. A New Wave time capsule.

Two complete stereo systems ensured the music need never stop for even so slight a gap as to flip the record. A gigantic American flag a full hundred feet long, stolen from somewhere, hung from the ceiling in bulbous downward festoons. It brushed the top of your head in spots and accented the strange paranoid effect of being in there.

On the wall was an Iggy photo, a giant Sex Pistols poster and a charming Donny and Marie shot. Next to all that was a framed Hound Dog Taylor album cover *(Natural Boogie)*. Kroger Cost-Cutter packages occupied one wall as a sort of theme. Six Cost-Cutter beer cans were attached to the telephone. They'd answer the phone and shake the receiver so violently that the cans clanged any caller into submission. They raised their mattresses off the bed frames with milk crates, so they could store even more stuff underneath: old 45s, flea-market items, old photos of people they never knew but thought looked cool, clothes, from New Wave chic to bizarre. Those guys could wear anything and make it look like you should be wearing it too.

And in one corner was a massive Fender Super Reverb. (An amp.) Ken ran his Gibson Melody Maker through it. (A guitar.)

From this meager cubicle, crammed and claustrophobic, Skot and Ken carried on an infectious New Wave Playboy vibe. In and out of the nun suits—which they'd wear at least once a week to some staid campus function—they were two Louisville Catholic-school reprobates out to cram four years of high-intensity college lifestyle into each semester.

Spicing their mystique for me was a musical lineage. They'd both played in punk bands. Ken was even part of a local Louisville compilation record. This is not to say they were good, but they did have loads of the charisma I felt I lacked. We sat in that dorm room amidst all the priceless junk, playing guitar together. Ramones, Pistols, Undertones, Chuck Berry, Little Richard, and others. A fave of theirs was Robert Gordon, the fifties revivalist. We used to do ''Lonesome Train'' by him, along with ''Pipeline'', ''I Wanna Be Sedated'', etc. We wound up in a ''band'' together.

The only band I'd been in previously was a frat band with a capital F. We'd worn ties and played Eagles tunes. The Cars was as New Wave as that band had gotten. I'd persuaded them to do a Clash tune once and they'd grumbled, so when I fell in with Skot and Ken, I got the rush you get when you meet like-minded types and finally know you're not crazy. They sent for Greg Curry in Louisville to play drums with us. He'd put rice on his toms and send it sky-high with his whacks. I'd never seen that one before. Two songs into the party, you'd have rice sticking to your sweat all over you. I liked that.

We played maybe once or twice a semester. We even did one show in the nun suits. I'd never dressed as a nun before. The suit was very hot and evidently hadn't been washed since a legitimate sister had owned it. It smelled like a cross between cattle and the dirt surrounding a ruptured septic line.

Skot, Ken, Mike Bailey and I took a house together on Dennis Way, across the tracks in the shadow of Pearce-Ford Tower. Three nuns, and me as the back-room bishop. The three of them managed to expand the aesthetic mutiny of their dorm-cubbies to a full five-room house, and it still looked cluttered as hell. They were fun guys, and I like to think I sort of bookishly hovered over their aura.

For the first time in my life, I routinely enjoyed myself. Parties were semi-regular and generally attended by interesting people. They were highly social and clean-breathed type fellows.

*Hello and welcome to the early eighties almost-athletes, but not quite, chicks dig us we're wildasses but smart about it how 'bout comin' back to my place let's have a shitload of fun 'cause in two years we start entry-level marketing jobs and the earrings'll come out and we'll shed this beatnik skin with an offhandedness that will shock and depress the true believers but for now we're bohemians and beer's cheap in Bowling Green so no thanks I really gotta study right now because I am serious about making money someday but tonight we'll drink a case of Cook's longnecks because a case of beer for under five bucks is truly hilarious and life is truly hilarious and dressing up as a nun is truly hilarious especially if you go to a football game that way and I'm truly hilarious and I know you shouldn't say such things about yourself so I don't I just live by example because life and titties are such great things and sometimes when things are tough I'll just close my eyes and picture titties and I don't know it seems to help dealing with . . . you know, life and shit, and you know life is there to be lived and man that's a bad jacket yeah I got it at St. VDP's for fifty cents dig these shoes hey I got a Pistols bootleg of the final show in San Francisco! No shit? Is this still Kentucky? College, college. Truly, truly hilarious.*

Ken got serious about pre-med, and Mike never did actually play an instrument, so that left Skot and me with the itch to form the "real band." Yes, the "real band." The type that stayed together more than two weeks in a row, actually played often enough to break a sweat, got publicity pictures taken and all that. The average attempt to start this next Beatles lasted about thirty minutes once a month. Those were painful half-hours.

Ten years of distance has made me plenty reminiscent for that house and the good times had, but I'm none too nostalgic for those afternoons trying to get through "The Wait" by the Pretenders with no drummer. Skot and I had not one whole person's gift of rhythm between the two of us. Neither of us could vocally carry a tune across the room. We made no *music*. We may have bashed the guitars a bit, and written lists of songs we'd like to play on scraps of paper, and we may have dreamed up band names, and even tried to write a song or two, but we certainly made no *music,* no sounds to caress and cajole the spirit. We weren't even close. We didn't even know where to start except to just, well . . . *do it,* make some ungodly noise, be disgusted with ourselves, take a break, and then . . . *make some more ungodly noise!*

Making music, no. Hearing it, yes. That house was a 24-hour rock and roll revelation, often while you were trying to sleep. These guys were eclectic. Bryan Ferry if the situation was closed-door and carnal. *Muddy Waters Live on Stovall's Plantation* is one we used to shave to. At the same time Jonathan Richman might be blasting out of the megaton speakers in the living room. The speakers were Skot's, the wires snaked back to his bedroom power amp. You haven't heard the Ramones until you've heard them on those speakers. It was through those sphincter-throbbers that I first heard what was coming out of Nashville, and came to know what that hog-farmer's son from Illinois was up to.

Nashville was our big Mecca one hour south. When Bowling Green got just too sleepy to deal with, we thought of Cantrell's and the Exit/In and Rooster's, and all the other decidely non-Opry places where dark-eyed, rudely hip people smelled of patchouli, slam-danced and gave us the once-over when we walked in. These dens in Nashville struck us as exotic and dangerous, accustomed as we were to Boring Green. There was genuine punk rock in that town, and one band stood knees, hips, and shoulders above the whole rest of them: Jason and the Nashville Scorchers.

Jason Ringenberg had packed up his cowboy hat and his finest silk western wear, and left his family's Illinois hog farm for Nashville, stumbling whole and pure into that dark side of Nashville. Jason wrote panoramic songs of good and evil, great American country music full of acoustic twang and plaintive harmonies, and he might have stayed simply an appealing midwestern songster had he not fallen in with the most dangerous rock and roll band in the South, which then unleashed some madness inside him and changed everything for everybody. Jason and the Nashville Scorchers. I think they got very tired of being called "country punk", but they did invent it, and country punk was a wonderful, beautiful thing.

Warner Hodges played a fast and loud Fender guitar, through an amp you didn't want to get too close to. Perry Baggs and Jeff Johnson were the rhythm section. Together, the four of them found what I can only call the Sex Pistols Thing, that Thing the Pistols had on "God Save the Queen" and "Bodies". That ferocious rhythm and growl, whatever that thing is that makes you legally fucking insane when you hear it. The Scorchers at Cantrell's in 1983 are the only band I've ever heard—outside the Pistols themselves—who completely, inarguably, had THAT.

The first time I saw them, Warner came swaggering onstage in an old T-shirt, jeans, and boots with big spurs on, his hair pulled tight and sticking out the side of his head, a cigarette in his nose, puffing away remotely as if that's how everyone always smokes them, as if you could pick up a People magazine and there'd be a Salem ad with two laughing preppy couples whitewater rafting, cigs jammed halfway up their nostrils. Talk about somebody who hadn't hidden his crazy side. This guy was waving a goddamn flag.

He had five Bud Lights in his teeth held by the plastic rings. He peeled one off and gave it to me. I'd never been to a rock and roll show where the lead guitarist gave *me* a beer. That was pretty cool. He put down the other three, shook up the fifth one, popped it and a foamy geyser shot down his throat as he balanced it on his thrown-back head, still blowing that nostril cigarette as he suddenly spun like a top on one leg and started ripping out *brilliant* dead-on chunka chunka power-chord mayhem. Somehow, in the midst of all this gymnastic indulgence of vice, the first song had started and Warner had been right there with the rest of the band, as if he'd been standing stock-still the whole time and wasn't in a million years going to be caught off guard.

Then, chaos. The crowd smashed into the stage and back again like surf. Warner and Jason, in his silk fringe shirt and cowboy hat, careened across the little stage like men possessed, barely missing each other, occasionally going balls-out crazy and diving into the front-line throng. It was utter madness.

They were a scary thing to behold, whizzing just above my head on a postage-stamp stage. To be part of a boiling batch of humanity, hugging a stage monitor for dear life and occasionally taking it with you, your body and face crashing against and away from your neighbor human flotsam, you got a Zen sense of being part of a human sea. To have rock and roll that hopped up in your face was to be part of a true moment. I wanted as many of those moments as I could get.

We bought the Scorchers' indie records and took them home to Bowling Green, where they sounded as if they were mixed to sound good specifically on Skot's apocalyptic speakers. After the breakdown in ''Both Sides of the Line'' when the band came crashing back in, there'd sometimes be ten people in that living room, jumping off chairs, flailing into walls and door facings, and generally trying to separate their skulls from their vertebrae. Then, when the moment was over, and everyone went their separate ways, I'd sneak back to my room and try to learn those Merle Haggard-meets-Johnny Ramone guitar parts.

I became obsessed with Warner's playing. I wrote him long, deranged letters, begging him to show me how he played. I followed him around in bars, asking him ''how do you play that one lick there'' questions. I'd bug him into showing me guitar licks in the Cantrell's parking lot. I'd be on the front row at Scorchers' shows, banging him hard on his boot should he ever turn his hands away from me so I couldn't see what he was doing. It's to Warner Hodges' eternal credit that he never actually hauled off and hit me.

Proximity intensified them. The Scorchers were near enough to touch, near enough to know that these people were real. Before them, rock bands had been unapproachable icons that appeared before us in great barns and sped away before their humanity was unveiled. The Scorchers, however, together with their friends in Georgia, R.E.M., were, by their close-up and familiar natures, making it all look somehow . . . *realistic* to want to do this sort of thing.

Ken began to worry. He saw my obsession and cared enough to take me aside a couple of times. First of all, I was in no way the rock and roll type, he said. Didn't I see that, he'd ask. Tommy, you're a short-haired, bespectacled intellectual type, and you're a GOOD short-haired, bespectacled intellectual type. There's nothing wrong with that. You're not gonna be Sid Vicious. You don't WANT to be Sid. Sid's dead, and when he was alive, he was rather stupid. You sit all afternoon after classes playing your guitar with this dreamy look on your face like you're picturing yourself years from now on a big stage. Don't break your own heart. Put it aside.

But I didn't. Ken's heart was in the right place, and the conditions pointed in every way to his being right. I paid no heed. For better, for worse, I couldn't be reached with something so flimsy as solid logic.

Like all lovely things, that fling at Dennis Way came to a close. We all went our separate ways in May.

1984. I found myself in that shitty apartment, an attic on the corner of 12th and Park, all alone. Well, Keith Etter was across the hall, but he was all alone too. We were all alone together. I spent that summer deejaying at night at the Alibi and tending a church camp in the daytime. In my free time I sat on the edge of my bed playing along with records a lot. Dreaming a lot. Playing Richie Blackmore's solo on "Lazy" over and over again. Listening to Robert Johnson's "Hellhound on My Trail" over and over again. Sitting on the edge of that bed, knowing what the Buddhist speaks of when he says all unhappiness springs from desire.

* * * *

# 2

# jaws of life

1984. I was inching towards graduation like that scene in *Jaws* where Quint slips down the sinking boat into the waiting shark's mouth. Everything was coming loose of its moorings, and I was hanging on to anything I could grab. Inevitable. A slow descent to some new and awful world.

College is a great cuddly womb. I imagine heroin is kind of like college. You're all warm and comfortable and feel like your parameters are broadening, when at the same time you're devolving into protoplasm. You think you're wise, but you're really just glib. Genuine wisdom's waiting down the street, crouched down behind a parked car waiting to jump your ass. They hand you a diploma, one sheet of paper in a faux leather binding, and give you a big smile full of bad teeth. Professors are sick bastards at heart. They love to watch the sheep get shaved and ground up and then there's just so much more chow for the system.

The worst part of the whole experience is that you know something's coming. Some new set of rules, and the end of the honeymoon and all that. You know this because your parents won't shut up about the fact that something's coming. Bosses and new shoes. Company cars, and alarm clocks set across the room so you definitely have to get your ass out of bed to shut them off. And you don't know what's worse, getting the shot or waiting for it. Mom and Dad are on the phone offering all these nebulous hints on what life's going to be like once you can't get up unshaven and hit class in your bandana/shades ensemble. Little koans and parables are all they give you to work with, and they act mystified when you don't miraculously grasp a parent-to-child thumbnail sketch of life's upcoming pistol-whipping technique. It's like describing royal blue to someone blind since birth, or explaining abstinence to a roomful of blood-caked, mud-covered rugby players. "C'mon boy! Git that resume printed! Kinko's is open late. Don't you know what's coming?" Uhhh . . . no.

My resume was a joke. Usually, you can lie a little—gussy it up. Make little bits of semi-experience sound like invaluable accomplishments. I didn't even have that much to work with. I had no lily to gild. In Tommy Womack's realm of workforce achievement, I had (A) pushed the food wagon in a hospital, (B) sold shoes at a Pic n' Pay, (C) delivered ice on a truck, (D) washed dishes at the Student Center, and now I was, for the second summer running, (E) custodianizing Dad's church camp. All summer long, tripping the light bucolic with a different truckload of good Christians each week.

Camp Koinonia. You see a sign for it on the Green River Parkway. Morgantown's the closest place with more than fifteen people. For two summers, '83 and '84, I lived at the place. One concrete room with an air conditioner that dripped inside the room onto my bed. A little black and white television that picked up Channel 13 in Bowling Green. The walls were so damp that posters wouldn't stick with tape, and it takes a better man than me to drive thumbtacks into cinderblock. Me and four mustard-yellow walls. The floor was cold elementary-school tile. Really slick. I'd put one foot on my throw rug and go flying.

For a cool two hundred a week, I listened to my Walkman, drove the mower in circles where it looked like it might need mowing, unblocked toilet bowls, changed light bulbs, flipped circuit breakers back on when fourteen old ladies and five preachers couldn't figure out how to do it for themselves, and basically convinced all the campers I was the Dark Angel sent to claim the children. I wore sunglasses inside and out, and played "Stray Cat Blues" off *Beggars Banquet* over and over again.

Most of what I know about guitar playing comes from those summers, since there was nothing else to do. The chapel had an old, wretched turntable (which I stole) that slowed down to 16 rpm, a lost godsend for young guitarists copping licks. Slow it down and get it right.

My guitar at the time was an old $100 Gretsch Rally I traded the Musicmaster for. It wouldn't stay in tune, but it looked great. For six to eight hours at a stretch I'd sit there with that old player trying to rip off Brian Setzer and Stevie Ray, lofty-goal stuff I couldn't hope to play then and can't play now, but along the way I did learn all the chords and the basic catechism. Chuck Berry (Play the top two strings and wiggle the third one). Scotty Moore's Sun stuff with Elvis. Those first Scorchers and R.E.M. records.

It should be noted that a summer alone in the woods might not have been the keenest bit of survival strategy for a twenty-year-old given to feeling *really bad* occasionally. Dad knew that. He was semi-retired by now, preaching a little here and there, and really getting old-looking to me for the first time. He didn't really have much business at the camp, yet he was always there.

He was trying to get close to me. We'd never gotten along great. There was a monstrous age difference. He was born under Woodrow Wilson in a shotgun house, and I was an air-conditioned Camelot kid. Dad was the old guy I passed in the hallway. We got the second television in '75, that somewhat portable black-and-white Magnavox, and I hardly ever saw him at all after that.

Now, here he was at camp all the time, looking after his occasionally suicidal son. He'd have no other purpose there besides to watch me mow the lawn, run his thumbs up his suspenders and say "You mowed a real good lawn there, son."

He'd watch me clean out the dumpster and say "Son, that dumpster hasn't looked that good in twenty years." He was even getting into my guitar playing, when it involved musical genres he could deal with. We got together on Jimmie Rodgers, and I remember him quite liking "Baby Let's Play House", but "Iron Man" didn't translate at all.

My resumes didn't have Camp Koinonia tops on my experience list, though. That honor went to the Alibi on Adams Street, in Bowling Green.

The Alibi was a masterpiece. Somebody in Bowling Green saw "Saturday Night Fever" 230 times and memorized the layout. It was the last true surviving "disco" in America. A real polyester and mirror ball Tony Manero Ah Ah Stayin-Alive time-capsule type place. The Alibi. Genuine aluminum foil crumpled up and glued to the walls. A strobe light and break tapes I could play that still had KC and the Sunshine Band on them. Tight burgundy carpet and a lighted dance floor. The last person in town who had any business being the disc jockey in a place such as this was me, and there I was.

Don't ask me how it happened. Somebody said the Alibi needed a dee-jay and it paid two hundred a week and all you had to do was give up all nights except Sundays and Mondays, and play lots of music you never in your darkest fantasies thought you'd ever play lots of.

In case it need be said, the place was way beyond its glory days. When I was a freshman, though, it was Mecca. You could be nineteen for dancing and twenty-one for drinking, and it took one helluva moron not to finagle twenty-oneness in *that* place. I got past the doorman once with a glaringly doctored birth certificate. It said I was 29 when I barely looked eight. I had four sloe gin fizzes and drenched my Nikes in pinkish pukum and Spaghetti-Os you could still tell were Spaghetti-Os. And I blended in.

I got along great with Bill and Catherine, the owners, but it wasn't long before the place affected my brain. The regulars, such as there still were any, didn't like me. I don't blame them. I suppose I played "Tiptoe Thru the Tulips" a few times too many for it to have been funny any more. I kept playing the B-sides of disco hits because I didn't know any better. Oh, *this* is the A-side? Sorry, man.

There was this one guy who'd really wanted the job. I mean, he'd outright campaigned for it. And here I'd walked in like a bastard and zeemed this major career-ladder rung right out from under him. He was pissed. Every night he would come in and wait endlessly for me to make a mistake, drooling for the moment when it would happen. He was always approaching the music booth and requesting the *latest, hottest big disco hit!* And then when I didn't have it, he'd sneer knowingly and walk away, shaking his head. He was the guy who knew about Sheila E. before *anybody*. He was cool!

The next night, I'd have the record he'd requested. When I put it on, he'd snort about how I hadn't a clue about the song until *he'd* brought it to my attention. Night after night, he kept unwittingly telling me what to buy, until he made me the hippest young disco jock in town. Poor dumb bastard, he'd have had me rapping before too much longer. All night long he'd stare holes in me. I'd cue up the latest hottest new artist (Madonna) and her big breakout hit ("Borderline"). I'd let the platter spin, face this guy—drinking his Shirley Temple at a table all alone—and envision his head exploding like that scene in *Scanners*. Every night it was like that. What a job.

The night I quit was when I realized I knew all the songs on *Thriller*, their exact lengths, what was up or down in tempo, and the order in which they appeared. I don't mean just "Billie Jean" or "Beat It". I mean I could flip the record over and drop the needle right down on "Lady in my Life" if you asked me to. I'd also realized I knew all the words to "Party Train" and "You Dropped A Bomb on Me"—and that I actually kind of *liked* "You Dropped A Bomb on Me". I'd feel my ass wiggle despite myself. That made my chest tighten.

I killed that copy of *Thriller*. I bought it from the club and stomped it to bits amidst a floor full of bemused dancers. What is the freak DJ jumping up and down on Michael for? Is this his last night? Thank God!

Quarter Beer Night was the last great night at the Alibi. Somewhere in the crowd most of those Tuesdays was a tall fellow named Billy Mack Hill. He had a lot of foreign student friends who still harbored home-country loves for disco. Billy would go there to hang out with them and get righteously polluted for under five dollars. I'm very surprised now that I can't remember him, as he has a very distinct dancing style, one where you move only from the waist up and your feet don't leave the floor.

I actually got through one whole attempt at typing my resume up nicely. I stumbled through those aforementioned disastrous job interviews. They were at television stations, since I was under some stupid delusion that, because I'd majored in broadcasting, I should therefore be expected to get a job in that field.

Skot was waiting tables at Rafferty's, which, at the time, was managed by four-hundred different people at once—none of whom had ever been described as cuddly—and working for them was what nice young college kids of my era did to compensate for no other Vietnam-type experience in their lives.

The Rafferty's waitstaff was the nicest, most wholesome-looking hearts and minds of Young America you'd ever care to see, and they all came home from work with gritting teeth and high blood pressure. The moolah was the bait. No table or bar gig in town touched the tip money you could make at Rafferty's. If you could half-pass as preppy, and wanted to make a C-note per night on the weekends without actually going to bed with anyone, then you put on your white buttondown, your nice khakis and your leather topsiders and you brought the cream of Bowling Green their quiche and salad, double nachos, Gold margarita or whatever. From a diner's point of view, everything was tony and relaxed. The only thing missing was a pianist playing "Misty" in the corner.

From an employee's perspective, things were decidedly starker. I never actually worked there, but I had several interviews. The last one was with a bar supervisor who is surely in jail by now. He fixed me with withering scowls and painted a super-bleak Ravensbruck image of how hard I'd work, and how quickly I'd be out the door should I be caught, as they said, "leaning instead of cleaning." They stopwatch-timed the waiters and waitresses, and would call you at home the next morning if your tip sheets divined that you had absconded with a dollar-forty too much.

Skot did what it took to get on board and he started making that big-ticket tippage. His world morphed into half-and-half 21 Club and triple-tiered Roman slave galley. I hadn't seen much of him lately, until one night we ran into one another at Airport Liquors, right across from Rafferty's on Scottsville Road.

His skin was all blanched and pasty, His eyes were blank. He looked like he'd sweated profusely ten times and patted it down ten times since his last shower. His tie was barely still around his neck, like a noose that hadn't been tightened up yet. One side of his shirttail was peeking out. He'd just left Rafferty's, looking like he'd gone ten rounds with Ken Norton. Skot Willis, staunch non-smoker, was sucking on a Marlboro like life itself was on the other end of that filter. He'd come straight across the four-lane and was blowing his money on any number of mind-soaking stress-quenchers. I think he may have walked across all those lanes of traffic, daring anyone to run him over. "Tommy," he said, "I just made ninety dollars in seven hours, and it wasn't worth it." And then he started laughing insanely.

We whiled away the fall afternoons at 12th & Park. Toby Myrick set up his drums in my little apartment so that the bass drum physically touched my bed. I borrowed a huge Peavey amp from Terry Utley. We were in the very top of a massive old house that had been broken down into about seven hundred off-campus apartments. For several weeks, we practiced up there. Actually, once again, "practice" is way too constructive a term for it. "Howl and Bash" more suits it. Repercussions from the other tenants were swift and non-negotiable. The landlord was good enough to personally drop by and assure me the New Ramones would have to be gestated elsewhere, thanks very much. And once again, our little combo fizzled.

Toby Myrick was an Owensboro native and therefore slightly crazy. Owensboro is a short distance from my own Madisonville. They've always enjoyed legal liquor there, as their Catholic-to-Baptist ratio is a bit more slanted to the Papacy. That, combined with the bluegrass music and the barbecue, and there did seem to be a bit more Fat in their Tuesday compared to the rest of us in the coal belt. Toby was a true rock and roller, and is a much better drummer now than he was then in my apartment. In those days, he could keep a beat fine, but halfway through any tune, he'd launch into some new exploration that took the song way off whatever course we were on. Everybody would stop and look at him and there he'd be, flailing away like the happy Toby he was, completely oblivious.

He looked a bit like Nicholas Cage in the eyes, and was always playing a drum solo in his head, even when you were trying to talk to him. He had the type of charisma where he'd show up at midnight and wake you up after having missed practice and he'd say ''sorry man, just wasn't in me today.'' And what good would it do to get mad at him? You couldn't. And then off he'd be, drumming in his head the whole time.

So, like some load of garbage kicked off the end of an interstellar craft, bagged waste left to float through eternity, I was graduated from Western Kentucky University. I was only one semester late, which was quite impressive at Western. The only way to finish up there in eight semesters flat was to know full well the direction life is going to take by the age of seventeen, and what kind of vapid, bloodless soul knows that? Not this one.

My good time in getting out proves doubly miraculous in light of the recklessness with which I'd plotted my degree program. I was almost a junior before I ever knew what General Ed. requirements were. I honestly had no idea that there were certain classes you *had* to have in order to graduate. Things worked out only by the sheerest coincidence. For the longest time, whenever registration reared its ugly head I'd just look through the catalog and select courses based on the name, or perhaps the *professor's* name if it was amusing-looking on the page. At least once, I recall closing my eyes and stabbing the catalog page with my finger. The course my digit lit upon was a two-hundred-level painting class. I got a C.

So they turned me loose to twist in the solar wind. A BA in mass-communication, and a minor in writing. A pithy piece of paper which they wouldn't even send to my house. They made me trudge up that hill one more time and skulk out the proper office where my diploma might be found, and then they held my transcript hostage until I coughed up the twenty-five dollars for traffic tickets. I've got the diploma somewhere around the house. I could probably find it inside of an hour. And I could sure use that twenty-five dollars.

So now that I'm a college graduate, I *can't* be a custodian or a deejay any more. I have a *degree*, now. What shall I do? Ah, *fry cook!*

Of course. That's the ticket. Lee's Famous Recipe Fried Chicken on the 31-W Bypass. Skot had a house a block away, on 13th Street, where he took me in like a wayward waif. I lived in one room—actually a large closet—for 65 dollars a month.

My newly acquired smoking habit disillusioned my roomies and got me banished to that cubicle to practice it. In that little space, I worked on new dimensions of fetid. My brand was Marlboro Lights. My drink was Kahlua and coffee, a best of both worlds beverage. It stretches your mind to the caffeinated breaking point, and gets you slobbering drunk at the same time. You get loquacious as any old cig-blowing beatnik, but it's filtered through the Keith Richards school of thick-tongued distinction, your elbow slipping off the table and all that. Hyper drunks wear out their welcomes real fast.

Skot saw himself going in solid directions. The band was a nice idea and all, but a job with a marketing firm, good friends, quality frolic on the weekends, ski trips, a truly bad sports car—those things would be nice too.

He started making friends in the marketing industry, however the hell you do that. He was the campus chapter president of APICS, which means American Production and Inventory Control Society (Hoo! Don't let me miss *that* office party!), and he was on his way to what the world interprets as legitimacy. More power to him. What could I say? Tommy Womack? Fry cook? Chain-smoking, rocket-fuel cocktail-swilling snarler that I had become in rather frighteningly short order? Good luck, Skot. Loan me a fiver someday, maybe?

Skot escaped Rafferty's one night. He dodged the searchlights, cut the wires, outran the dogs. He got out. He went to work at Nat's, a sporting goods store, ostensibly to gain some sort of marketing expertise. I think it was more to get Patagonia at cost.

Nat's was as much a way-of-life sanctuary as a mere sporting goods store—a tranquil maze of top-quality racing bikes, electric socks and genial, left-of-center employees. You just had to walk into Nat's and suddenly a calm enwrapped you. I liked it in there, although I began to suspect I was embarrassing Skot. Here's this hyperactive, blinking guy invading Skot's oasis of cool, acting like he knows him in front of all these people, and, as we were still supposedly forming a "band" together, I was in and out of the store all the time.

Billy Mack Hill had me pegged as nuts from the minute we met.

There he sat across the living room from me. It was a cold cloudy January afternoon. 1985. I was on the ratty couch and he was on the worse one. Between us was the coffee table rescued from someone's trash. The hardwood floor was all battle-scarred, dotted with haybales of dust. Guitar cords snaked through the linty tumbleweeds to a couple of cheap off-brand amps. My beige Telecaster was leaning against the wall. Skot's lay unceremoniously on the floor. His was also a beige Telecaster. We could tell them apart because Skot's guitar had a Bigsby tailpiece, and, on the back, an immense *KISS ARMY* sticker stained into the enamel. Elsewhere on the floor were strewn magazines, overturned beer cans, a lone ten-pound dumbbell, a spit-up furball from the cat. Hovel sweet hovel.

Billy sat, all six-feet-six of him, while I tourette-twitched and chain-smoked. I was explaining to him how we were going to form this monstrous band that was going to do this and do that and go here and go there. He was fairly incredulous, and fixed me with a steady, impassive mask of a face in the interest of plain courtesy.

Skot had invited him by the house after meeting him at some party, where Billy was holding court over a keg of cheer. Billy'd been headlong into his Southern preacher's fire and brimstone routine, and the topic was salvation through proper dry-cleaning. "Now brothuhs and sistuhs! I woncha tuh tuhn tuh page toohunnedfawtysebben of the South Central Bell phone book and say it with me now! *Martinizing! Martinizing!*" Perhaps you had to be there.

Anyway, he was making Skot laugh, no mean feat in itself. And in an ensuing conversation it came unveiled that Billy Mack Hill of Horse Cave, Kentucky *owned* a bass guitar.

There was no audition. He was hired. In those innocent times, it was far more important that a fellow own a bass than whether or not he could play it. To ask that he be a true bass player was just shooting for the moon. The bass player was always the guitarist who was shittier than the other guitar players. If you actually possessed a bass, you were hired. And, as bad as Skot and I were, Billy would have to be pretty damn bad not to have worked out.

Billy Mack Hill of Horse Cave, Kentucky. He played my future wife's homecoming dances. Two years my senior, he was as honest and forthright as they came. His height afforded him unfair advantages in arguments, as he could loom over you while stating a position, as well as cloud the fact that Billy could be as nervous as a tomcat. There is no one who knows him who does not like him. Instant thumbnail sketch.

One night, years later, after we'd become Government Cheese and were literally famous for blocks around, Billy was leaving a liquor store with his nightly ration. As is usual around such establishments, a phalanx of pimply Camaro kids were in their rod out front, scoping out the first easy mark who'd go in the store and buy for them. The boys knew Billy from Government Cheese, and Billy knew the boys, basically, because they knew him. A bit of conversation ensued, and Billy was coerced into reentering the liquor store to purchase, I believe, one fifth of Bacardi Light.

The transaction was done, the goods were transferred and the boys scrammed. Billy went home with his own libation and found himself unable to enjoy it. The ramifications of his deed with the youngsters appalled him greatly and wouldn't leave his mind. He curled in horror, a rampage of gnarly scenarios speeding past his mind's eye:

*The kids will spin out in a drunken interstate fatality. The officers will question the one surviving youth, now condemned to a wheelchair for life, paralyzed and learning to paint with his mouth. The cops will ask "Where did you KIDS get the booze?" The young ruffian will reply "Sir, it was Billy Mack Hill, 1373 Center St. Apt. D." Billy would be pilloried by the good people of the town once he left prison a decade later, a shell of his former self. By then, his parents will have long ago committed double suicide in their shame, and his siblings would shun him. The horror . . . The horror . . .*

So Billy made up his mind to find the kids, whatever it took. He left his place and, amazingly enough, traced these unfamiliar fellows down to a young collegiate squat. He burst into their apartment and literally snatched the just-opened bottle from the clutches of its deflowering inebriates. To the slack-jawed amazement of all, Billy threw the exact price of the liquor down on the table, a smack of silver and paper aflutter. Billy mumbled something between an explanation and an apology. Then, he took the bottle home to his lair and drank it quickly, by himself, before its harm could clutch another in this world.

This deed done, and then undone, Billy was once again at peace with his life and surroundings. The sun shone on a bright tomorrow.

Billy had the most raw talent of any member of Government Cheese. His voice was limber and tremulous. It climbed high into

Neil Young territory, then dove into crooner land, far and away the best voice in the band. The bass was never his main instrument. He was an acoustic guitar picker, with a bright, loud, fingerpicking hand. My songs might have been funnier, and I might have written more rockers, but Billy had the poet's touch. Songs we recorded, such as ''Mammaw Drives the Bus'', ''The Shrubbery's Dead'', and ''No Sleeping in Penn Station'' are only the most obvious examples. (Though, unless you're one of the few and the proud who bought those records, none of them are obvious examples, I suppose.)

Billy started like any of us in the '70s, only more so. There's a photo in his high-school yearbook of him playing guitar with some friends at fourteen. His long, limp, dirty-blonde hair hangs blunt-cut just below his eyelids. He looks stoned out of his mind. His jaw is hanging loose, and the basic bell-bottomed impression is that he's just smoked about seven joints, and here he is singing ''Needle and the Damage Done'' with some friends.

Between him and his brother Ned (a talented singer/songwriter in his own right), they had an immense record collection, ranging from the essential Alice Cooper, Black Oak Arkansas and Elton John through the sublime Patsy Cline and Ray Charles, to the inexplicable devotion Billy has for Bobby Goldsboro, notable for such hits as ''Honey'' and ''Watching Scotty Grow''.

Billy had fun as a teenager. He missed REO Speedwagon completely at one Louisville festival and only vaguely remembers Ted Nugent opening the show and screaming *''Loueeville, you muthafucka! Loueeeville, you muthafucka!''* Billy was yet to forgive his oldest brother Randall for getting married the same weekend as Kiss at Freedom Hall. That was in '75. The *Alive!* tour.

In his senior year of high school, Billy's raving came to a decided and very nearly tragic end. One day, as occasionally happens with very skinny folks who smoke, one of Billy's lungs collapsed.

He was rushed to the hospital. The lung was repaired, and permanently attached to the inside wall of the rib cage. While still there in the hospital, the *other* lung collapsed, and the whole reinflation and attachment process had to be repeated.

When he recovered, Billy never got back in the swing of things. His old smoking buddies were anathema now, since nothing smoky—pot, tobacco or otherwise—could ever again infiltrate Billy's fragile sacs. He finished high school all alone, way behind his friends, who'd all split for college. He wound up joining a band, a legendary one for us

Cheesers. All we know is Euphoria was their name, they wore kimonos and played lots of Bachman-Turner Overdrive.

Playing the VFW in Munfordville meant adding a preponderance of Hank Jr. to the set. Billy used to stifle giggles and throw himself headlong into "A Country Boy Can Survive."

Billy bailed out of college to do Euphoria. Mom and Dad weren't happy. His fortunes sank lower when he was edged out of the band in favor of another guitarist. This new fellow actually asked to borrow Billy's Ibanez Les Paul copy, as he himself had nothing so magnificent. Billy, good-naturedly, did loan the Ibanez Les Paul copy to his usurper, who did not return it for a year. When the fellow did bring the guitar back, he had taken the strings off—because, the fellow explained, they were brand new and he wanted to use them on his next instrument as well.

With contemptibles such as that guy to contend with, and doubtless others like him down the road, who needs the music business, right? Fuck that buncha noise! Billy just wound up going to school, at WKU down the road from home, and he set his sights on being a park ranger. Yes, a park ranger, living in a fire tower for eight years at a stretch. He majored in geology and joined the geology club. He drank beer with his buddies, and life got to be essentially all right. It never took much more than good friends and those old scratchy Bobby Goldsboro records to keep Billy reasonably happy. Sure, he would have liked to play in a rock an roll band again, but he didn't *need* it. In the spring of '85, just one semester behind me, Billy Mack Hill was getting out of Western with a BS in Geophysics, and the absolute last thing he needed in his life was any hassle with a rock and roll band.

On that cold cloudy January afternoon when Billy Mack faced me from an opposite couch, he was, best as I could tell, light-years from the easygoing stoner sort he might have been in his youth. It had been a hard, lonely slog since his lungs popped.

Billy Mack Hill, at 24, had hit that horrible period when you question everything and wonder what to put your faith in the same way you travel from bank to bank for the best interest rate. That's a suck age, when you're definitely not a child, not an adolescent nor even really a young adult any more. All you are is a person the same age as other people who are already independently wealthy, or married, or in jail, or dead. And that Billy Mack Hill sitting on our ratty couch was a cautious, nervous man, who got the hell out of the house the minute I stopped talking.

Days went by, and the wily Willis charm lured Billy back to our lair. At last, he agreed to drop by sometime for an informal jam. This commitment came about when he couldn't conceal his joy at finding out all three of us owned *Catholic Boy* by Jim Carroll, and that "People Who Died" was on everybody's desert-island-disc list.

Billy came to town one day with his big Sound City bass cabinet and his runtish Fender Musicmaster bass. He piled them into the seat of his huge, ten-year-old, beat-up Lincoln hillbilly pimpmobile. Billy always drove cars you could fit two other cars into. He's so tall and lanky that he can't fit into anything else. He swung the big black bomb out onto the interstate, the massive bass-amp cabinet rocking forward and backward in the back seat, the bass in the front seat with no case, anchored among tossed-off styrofoam coffee cups in the floorboard.

Horse Cave is thirty miles from Bowling Green, and that gave Billy ample driving time to convince himself he was crazy to even consider this music thing again. *No way! What was I thinking? I'm going home. Straight home right after class. I'll come back home and study, or drink ten beers in front of the television, but no band! I'm not going over to that house!* He vacillated on that point throughout his mid-morning classes. By the end of his short student day, he was fairly committed in his own head to standing us up. Another rock and roll band? Four months before graduation? Hmmmm (Billy thinks very carefully, when he thinks). *NO! Uh-uh! No way! Absolutely not! Been too long! I'm 24. No band! I'm going home and I'll phone apologies. I'll fake an emergency. But NO BAND!*

After classes, he threw his books in the front seat and spun the Lincoln out of town. He got out onto the interstate and made it five miles back toward home. *God, what was I thinking? That was a close one . . . No way. No band! . . .*

He drove a few miles in silence, thinking carefully, like he always tries to.

"AaaahhhSHIT!" He spun the Lincoln in a spray of gravel at one of those U-turn spots with a "No U Turn" sign stuck in it. With a screech of the radials, he headed back into town.

Life can turn on a hairpin, and just as easily on one of those gravel I-65 turnpike capillaries. As the winter sun died early behind Kentucky snow clouds, Billy Mack Hill consecrated that spot in the road and ricocheted his life wild from it. He thought he'd been through the mill already, yet the rollercoaster was just warming up. He came to his first practice.

Right about a year later, on or near that nefarious decision-making spot, Billy's huge mondo pimpmobile stalled out and burst into flames on the side of the road while he frantically rescued his possessions from inside. Make of that what you will.

\* \* \* \*

# 3

# the bay of gigs

Billy had immediate reason to regret his decision. From the first, rehearsals were their usual ragtag, chaotic affairs. No drummer again, since Toby'd drifted away for some reason. We just made a lot of noise as the three of us, in the kitchen. Skot and I, Billy discovered, would forget to turn our amps off, leaving them humming next to the fridge all night long, their little red lights glowing in the dark. Much to Billy's astonishment, Skot had booked a gig almost immediately: the Sigma Phi Epsilon basement, Thursday, January 25th, 1985.

He couldn't believe it. We knew not one single song all the way through, and the gig was less than two weeks away. Guys! I hate to be the new guy turned asshole all of the sudden, but we don't have a *drummer yet. Hello!*

Skot and I couldn't care less. Okay, no drummer. We'll work through that one. We'd been so close so many times to having a real band that we'd become all too aware of the Catch-22 involved. You can't get gigs without a band, and you can't start a band without the lure of gigs. This time, by God, *there would be a gig!*

The name came from a humble block of U.S.-surplus cheese sitting on the kitchen counter. Tommy Bray, a third roomie in the house, had gotten it from his grandmother. She was always giving us government surplus stuff—butter, cheese, peanut butter. It was just another brand. If it wasn't Parkay, or Cost-Cutter, it must be the government stuff Bray was getting. No long-term thinking went into it. It just sounded good at the time. *Government Cheese.* I thought it had a nice ring to it. It's easy to remember. We later won a best-band-name contest in a Nashville newspaper critic's poll. Also, at the time, it sounded *political,* and therefore *cool.*

Years later, I'd go through a massive sociopolitical guilt trip, since the name was a poverty metaphor slapped on four suburban white college guys who hardly merited such a tag. In that sense, it made us look crass to folks who sniff out metaphors at that level. People from northern climes caught onto that more quickly and vehemently than southerners. I certainly didn't think about it at the time. To an eastern seaboarder, perhaps, a block of government cheese is a graphic illustration of urban deprivation and economic despair. To us in Kentucky, it was the stuff Grandma gave you, and it was great on Ritz.

Incidentally, we were never alone on the idea. There have been bands named Government Cheese: in Colorado, Chicago, several in California, one in Ohio called Free Cheese, and of course, our old nemeses, *those adorable tykes,* Government Issue.

Their logo, by utter coincidence, was frighteningly similar to ours, with military block-letter feel. I guess it was the obvious way to go. Skot met the lead singer once in New York City. He was crouched in an alleyway, scowling and looking away, and all he would say was "Yeah, I heard of you guys. We've sold more records than you." Harrumph.

January 1985. Government Cheese debuted on the aforementioned Sig Ep party date. We knew ten songs, no endings, and pretty much cleared the room inside of ten minutes. Only a couple of loyal standbys made it through most of the "performance" and absolutely no one was there at the end.

I'm sure many bands have appalling tales to tell of their debuts. Horrific, embarrassing comings-out where the first and foremost emotion is regret, wrapped like a python around you, squeezing all confidence and optimism out of your soul before the first chorus comes around. Ha! I say. I'll stack Government Cheese's beginning against anyone's as one of the true worsts in mankind. It was not just a bad GIG. It went beyond mere gigs or gigness. There was an intensity of "worst" in that room that connected me to history.

The Government Cheese debut was Bay of Pigs bad. It was *Lusitanian.* A true awful. It might take a history of clinical depression to understand how something that macabre, that dire, could also be . . . *fun,* in a strange way.

The temperature in the room was right around forty-five degrees. We played in our coats. The lights were dim, and, from the first notes, shadowy figures headed for the doors. The next two hours were a gothic horror tale of clangy, out-of-tune, untogether sounds kerranging from uproariously misdialed amps. Grown men were reduced to little boys barely making pathetic, gnarly, vocal croaks into the two microphones we had.

The drummer that night is a lost chapter in Cheese lore. His name now twists down the street of Cheese history like a thrown-away newspaper.

Brett Ballard was an old friend of mine from high school, another Madisonville escapee. He was quite a jazz drummer. A jazz drummer, mind you, with brushes and suchlike. He didn't listen to rock and roll; Show tunes and pop standards were more to his liking. He and I had a mutual admiration for Bobby Darin, particularly the great song "Artificial Flowers" which ought to have been a bigger hit than "Mack the Knife". Brett stood about five feet four, kept his hair neatly cropped, and, with his wire-rimmed glasses, looked to be much younger than his twenty-four years.

He barely spoke, and kept a dry, tangy wit in the corner of his brain. He'd never heard the Clash, except for the two big hits. He'd never heard of this "People Who Died" song we were doing. His forte was the Manhattan Transfer. All that night he sat behind his elegant little jazzer's trap kit with this look on his face like a deer caught in headlights. It was the look of a man completely mind-blown that we were actually doing this in front of people.

U2's "I Will Follow" was at least a song he'd heard of, but nothing prepared him for the anti-jazz disaster it devolved into that night. It started out okay—the intro's hard to screw up—and then took a left turn into bad Dead-jam land. It hadn't been intended that way, but no one could remember the arrangement, and no one took charge. The jamming got worse and worse, and wouldn't end. Just when you thought it was over, drawing to a merciful close, the damnable thing would whip back up again. I was playing the two blues licks I discovered I really knew how to play. At home I knew around forty. In that cold basement, it got whittled down to two really quickly.

Skot was standing stock still in front, not moving a muscle. Far from a front man yet, Skot was merely terrified this particular evening, terrified and cold. Billy Mack was furious, blaming Skot for the whole debacle, since his personality seemed to be the dominant one between the two of us. Billy had to be restrained from going at Skot at one point in the evening. I was dipping my hands in a bucket of warm water between songs, trying to keep my icy fingers from stiffening any further than they already were. I was hearing the toilets of time flushing in my brain.

On top of everything else—bad playing, friends leaving in droves, near-freezing temperatures—Brett Ballard had to deal with something else: Toby, who'd come primed and ready to "sit in". Midway through the gig, this was seeming like a damn fine idea, too. Toby would liven things up, at the very least. Sometime in the second set, Toby got his wish, while Brett went off to find something to slit his wrists with.

Toby thundered into Brett's delicate little kit with a terrifying ferocity. He made short work of a snare head Brett probably hadn't changed, nor had to, in five years. Then he went after the high-hat, the kick-drum pedal, the whole works.

Upon hearing this calamity being wreaked, Brett rushed back in the room with an expression on his face like your neighbor would get if you just went next door and started clobbering his dog with a mallet. In a loud, tremulous voice, he relieved Toby of the drum chair, effective immediately. An brief altercation ensued, and—once it had blown over—Toby was relegated to singing backup. Every other verse, he'd turn around to Brett and say "C'mon man, give me one more chance."

After two hours of all this, Brett just all of the sudden jumped up and quickly packed all his gear. I've never in ten years of playing seen a drummer pack his gear that quickly. He was out the back door, slipping across the icy parking lot, thrusting the cases into his car, and then he was gone. I didn't see Brett Ballard again for a year. On a campus of ten thousand students, he disappeared better than a government witness against the mob. He returned no phone calls and skulked furtively back and forth to classes, hugging walls and looking over his shoulder lest we find him.

And it was over. One gig. That's all we got. We couldn't even break up right. I suppose a band has to actually be together a while before it can break up. Brett had run away, and while Billy stayed in touch socially, there seemed to be an understanding. It was done and over.

January became February. February became March.

I found my time at Lee's Famous Recipe to be mercifully short. I actually recall thinking it a slight pity to be leaving the place, as I was just getting the routine down. I could put the chicken in the bag with all the extra-crispy ingredients and shake the bag for the exact length of time and I finally knew how to take the drippings out of the bottom catch-pan beneath the deep fryer and make the next day's gravy with it.

I left Lee's because I'd fulfilled that aforementioned silly notion of finding a job in my college-bred career field. I nailed a nighttime disc jockey job at a country AM station.

It was the first and oldest station operating in Bowling Green. WLBJ. That stood for (so they said) "Where Life Brings Joy", as if anybody'd decided that ahead of time, before they'd actually gotten stuck with the call letters. A pastime was to think of better things it could stand for. You're already thinking of the obvious one or two.

1985 was the lowest point in the history of country music, and I got to hear every goddamn bit of it. Nashville had just discovered the synthesizer, and the Old Guard were falling asleep at the wheel. Lots of undeniably great artists were making the worst music of their careers, all at the same time. I was amazed at the obviousness of it all. Every song sounded exactly the same. I don't mean obsequiously similar, stuck in a safe rut. I mean *exactly the same!* People who complain too much about today's cookie-cutter country music don't remember 1985 as well as I do. There are reasons that all those young new acts burst on the scene at once. True, they're easier to look at, but it's also because the old artists were flatulating Pompeii dust in twenty-four part harmony. I don't mean to be so dogmatic about it, but I had to listen to those records five times a day, six days a week. It damaged my brain, and so, to this day, I have a bit of a horse to flog regarding it.

All the songs had "heart" in the title, which is a universal music thing that has forever mystified me. The only thing good about the word "heart" is that the middle of it sings really well. You still have to end the syllable with that problematical "T", though. And from a reading standpoint, it's an ugly word. Look at it. Heart. Heart. Heart.

While I ran this live country station at night, there was also an automated easy-listening FM monstrosity to watch over. Four huge reel-to-reel tape decks stacked six feet high, with two cart machines and a computer. We called it Darth because of the Darth Vader helmet set atop the whole thing like some Polynesian idol. Darth's eyes lit up when it was time to record network news off the satellite. When reels of music ran out, you replaced them and refiled the spent ones on the shelf so that they could be played all too soon later on. That was BJ-97.

A good dee-jay would be listening to both stations simultaneously and keeping a good watch on the FM. Not me, buddy. The FM was always "silencing out", which was what happened when the computer went to two sources of sound in a row, and there was nothing to play on either one. Then, a buzzer went off, and the computer began spitting out paper.

The station manager was an old Navy radio engineer, R. Dean Maggard. He looked exactly like an older Major Dad, with a thin mustache seemingly painted on his upper lip, a military haircut and bearing, and a severely no-bullshit facial expression all the time. He was hyper as a jackrabbit, and by turns conciliatory or harsh. One minute he'd be laughing uproariously at a joke you don't tell in front of the women, the next minute he'd be so pissed off he'd race through the control room without saying a word. His office was ingeniously placed on an unavoidable trajectory between the control room and all the other offices. Whenever the microphone was on, it was quite common to hear doors slamming and people walking by, jabbering on in whatever four-letter dialect felt right for the moment.

Dean Maggard was not a bad fellow, but he was not a well one either. He was a casualty of the filterless Luckies generation, and his lungs were barely working. He was in and out of the hospital, and he kept air purifiers quietly humming in every room of the station.

When he was in action, though, it was hard to look at him and think he ever needed a hospital stay. He was a thunderball of energy, especially when working on that old AM transmitter, an immense, tube-driven relic from the fifties. I think he might have thought that as long as that transmitter kept its big tubes glowing, Dean Maggard himself might go on another day as well.

Sometimes the air purifiers didn't suck dust hard enough for him, and then Mr. Maggard used to vacuum the walls. He'd walk up and down the hallways with his Electrolux hose attachment, running the nozzle from floor to ceiling over the shiny painted cinderblocks. After a few months, I learned that a day when he vacuumed above the floor was not the day you wanted to talk to him. And on a day when he put on the sharp-edge attachment and got those hard-to-reach corners, you stayed way the hell out of his way.

The program director was a saint. Rich Ryan was his real name. His air name was Keith Richards, and I don't think much of our listening audience got the joke. Keith who? He did the mornings, pretty much ran all the programming aspects of the station, and was a genial smiling good-cop balance for Mr. Maggard. He was in his late-thirties or early forties and seemed not to do much except run that station. He looked amazingly like Robert Tilton, the televangelist, more so even than Maggard looked like Major Dad. Unlike Bob, though, he was basically a nice, smiling, unmarried guy who probably phoned his mom twice a week, was in bed by nine, and didn't have the time or money to do much more.

It was Maggard's sad fate that his right-hand man smoked two and a half packs of Pall Mall unfiltereds per day. Keith said he was glad I smoked, because he'd been feeling a bit lonely at the station, vice-wise. Between the two of us, poor Mr. Maggard had to gulp a mouthful of fresh air before dashing through the control room.

The sound of that AM was so spooky. You could be half a mile from the tower and it sounded like you were barely picking the signal up over thirty miles of Texas plain. It was a lovely, warm sound, really. On night power, we barely covered most of Bowling Green. After ten at night, I'd play anything I wanted to. I used to play Jason and the Scorchers (who'd signed with a major label and shortened their name, to everyone's indulgence and understanding) and Arlo Guthrie (with whom I'd sign off on Friday nights with the entire "Alice's Restaurant"). It didn't matter, because it would have been a true miracle for more than a few hundred people to be listening at that hour with that wattage. The sound of that station suggested you were listening to thirty-year-old signals being bounced off a UFO back to earth. And I was Tommy in the Evening, your friendly Ranch Party Martian in the Night.

Joe King's name seemed to keep cropping up. He was one of those guys I knew in the halls. When you have the same major, you become at least a face to all the other faces. He was a nice guy, good-looking. Everybody liked him. He was competitive, fiery-tempered, but also friendly and gregarious. If he was in a room, you knew it usually. He ran six miles a day, quite the Olympian, all blonde hair and cheekbones. Guys liked him because he was a real guy. Girls liked him because he was a real guy.

He played drums in Western's marching band (where he knew Brett Ballard), he was president of his fraternity, and he was a double major in speech and broadcasting. Solidly on the way to some sort of financial success somewhere, the kind of student that *teachers* stopped in the hallways to chat with, the last thing in the world Joe King was was any sort of sneering, finger-snapping upturned-collar type rock and roll rebel. This was no malcontent punk. Not that the crowd I was running with were nihilistic Sid Viciouses, but we *were* dressing as nuns a bit. Joe King was as normal as normal gets without being abnormal.

I was already out of school and had no business on campus, but I started showing up in Joe's classes—this rapidly blinking skinny guy Joe kinda knew—pulling up a desk next to him and passing him notes. "Wanna join a band, man?" "Here's our set list." "My name's Tommy, you know." With the typical degree of subtlety I was known for, that's how I first approached him.

Well over a century ago, the first Joseph Warren King settled in Cincinnati and started making, among other things, gunpowder. The Civil War came along, and the King Powder Company became a primo source of nut-busting Yankee firepower. Quite the industrial complex arose out of this, with several side businesses. The powder company became the core of a small but profitable empire for a succession of Joseph Warren Kings.

As mills were needed for this sort of business in the beginning, the complex took root next to the river, on an island. King's Island.

One day, generations later, the final King left the property. The powder company is long gone, but the name of the island has stuck. Someone in the family tree sold the property to a development company and the King's Island Amusement Park was built. The modern-day Kings make no cabbage off your riding The Beast, nor does your consumption of Little Kings Cream Ale do anything for their pocketbooks. It's just the name on a bottle now.

Joseph Warren King III first came to know things in Wilmington, Delaware, just across the river from Philadelphia. He was actually the sixth or seventh JWK, but someone down the line had named his son Warren Joseph or something like it, and you have to start over if you miss one. Executive promotions moved the family to Hendersonville, Tennessee while Joe was a sub-teen. Hendersonville is a bedroom community of Nashville, with a country star taking his or her suburban bliss approximately every three hundred yards. Joe played the piano and marching band drums, and worked at Twitty City, Conway Twitty's tourist Mecca right up the road from Joe's house.

The late, great Conway lived with his family on the grounds of the whole tourism complex. Occasionally, as is a successful man's right, he liked to stroll about in his front yard. In those days, the differences between Conway's front yard and yours were staggering.

You couldn't buy cotton candy in your front yard, nor did eighty middle-aged women from Wisconsin lose their collective shit when you stepped out your front door. Things like this happened every day at Conway's house. And when The Best Friend A Song Ever Had took it upon himself to stroll around his grounds, Joseph Warren King III would pull duty as one of the big-boned young men charged with peeling Lucy Mae Citizen off the man, and shielding him as well, from the jealous husband who wanted to be down the street at Barbara Mandrell's One-Hour Photo because he was sure she showed up there every day. Joe would also go on the road and sell T-shirts at Conway's arena shows.

The original CMT (Country Music Television) was part of Conway's front yard as well. At the time, CMT bore no more resemblance to its modern self than any embryo newly latched onto a tele-uterine wall. CMT basically fit into a closet is what I'm saying, and, when Joe became—like me—a broadcasting major, he gained that all-important resume experience by running the switcher for some of CMT's maiden telecasts. For those without my peerless broadcasting experience, let me explain that a switcher is a big board with lots of knobs and buttons and lights and joysticks and doohickeys, and you play one video on one screen while you cue up another video on another screen.

Then there was that special place on the board where you kept the Darvon bottle handy, because in 1983 there were only five country videos, and they were all the worst bunch of shot-on-videotape garbage you'd ever not want to see. A twelve-hour shift at CMT was blessed assurance you'd see everything thrice. You'd know all the lyrics after the first day. You also got to see the same mail-order commercial for Cristy Lane's *One Day at a Time* album enough times to memorize the segues between songs.

Somehow it was borne out that Joe knew all of Journey's material on the piano. He could play "Faithfully" rather, well, faithfully. He'd learned early how young maidens get hot when a young blonde guy sits down at the spinet and tinkles out "Three Times a Lady" or some tripe like that. When I learned this, I briefly considered life without Joe.

Skot wasn't without trepidation either. This was a major sin. Of course, none of us were in any superb position to label anyone Mr. White-bread Mainstream. Skot was barely cooler than Joe, and that boiled down to a choice in sunglasses. Me? I was spinning T.G. Sheppard records every night 'til midnight. Who was I going to criticize?

I got him to come over to the house eventually and set up his drum kit in our kitchen. The first song we ever played, I believe, was "Tell It To The Judge On Sunday" by the Long Ryders. Joe had never heard it, but it's a real count-it-off-and-go sort of thing. The minute I heard him drum wiped out any Journey worries. It was one of those moments you get in life, when you'd better have your antenna whipped out and shiny, ready to savor.

We played all afternoon and into the evening. Any doubts about anything went out the window. I felt in all my overweening heart that I'd finally found the rock upon which to build my church. It was a completely positive wash. The whole kitchen was a big loud barrelhouse of possibility. The windows rattled. Things shook off the shelves.

It was a sunny day, in that first completely warm week of 1985, that week when you can look at the bare branches and know buds will be there in a matter of days. You can smell April showers coming. You know you can get the short pants out. It won't be long now. In the kitchen then, on 13th Street, two blocks from Lee's Famous Recipe Fried Chicken, in Bowling Green, Kentucky, my band, *my band*, that fabled thing I'd been looking for, grasping at, since I was thirteen, was born.

\* \* \* \*

# 4

# defibrillation

We played the Alibi, of all places, a couple of weeks later. For some reason, we wore matching Michael Jackson *Beat It* T-shirts. By this point, in '85, you could get them on mark-down for fifty cents each, I believe. How the mighty fall. How soon Big Brother moves on.

A band at the Alibi was a rarity, for several damn good reasons. There was no PA system, and for that matter, no stage. The place was designed for the dancers to be the stars. Ah ah ah ah stayin' alive. We played on the carpeted floor next to *and below* the dancers, looking up at them. People, in the course of the evening, fell off the dance floor and onto us. How the mighty drunk sorority wenches fall. How soon big brothers help them up and offer to take them home. It was another fraternity function, but this time one of those affairs where members had to stay. They couldn't leave. If they left, they got fined. Really. Good for us, bad for them.

I was growing my hair, chain-smoking Marlboros and cloves, staying as jacked on Kahlua and coffee as I could afford to, and bashing my trebly guitar *while they couldn't leave! HA! HA!* I remember hitting a chord that night at the Alibi, and this girl screamed, put her hands over her ears and even doubled over a little bit. Ooops, I guess I had the treble on 10. Sorry, honey.

I'd already totally brainwashed myself into believing this band could work. It's amazing what a man can convince himself of when he wants something hard and bad enough. We didn't sound like shit. We sounded *utterly* like shit. It was vile. Tempo, pitch, tuning, harmonies—name a way a band can be bad and I guarantee we were pegging the meter.

And to me, it mattered not. I could hear nothing other than what what we *could* be. What we actually sounded like *at the moment* was immaterial, the sound in my head was the first Clash album in a sea of the sweetest tea. I saw strength and gray matter among us in doses enough to hurdle such trivialities as whether or not we—at the moment—sounded like tone-deaf, cloven-hooved, braying ruminants playing instruments in separate rooms. I was grooving on the future, baby.

I was *giddy* about that band, and for other reasons as well, notably sleep deprivation.

I was now the WLBJ morning man, getting twenty extra hours a week and job security, knowing I was the only person in town stupid enough to take the job for minimum by-God wage. They couldn't fire me—who'd possibly replace me? I'd make them wish they could, though. I was playing records on the air and leaving my mic open, offering running commentary on anything from the banalities of the arrangement to the cliches miring the song itself. I'd play Anne Murray's "Time, Don't Run Out on Me" and breathe heavy throughout it. Old ladies were calling me up and cussing me out.

The turnover was ridiculous at that station, even by broadcasting's notoriously nomadic standard. Four months into the job, I was a goddamn senior member on staff. I was morning man, interim news director, gardener, you name it. I once mowed the yard and cut the cables to the south tower, knocking both stations off the air. I thought Maggard was going to vacuum the roof over that one.

I didn't care. I would work in a bathing suit and sunglasses and never explain why. I'd run the copier dry making Government Cheese posters. I'd suck helium and read the weather forecast sounding like Donald Duck. Village idiocy as a serious long-term art form. If success in this genre means that you become an idiot, I guess I was going at a fair clip.

As a true idiot might, I believed my band was GREAT and we'd KICK YOUR ASS. Chaos philosophy. If we suck, then by God, let's go out there and SUCK! Let it be bad, and let it be bad where people can PAY to SEE it! Maybe some folks will come just to see HOW BAD IT IS! If people were going to be appalled by this band, then let's make them frightened, so deeply nauseated, they won't ever forget it, and they'll tell all their friends about it. And, as in chaos, some pattern will emerge. The telltale spirals. The possible proof of God Herself.

I'd come out with slices of cheese and pelt the crowd. I'd yell things derogatory to anything or anybody white-bread and Journey-loving, and then I'd start playing guitar without looking at the other

guys. They'd haplessly plunge in. What else could they do? One guy
had jumped from the jetty with his rope looped around everyone
else's belt. If one was going to drown, everybody was going to drown.
*HA! HA!* Skot would flail about, as he was starting to move around a
bit. Joe would plunge blithely in. Billy would scowl, convinced we
were all nuts.

At the time we had a sort-of floating fifth member, Scott
Brantley, a par-excellence conga/timbale/every-weird-Latin-percuss-
ion-device kind of guy. Years later, I would have really dug what he
was adding to the sound. At the time, though, timbales and Ramones
covers didn't seem to be jelling. A few gigs later, Scott drifted away.

We played the intermission entertainment for a staid Greek Week
Spring Sing competition. They'd expected something nice, and here
we were. I threw more cheese and it came back unwrapped, squares
of processed American sticking to my sweaty cheeks. Don't ask me
why I was throwing cheese in the first place. All I can tell you is that
it seemed like a good idea at the time.

Billy had a—I swear—four-foot long guitar cord. He couldn't
reach the mike and still play from where his bass amp was. He had to
sing two numbers, and he kept unplugging himself. I kept unplugging
myself as well. At one point, I remember—during "I Will
Follow"—we both unplugged ourselves at the same time. Suddenly
there was just vocals and drums! I began doing some strange duck-
dance across the stage, screaming "Fuck it!" at the top of my lungs.
In the future, remember, screaming the "F" word at a Greek Week
Spring Sing gets a lot of Buffies put out with you. I'm not saying you
should care; I'm just saying that's what happens.

I managed to lose the only guitar pick I'd brought, and I wound up
raking my forefinger across the guitar, sending little spraylets of blood
all over my instrument and all over the stage. I saved the bloodstains
on my guitar for weeks, all brown and grotesque, as a kind of talisman.

We finished up our little six-song set with "Louie Louie" as was
only fitting. They all got up to dance, because "Louie Louie" is a
trance-inducing hymn for the legions, and it's hard to play it so badly
they don't dance at all, though I'm sure we brushed up against that
barrier. It is, however, *all* they danced to. Otherwise, they shouted
"You suck!" and wondered why on earth we were playing a country-
western version of "Jump" by Van Halen.

May 9, 1985. Thursday of finals week, we played the Alibi again.
This is the first show of which an audiotape exists. (A video copy of

the Van Meter show is now long lost.) It was the first show we ever did where we just booked the club and promoted it. It wasn't Alpha Kappa Whatever presents Government Cheese, it was Government Cheese, period.

School was over. Billy and Joe were both graduating. Skot should have been, but it looked like it might take years for him, at the rate he was going. Joe and I talked as we loaded out. I was telling him for the thousandth time that I was game for keeping the band going over the summer if he was keen in like manner. I mean, I was into it, you know, if, like, you were too, and maybe we could, like, keep it together and, you know, play some and, you know, uh, like, keep it together, maybe, I mean, I'm into it if you are, man.

"Of course." Joe replied. I'm pretty sure he didn't mean it. If he had a brain in his head, he didn't mean it.

We booked a gig playing Billy's Geology Club picnic, the Geofest. Commiserate with cavers. Heft a hearty stein with dye-tracers. Oh, the humanity! Joe couldn't make it because of a—ahem—job interview. To hell with him, I thought. We don't need *that* traitor. We'll play the gig anyway, *sans* drums. Where's it written you need a drummer? (Somewhere, I'm sure.)

You haven't lived a full life until you've heard a five-minute version of "I Will Follow" without any drums at all. You think you've known suffering. You don't know a damn thing 'til you've sat through that. We vowed to play until no one was paying attention to us at all. It took about twenty minutes, as I recall.

Joe had his spin in the road just as Billy had, that moment when he chose life as a Cheesed person on this orb, when he cast his lot with greasy bosom butt buddies and turned his back on civilized options.

His interview was for a job in Oklahoma, where the wind comes sweepin' 'cross the plain. It was a television station. Joe was doing what I'd done, that same old "Well, duh, I majored in broadcasting, I'd better find a job there *ho de do de do*" sort of attitude. That kind of thinking gets you signing-on a country AM for minimum wage. That's where that thinking gets you.

Everyone at this Okie television station wanted to die. Skot at Rafferty's had been in heaven compared to these unsmiling dacron-neckwear types. Joe found himself being taken from super to super, meeting everybody. He was being *shown around*. He had the job. He wasn't being interviewed, he was being piped aboard. Welcome to our unsmiling suicidal Oklahoma television station. Report our news. Smell our wheat. Tornadoes! Rodeo mishaps! Oh my!

Joe had quit the band. Of course, he hadn't bothered to tell us that yet. All things in good time. I suppose he was going to call me from Tulsa and say ''Nice knowing ya . . . '' But, best as I can tell, I looked a damn sight prettier when Joe left that station.

He never mentioned quitting, I knew nothing about it for years. He simply came back home and we just kept practicing, and somewhere in the recesses of Joe's mind, he'd decided that this Government Cheese thing was going to have to work.

Joe decided he saw something to believe in. We weren't too alike—we'd have hated each other in high school—but something clicked. We filled in each other's cracks. We never talked about it, but we felt some sort of commitment accrete.

In the early eighties, a regular family of jammers travelled from club to club in Bowling Green. Everybody knew everybody. When one band got tired of playing, or lost their regular gig for whatever reason, then next week you'd see a new band, made up of the same folks, plus whoever else needed a gig too.[1]

Los Juages were B.G.'s chops band. They played the Lit Club week in and week out. A favorite trick of theirs was to get people dancing by playing something they had to just to keep the gig, and next, they'd swing into ''Long Distance Runaround'' and there would then be a floorful of dancers trying to figure out a step that goes with *that* prog-rock monster. Smart folks got off the floor immediately, and it would whittle down to a couple of Fort Campbell soldiers trying to impress their dates by acting like they knew how to dance to Yes.

Sgt. Arms put out a single. Their singer, Bill Lloyd, took his guitar and moved to Nashville, where he'd eventually become half of Foster and Lloyd and have success with his own solo pop records. Others would make it down to Nashville to test the big waters as well.

---

1. Previous drafts of this section had me attempting to name every single talented and deserving musician in Bowling Green. It ran many pages. All editors assured me it was a sweet gesture and lousy reading. So there you go. Paper beats rock. Readability beats gesture. The cited talents are mere examples, a few among many.

Itchy Brother played around some. That was the group of cousins and friends from Metcalfe County who, according to local lore, had come within a hair's breadth of being signed to Led Zeppelin's Swan Song label about ten years before. Now they mostly had paying country gigs. One of them drummed for Sylvia, two of them played behind Ronnie McDowell, they got by doing whatever. When time allowed, they played together. In the future, they'd junk all the side projects and change their names to the Headhunters, and, eventually, the Kentucky Headhunters.

New Grass Revival boasted what may well be the best mandolinist in the world. I don't know much about mandolinists, but I have heard Sam Bush, and if the world can produce evidence of a better mandolinist, I want to hear it. NGR was a host of stalwart musicians, including Bela Fleck on the banjo. Their gigs in Bowling Green were like going to church. The world's only bluegrass/reggae/jazz/gospel/R&B/vocal quartet. John Cowan's soul vocals were a quantum leap for bluegrass. Pat Flynn was one of the top acoustic guitarists in the nation. A New Grass gig meant you'd see every hippie from Edmonson, Barren, Hart and Simpson counties that you hadn't seen since the last show.

Then you had the Ken Smith Band.

Ken, Byron House, Jonell Mosser and Jeff Jones. Weddings, parties, anything. They played anywhere, anytime. Ken was a true blues man, the guy who'd show you the difference between the Albert King style and the Freddie King style. Byron was a bass playing savant. He could do that Entwistle thing where his fingers produced absolute thunder but his body didn't move at all. You look at it and it doesn't seem possible.

Jonell Mosser was already a legend. The same way people talk about Robert Johnson selling his soul at the crossroads, folks openly speculated whether Janis Joplin's soul had bounced across a continent into Jonell's receptive bosom at the instant Janis' junk and Southern Comfort-frozen body had hit the motel-room floor. That may sound overly dramatic but it's the truth. When Jonell sang, people shut up and flowers grew faster.

The Ken Smith Band became tired of trucking from date to date, and so Ken took it upon himself to make that unholy transformation, from musician to clubowner. In '83, he opened up his own place in a building behind Mariah's on State Street. He called it Picasso's.

You sunk down a flight of steps to go in. The 'Picasso's' signature, underscored with a paintbrush, was everywhere. A couple of dozen tables, a mirror ball, lights, mondo PA, a black-and-white tiled dance floor and a small, barely adequate stage in the corner. That was Picasso's. It was loud, smelled of spilt beer at all times, and was instantly the best place in town.

Five nights a week, the Ken Smith Band held court there. Freed from the rigors of putting their equipment up and tearing it down endlessly, they dug in and entrenched themselves. Within six months of setting up shop, the Ken Smith Band swelled from an amiably spartan combo to a true eighties monstrosity. Banks of keyboards anchored each side of the tiny stage, along with electronic drums, lights and foot pedals—Jonell barely had room to dance around.

Monday nights at Picasso's were up for grabs. Ernie Small might play. Tim Krekel would come up from Nashville. Maybe Clayton Payne would bring his acoustic guitar in. It was an easy gig because the Ken Smith Band were loath to move any of their gear. You walked in, plugged into their stuff and wailed. It was a breeze.

Ken and I had known each other since the summer of '84, when I'd won a Picasso's joke contest singing a novelty song about Michael Jackson. He knew my weakness for rock lore and he'd hold me in thrall, telling me stories of how he'd seen *Zeppelin in '70 at the Atlanta Pop Festival* and how he'd seen *Hendrix . . . twice!*

We ran into one another in Fountain Square Park around lunchtime one early summer day. By this point Government Cheese had played the Alibi, played on campus a couple of times, been featured in some TV student's video project, and were making quite a rep for ourselves as Bowling Green's (gulp) *PUNK* band. Ken was intrigued. Hell, he was thinking, if it sells drinks, it sells drinks.

Monday, July 8th, 1985. The beginning of a great adventure, the ribbon-cutting on the longest-running bar tab I've ever maintained.

I think Ken expected us to put about forty people in the club, all coming to see us the same way people slow down when they pass a car wreck. They want to see the carnage. It's not cool to admit it, but they're looking and thinking *cool, man! Blood!* Well, word of our carnage must have spread. The club was crammed. And it was a toss-up as to who was more surprised—us or Ken.

Skot was turning into a front man to be reckoned with. Always athlctic, he had stamina not usually seen in musicians. He cycled a ridiculous amount of miles every day. Don't call it bike-riding. It's cycling, with tight black pants and water-bottles and air-pumps to bludgeon untethered Great Danes with. Cycling. Skot and Gus Moore and other Nat's type people would be doing insane cross-country *cycling* trips when they could have been home smoking cigarettes. Different strokes.

The benefits of such aerobic thigh-tightening showed in Skot's performance. He shrewdly masked any and all freshman vocal shortcomings with a boggling jump-spin-dive stage persona. Looking at him, it was tough to believe that six months ago he'd been too terrified to move. He was all over the place, as often off the stage as on it. Leaping on table tops, flailing about on the floor, spinning on his back, doing the split-jumps. I got winded just watching him.

Billy was doing his bizarre innate dance. From the knees down he was completely still, but his torso spun like a whirly top, his hips made one circle underneath his shoulders, which were circling a half-turn behind his hip swivel. Sometimes, he'd lean against the wall and bend forward from the waist, flying back straight up again in time with the music, like one of those plastic birds with colored water in their bellies. You tip them to get started, and they dip in and out of a water glass indefinitely.

Joe was the smiling straight man. Blonde hair and a muscle shirt. I found my presence up front was an obstacle for lacy nubiles dancing and preening for His Joeness.

Joe said he liked watching me "rock out" because it was amusing, in the same way you might like watching a nun try to mount a Harley. I didn't take to the physical part of it instinctively, in other words, but in my defense, I must say I did throw myself wholeheartedly into the affair.

My dance was a combination of the classic up and down pogo with whatever body position I could put myself into. Being onstage kicked my mild Tourette syndrome, mercifully fading as it had over the years, back into high gear. To mask the eye-blinking and head-jerking, I took to making whatever funny face I could conjure. Weird Marty Feldman smiles and bugged-out Charlie Manson eyes were two standard riffs for me.

I came home that first Picasso's night with the board tape and played it over and over, digging our slamfest melange of obscure covers and things we'd written ourselves. I was on cloud nine. It's hard to describe now what it meant to play that beer-joint downtown. We'd played a *real club,* where people went to *hear music.* We'd played original material and put maybe two hundred people in the place. We almost certainly were going to be asked back. It was like we'd just played the Garden or something. It was that big a deal.

I'd never heard a PA-system board tape of the band, with all that reverb on everything. We sounded so big league. You could barely hear my guitar, because on a board tape you hear only microphones fed into the sound-mixing board, and the loudest thing onstage has the lowest mike send signal, and I was pretty much the loudest guy at every Cheese gig.

I floated into bed having to be up in two hours to wake up a whole different segment of Bowling Green, give 'em their rise-n-shine T.G. Sheppard and the current temp. I felt we had done one unthinkable, actually bringing our brand of controlled idiocy to a real place like Picasso's. Now it was time for the next unthinkable.

A record.

From all those first gigs, we took out only enough money to buy something needed: a guitar cord, sticks, strings, etc., and all surplus wealth went underneath Skot's turntable. A forty here, a fifty there. It added up.

I'd gotten to be friends with Byron, which was a treat. His prowess on bass was formidable, and anyone who chose in Bowling Green to braid the bottom third of his hair—and dye each braid a different color of the rainbow—intrigued me. Now that the Cheese was doing every other Monday at Picasso's, we had occasion to get acquainted.

He took me over to Marc Owens' basement, to the studio Sgt. Arms built. Part of Bill Lloyd's *Feeling the Elephant* was recorded there. Marc was another fellow who'd intrigued me from a distance. A tall fellow with mid-sixties pop-length hair, not quite to the shoulders. I remember first noticing him because he always drummed like he was listening for a train. He would have this expression on his face, mouth open, brow furrowed, head slightly cocked to one side, like he could hear the 9:35 to Barstow coming over the prairie or something.

Byron took it upon himself to occasionally keep me cheered up that summer of '85. The band would play every second week at Picasso's, and once in a blue moon we'd rehearse. Other than that, life was what life is in Bowling Green, a college town in the summertime, when you have to be up at four and on the air playing synth-driven country records.

For the first year and a half of Government Cheese, I'd get a full night's sleep maybe every four days. More than once, I went three solid days and nights with no sleep at all. No naps, no nods, nothing.

I'd walk into walls, lose track of conversations and skitter off into stream-of-consciousness. Sometimes I'd fall asleep in mid-sentence, like Keith Richards and Jerry Garcia are both said to occasionally do.

By mid-summer, it was settled that Byron was the producer for Government Cheese's debut vinyl, whatever the hell that was going to be.

He was always playing this new band he was crazy about. The bass player in the band appealed to him. The Red Hot Chili Peppers was their name. I remember Byron going to see them in Louisville, at Tewligan's, and coming home rather amused. "How were they?" I'd asked.

Byron replied very slowly because Byron said everything very slowly. He talked so slow and mellow that before long you'd always find yourself talking slow and mellow back to him. When we got going, it would take ten minutes to get five sentences exchanged.

"Tommy," he said, "it was really interesting. They came out for the encore with *socks on their dicks* and nothing else." He paused, and then slowly added, "Never seen that one before."

A long pause. "No, Byron . . . ," I'd say, "never seen that one before."

(Pause) "Nope . . . " he'd say, "Nope . . . that's right . . ." It would go on forever like that.

Billy was living on pins and needles. He'd taken the worst off-campus apartment I'd never seen, one impossibly damp room in the basement of some courtyard apartments. It was more a cell than an apartment. You had to descend a concrete staircase full of muck to get to his door. You could clean it, sweep it, mop it with hot Lysol water, and it was still muck.

He was in the back corner of the place, facing a rear gravel road and some underbrush. You could get murdered back there and no one would hear your cries for help. Somebody might find you by smell in a week, maybe, if it was warm.

Pipes ran all along the ceiling carrying the entire building's sewage, which was quite a few apartments. If anyone took a dump, Billy could listen to it travel over him. He had to share a tiny bathroom with two student types in the comparably squalid hole next door.

He was down there with all his Billy possessions, most of which he carried with him from place to place without alteration through the years. His precious rocking chair, where he'd sit for hours, listening to a scratchy old stereo with tiny speakers. One little table and two chairs, a crooked bed with a moldy mattress, a kettle, two coffee cups, one teaspoon and a jar of Taster's Choice. One saucepan and one can opener. That was it.

He'd snared a part-time job in the Sears Lawn and Garden Department, and lived in a state of perpetual irritation, a smoldering resentment of his by-the-book boss. The chainsaws had to be set up HERE, dammit. Not over there. Listen, Hill, I don't care if they get in the way of customer traffic flow, the home-office directive says do it like THIS. Don't THINK, Hill! Just do it like this!

He'd given up everything for the band, even though he wasn't quite sure about some of it. He *told* me he was totally devoted, but his eyes and body language told a very different story.

Both of us were very self-involved people, and while we weren't fighting at all, we weren't a love-match either. Billy's a fairly regular guy with an introspective streak. I was just as introspective, and determined *not* to be regular, regardless of any contrary instincts towards normalcy. If I was in a mood to talk, I blurted out anything on my brain straight away, with little opportunity for anyone else to get a word in edgewise. Billy's get-to-know-ya skills were a bit subtler than mine, and he often just didn't quite know what to make of me.

Nevertheless, we had a situation. Billy was playing guitar and writing songs, and I was playing guitar and writing songs. It was two guys, in the same band, who'd better make it work.

I was heavily into doing songs with harmonies, oohs and ahhs, stuff of a complex and scientific nature of which none of us—especially me—had the slightest knowledge. I'd just heard R.E.M. and thought I knew everything. I'd try to get Billy to do these complex harmonies I knew nothing about until he'd throw up his hands and just leave, saying he'd had it with my "Gregorian chants", as he called them.

Meanwhile, I'd be losing my patience with his bass playing. I'd play him a new song, and he'd just hold his bass and look at me. I was hoping something sparkly would happen, that he'd just see the chords I was making and start playing. It wasn't happening. He'd get exasperated and say "Well, what do you *want* me to play?"—I don't know, man! Just play *something*. Geez.

And then again, there were the very good things. In that awful basement apartment, driven by fear, passion and wonder, Billy began to churn out some beautiful ballads. His voice wrapped around the acoustic guitar; we'd sit there and drink Taster's Choice or Cook's beer, and he'd play me his ballads. Some of them got bastardized into blitzkrieg Cheese stage material. Others remain just pieces of time from that basement, unheard by all but a few.

Two guys in an off-campus Bastille cell, the smell of mold and Lysol, the sound of everyone's sewage whipping through the pipes, crickets outside the screen door. Funny how I have such great memories of it now, 'cause it pretty much sucked at the time.

*   *   *   *

# things are more like they are now than they've ever been before

It was all so new. None of us in the band had ever been in a recording studio before. And let me tell you, there's little in life I've found to match the thrill of hearing your guitar come out of studio monitors for the first time, with all that trickery they can do to make *anybody* sound cool. I demanded it be cranked up really unprofessionally loud. This had been a long time coming, and I was a slut for the experience.

We did that first four-song E.P. in three weeks, working in Marc Owens' basement. Three rooms, one barely big enough for the drums, a washer/dryer in the corner, and somebody always smacking their skull on the low ceiling. We titled it *Things Are More Like They Are Now Than They've Ever Been Before*, which is an especially senseless thing Eisenhower said in a speech once.

In some ways, it's far and away my favorite of all Cheese work, because it's just such a hale and hearty polished turd of a record. There's a purity to it that none of the other stuff gets close to. A couple of the songs are decent. A couple are appalling. Performances range in tone, form and content from mildly out of control to screaming psycho bloodlust, from agreeable to absolutely unlistenable. It may be rough in spots—most spots actually—but there's not an insincere note on it. It's one of the most earnest records this side of Jonathan Richman. Four guys rocking as hard as they can with absolutely *no idea* what they're doing, and no one had less idea than I. The effect of that vibe is that for moments at a time on that record, things get pretty joyous. They do for me, at least. If you don't hear it, I'll understand.

The record-making process was a revelation. I'd never had anyone stop me in mid-performance and tell me I was *out of tune* before, or that the *tempo was bad*, or all these things musicians just naturally deal with. After three weeks of making that record, my whole consciousness changed. Previously, I'd just kerranged the guitar with no thought of whether I was out of tune or sloppy or whatever, but after this recording, and being around these guys and their ears, I'd play my guitar and KNOW I was out of tune and sloppy. A small step, but you have to start somewhere.

I also taught Byron and Marc a thing or two. One afternoon we were doing the lead break at the end of "Face in the Crowd", and I broke the D string. It was the only one I had. I recall not thinking anything about it. I just did what we'd always done ever since we played in the nun suits. I got a pair of needlenose pliers and took some extra slack from the peg end of the string. (We never cut our strings back then. We left extra string sticking out off the neck just in case we had such emergencies as this. The headstocks always had punk haircuts in those days.)

Using the pliers, I tied the string off at the tailpiece bridge, having taken some of the slack from beyond the peg at the neck. After about five or ten minutes of this low-rent hocus-pocus, stretching out this mangled curlicue guitar string with the first three inches of it having just been tightly wound at the tuning peg but now forced to lie straight and be very metal-fatigued, generally uncooperative and very tuneless, I was satisfied I'd fixed the string. Bob Vila meets Mick Jones at Les Paul's place.

I looked up and Byron and Marc were staring at me like I was a man from Mars. Safe to say they'd never seen that one before, and God forbid in the recording studio, but that's how that lead break was finished. And I rather like the result. It's manic, fast and naive. What more do you want?

We took the finished tape to NRP (Nashville Record Producers) to be mastered, which was the delicate process of making a needle-cut lacquer negative from which the vinyl records would be pressed. For you youngsters, this was long before CDs were considered a given. Vinyl was still the mode of transmission. I remember the engineer who did the mastering, while we watched, telling us all about what *kids today* were into. He kept citing "She Blinded Me With Science" (dropped off the charts two years prior) as an example of what was hip and happenin'.

He ran the signal through what we learned was an "aural exciter" which made the record, you guessed it, aurally exciting.We were given a test pressing to take home and listen to, which we did endlessly, and were told to check back in two weeks to pick up our thousand records.

Billy Mack and I went down in his monster Buick, or Lincoln, or whatever Jurassic automo-castle he was careening around in at the time. He would get them used and spend all his Sears money on gas. He'd burn a tank going to the store and back. Billy had neither the budget nor the aptitude for maintenance, and the results got hilarious. The chrome stopper-flange was always gone on the cig lighter, so when it heated up, the lighter would pop out and fly under the seat, setting things on fire. You'd pull the door shut, and the handle would come off in your hand. Billy Mack's mondo gangster car jerry-rigging masterpiece was his wiring of the muffler to the underframe with a fascinating network of coat hangers.

All his monster cars had electronic window-openers, and when the electronics died, so did your ability to open the damn window at all. You'd have to stand outside the car and place palms flat on opposite sides of the window, raising or lowering with enough force to wrench the tendons from your wristbones.

I remember one day getting in the back seat, slamming the door, and having the entire naugahyde inside panel fall off the door frame into my lap, just like a sight gag in the movies.

So Billy and I headed into Nashville one afternoon in late October '85, just praying we'd make it there and back. The rain was pounding. I remember listening to the radio, which indicates it must have been working at the time. We heard the premiere of the new Van Halen—Van *Hagar* if you will. "Why Can't This Be Love", if that helps you date things for yourself.

With the rain still heavy and the day growing dark, we loaded a half-dozen little *boxes of our future* into Billy's room-for-eight backseat. We took it back up to Bowling Green, and our first stop was the mall, specifically, the Record Bar.

In most college towns there's a supercool out-of-the-way record store/headshop, and true enough, when I first came to Bowling

Green, we'd had exactly that in Headquarters on Russellville Road. In the mid-Reagan years, though, we had the Greenwood Mall, and the Record Bar, captained by Jeff Sweeney, the stalwart flag-bearer for anything that was approaching musically hip in Bowling Green at the time.

Jeff was always agonizing that his was a chain store, and chains only order the top 40, and it's a bitch to get them to send more than one copy of the new Let's Active record, or to try to get some of those R.E.M. import maxi-singles, and a *local selection?* Get real, Jeff. But he pressed on with vehemence.

We set up a little consignment deal to sell the record from their counter. Davie Reneau made up a little cardboard display for it to sit in. Our little 7-inch, in its little white sleeve. Our little dream.

The cover was a photo, taken down the street from my apartment, of Bentley Tittle—a friend of ours—wrapped in an overcoat, his head buried in his hands, looking like any indigent with no place to go. The band's name was at the top, the title at the bottom. Black and white, very spartan, very cool, we thought. We didn't know what it meant, or if it was supposed to mean anything. But it suggested an image of isolation and desperation, and most of the songs were about that, except for Willis' tune "Rebecca Whitmire", which was about transvestism primarily, as so many great rock tunes are.

\* \* \* \*

# 6

# schkip

*Things Are More Like They Are Now Than They've Ever Been Before*
made its debut to the world later that evening on WBGN-AM, one of
the last top-40 AMs in the country. Meredith Ludwig was working
that night. She had been through WLBJ with me. We gave her a copy
to play while we ran out to the car to hear our own record on the
radio, like the scene in *Coal Miner's Daughter.*

Skip Walker was managing Michael's Pub at the time. He'd been
a presence at our Picasso's shows for a while, the always-resplendent
guy with the bright blonde hair and the glasses. Most importantly, for
us at the time, Skip didn't hear too well at all. He didn't pronounce
his s's or r's because he couldn't hear them. Skip Walker became
*Schkip Wawkuh.* It struck me as fitting that the earliest, most loyal
and fiercely dedicated supporter of Government Cheese's music was
himself unable to hear the phone ring.

I would see him mopping up in Michael's Pub. The phone would
be ringing off the hook right next to his head, but Skip would never
hear it. I could then presume that all the clangy high-end, out-of-tune
frequencies—the ones that made us a test of resolve for most
listeners—just sailed right on by Skip.

What he loved was that our energy was pure. A lifelong defender
of the underdog, he took to us because we were just that, the ones
least-likely-to. Right after buying our record at the mall—the first
Cheese sale ever—Skip pulled out his datebook and booked us then
and there for New Year's Eve at the Pub.

Skip had rolled into Bowling Green from points unkown. He was
in his mid-thirties and all we knew was that he originally hailed from
southern Indiana, that his brothers were successful professionals and
that Skip was a bit of a rebel. He was a published poet, and he'd done
a little bit of this and a little bit of that to get by over the years. Past
that, we didn't ask and he didn't offer.

If Skip loved you, he loved you, and would spend his day doing nice things for you. If he hated you, stay out of his way. He paid 75 cents for his suits and had them altered so you couldn't tell he hadn't paid $200 at a vintage store. He chain-smoked brown More cigarettes, lighting each on the dying ash of the prior one. He smelled like patchouli oil and, like any patchouli-wearer, one handshake and you were destined to smell like him for the rest of the day, too.

He used to say "The Cheese is happ'nin'. I know the street, and it's happ'nin' on the street. Everywhere I go, people are saying 'Skip, the Cheese, it's happ'nin'." The way Skip would pronounce it though, was "Da Cheeshe ish happ'nin'! I know da shtreet! And itsh happ'nin' on da shtreet!" And on and on.

Skip was destined to be a club owner. He'd been a street-level wheeler-dealer, moving from town to town, so long that it had to happen. Somewhere, there was a nightclub with Skip's name on it. He came into Bowling Green and wound up managing Michael's Pub, which was the very nice bar section of the Briar Patch Steak House on Fairview Avenue. The two businesses were small, old separate houses joined by a walkway. The Briar Patch was the pleasant steakhouse you took the wife and kids to once in a blue moon, or the place to take your prom date. Businessmen lunched there. And while you waited for a table, or were wrapping up the night, you went next door to Michael's Pub.

It was a very subdued, nice, mellow place, and still looked a bit like someone's old house, only with some of the walls knocked out. Clayton Payne would play his acoustic guitar there. Light jazz bands played there. Quiet, tasteful cover bands with Joni Mitchell in their roster were candidates for gigs there. It had been that way for years. What had also been that way for years was the fact that Michael's Pub had long been the closest thing B.G. had to an out and out gay bar.

And that was only one section of the place—three tables next to one side of the bar off in the corner. About ten by fifteen feet of level same-sex-union playing field in a town of thirty thousand. That was all an honest gay fellow in Bowling Green had back then. And because of this, these three tables, there were people in town who wouldn't be caught dead in Michael's Pub. Strange what frightens people.

I never understood how Skip got the job managing the Pub. I can think of absolutely no reason why the conservatives who ran the Briar Patch could have possibly looked at Skip and thought he was going to toe any kind of yuppiefied company line. Best as I could figure, someone high up took one look at Skip and thought he might at least *scare those kinds of people off, don't you know.* Beneath the bleached-blonde mop and the earring, Skip was—after all—one tough guy, with considerable bulk and an obvious, implied ability to pound anyone who displeased him ten feet into the ground, should he ever choose to do so.

The powers that be couldn't have been more wrong, however, if that was indeed their aim. Not only did Skip refuse to intimidate any gay clientele, he encouraged their friends to stop in, and to bring along every other fringe element from underneath every rock in three counties. Government Cheese turned out to be the house band for the whole damn social experiment. All I can know for sure in my heart is that God made Skip manager of the Pub so that the Cheese could have this dream gig that in any rational world shouldn't for one minute have been happening.

Skip came into the Pub and singlehandedly wrecked its pleasant yuppie atmosphere. He painted the walls black. He strewed glitter all over the floor and put colored light bulbs in everywhere. The pleasant ship engravings came down and rock posters went up. James Taylor came off the tape player and the Buzzcocks went on. It was insane. Right next door was Joe Family-Values' flesh-eating, tie-wearing Nice Place; over here was Cantrell's North. And if it looked a fright, it *sounded* like World War Three.

Skip would book us in the Pub as many as five nights a week, paying us more than we could ever make at Picasso's. There was no stage, so we set up in the corner. We brought in ridiculous, gargantuan PA speakers—horrifying huge noisemakers.

Picasso's user-friendly PA and soundman were gone, along with all the prettifying elements they had brought to our sound. In Michael's Pub, in November '85, Government Cheese was up close and ugly. From our debut there through to the next April, we went to school, learning how to sound good *as a band alone*, without any sophisticated sound or lights. It was slow going for a while, too.

First of all, we were loud. I don't mean annoyingly loud, where you can't hear the person across the table from you; I'm talking *INCREDIBLY FUCKING LOUD! TWO BEERS PLEASE! WHAT? TWO BEERS PLEASE!* Piercing clangs of treble at Boeing-test decibels. Industrial shrieks and factory sounds.

I used a big Fender Twin amplifier, a rock and roll classic. Trouble was, it was the worst one they ever made. A real post-CBS silver-face piece of rubbish, and *even then*, it wasn't intended to be used the way I used it. The amp would be set up beside me instead of behind me. I'd adjust the treble to where it sounded right to me *adjacent to* the amp. This meant that the person with the misfortune to be directly in front of the amp got an unholy, eardrum-slicing caterwaul.

Billy's big Sound City bass rig we renamed the Sound Shitty. Joe was in the back corner just trying to hold us together. Skot, by now, was simply lead singer, and sometimes didn't bring his guitar rig to the gig at all. He'd go crazy, leaping off the rafters, jumping up on top of the bar, slam-dancing with patrons who may or may not have been in the mood for such interaction, and I remember one night when he just rolled on the floor most of the night, writhing and screaming to whatever we played, without actually standing up at all.

The regulars were either revolted or enjoying the hell out of it, and our crowd, growing steadily, flocked in. The cash register was wearing out. However rotten tippers they might have been, our people were terrific drinkers. In consideration of their libation, at least for a while, the powers that be next door at the Briar Patch simply saw the liquor sales and left us alone.

With the gig money coming in, we bought equipment as fast as we could. Everything we bought was one more thing we wouldn't have to rent night after night any more. Bands routinely get reamed by music store rentals for such things as PA systems. We bought our own power amp, and our own (grotesque) speakers. We bought mike stands, guitar stands, floor tuners and cords. We saved more money for further recording expenses. We even had money to split up afterwards, which was a first. Piece by piece, we acquired an entire mix n' match PA. It didn't look like much, but it sounded pretty good. We didn't always, but it did.

The waitstaff at the Pub were initially scandalized by their boss's favorite new band. Elizabeth behind the bar cussed regularly with earplugs snugly in place. But then, within a month, she took the plugs out and became a staunch fan. It was a combination of our steady improvement and the fact that close-quarters punk rock is an acquired taste once you're a thirty-year-old mother of two.

Her husband James worked the door. It was his night job. He always came into work worn out from being up all day. He ran lights for us. I kid you not, his job amounted to turning the two light switches on and off constantly, while also operating a fader dial that brought the lights up and down. And he didn't do it because he had to. He loved it.

We'd be in the corner by the windows, rocking like mad, and there would be James next to us, just inside the foyer, between the front door and the cigarette machine, with his fingers on the light switches, his necktie flying up in the air and his glasses getting steamy and slipping off as he threw himself into flipping two lousy light switches up and down, this completely maniacal grin wiped across his face the whole time.

Michael's is the only club Government Cheese ever played where I can honestly recall patrons hunching over in pain, clutching their ears and diving for the exit. I remember one guy walking in and being knocked sideways by the noise, grabbing his head in shock like he was having a 'Nam flashback or something. It got ugly at times.

We had nice friends who would come see us, unprepared for the onslaught that we would be. These friends would sit at their tables, enthusiastic at first as we plugged in, thinking that we would be something pleasing to listen to. Then, suddenly, we were *UNBE-LIEVABLY LOUD! TWO MORE BEERS PLEASE! WHAT? TWO MORE BEERS PLEASE!* and jumping a foot in the air in unison to make the spring reverb in the soundboard rattle throughout the speakers, spinning, laughing, screaming into microphones. The expressions on their faces would change predictably—first perplexion behind fake smiles when we looked their way, then an honest horror they couldn't mask. Then it would all be too much, and they would run for the door, leaving little puffs of smoke like a Warner Brothers cartoon.

Michael's Pub was the only club we ever gave money back to. One Saturday night early on, when we had just about driven off everyone, the guy who paid us handed over the guarantee; Skot and I then handed some back, saying we felt bad about how bad we'd been. We totally stunned the guy. No band had ever done this before.

It must be stressed that Joe hadn't been consulted on this impulsive move by Skot and me. Joe's innate music business sense told him rock bands did not give rebates to club owners, no matter how bad they suck. Anyway, it was a one-time thing, and we grabbed every penny that came our way from then on.

General bizarre behavior took place. I thought we needed smoke for atmosphere and, since we couldn't afford dry ice, I took to puffing baby powder into the air, often when I was supposed to be playing guitar. It gunked up the power amps and made the dance floor (which was little more than the hardwood entry way) dangerously slick.

One night, for some reason I can't fathom to this day, Skot cut my hair onstage. We were both careening around madly and he was stabbing the air around my skull with a huge pair of pinking shears, little clumps of hair snipping off and floating away. We were bopping around and everyone was expecting him to sink the blades deep into one of my eyeballs any second. It did keep the audience riveted, if nothing else.

Billy began giving away free oven mitts to the first five people at the door. I remember autographing an oven mitt for someone and thinking it was a rather unusual thing to be doing.

We began scoping the horizons, looking out of town.

KDF, the big rock station in Nashville, would take a riverboat cruise with a band every Saturday night. We swung the gig one December night, and it went really well. Word spread, and we played a return engagement a fortnight later, for which a bunch of Nashville rockers came over, having heard that we were worth seeing. This time wasn't so great. As fate would have it, we blew chunks in dismal fashion. We had what appeared to be half the Nashville rock scene trapped aboard a moving barge watching us breaking strings and trying to get it together.

We tried Louisville for the first time, opening for Walk the West at Tewligan's and going down a storm. On this night I hadn't slept in three solid days or nights, because I was playing the Pub every night, signing on the radio station every morning, and just not finding any time to bed down.

I remember sleeping between sets one night at the Pub, curled up under the sound board. One night, I played in my pajamas, just to nap a little quicker.

One night that winter, we got our first encore—that first time when people were clapping and yelling "One more!" Around that same time, the first person popped up with a homemade button saying "I'm a Cheesehead."

From winter to spring, we practically lived at the Pub. We ate there. We rehearsed there, in the afternoons before they opened. It was a glitter-strewn, black-walled second home. We were starting to play at the Exit/In and Elliston Square in Nashville, and still doing Tewligan's in Louisville. We played the occasional Monday night opening for someone at Picasso's, but we were otherwise at the Pub, *our place.*

We went to Lexington for the first time in April, playing the Bottom Line, which later became the Wrocklage. We were scheduled to be the opener but wound up headlining. The original top band, Not Me and the Alibis, some frat boys from Centre College, offered to switch billing when they saw how our show was a dangerous cross between a rock performance and a rugby scrum.

These were the pre-van days, so we'd had a motorcade up to Lexington. Skip and I shared a vehicle. The next day, everyone thought I was in the other car. Hence, I got left in Lexington. It took a bit of doing and several phone calls to get someone to wire me a bus ticket out of there in time to make it back for that night's show at Michael's Pub.

The old adage is true. Not everyone who takes a bus is a freak, but when a freak wants to go anywhere, he takes the bus. For four and a half hours, with stops in every piss town between here and there, I sat next to a biker who smelled like the inside of a gorilla's stomach and a military grunt who sat with his bag in his lap as if he were telling the world "Don't anybody dare touch the *five pounds of pot I have in this big duffel bag!*" And then there was a woman with a Jersey accent who apparently needed to talk in order to draw breath into her body. She didn't shut up from Lexington 'til Louisville, where our paths mercifully separated.

I made it home just in time to play the gig that night at the Pub, and sometime during the second set, a great big fellow who looked like Santa before his hair went white came in. He outfreaked anybody I'd seen on the bus all day, with hair past his shoulders and a black beard halfway down his chest. It was the untrimmed type of beard where you can't even see the guy's mouth, but you knew this guy had a mouth the minute you encountered him, because it was in constant engagement. He wore glasses thick enough to take a bullet.

Fast on his feet, with a witty repartee designed for Mensa members, he said things like "If I get any fatter, I'll have to run for sheriff!" and other bits of Zen humor. He was a sight from head to toe, wearing an old 50-cent thrifter shirt, highwater Sears work jeans girding his 42-inch belly above the navel, I estimated from the looks of it. The pant legs ended a good two inches above his ankles. He was from Athens, Georgia, we were told, as he looked around him and wrote down every single thought he had in a legal-pad clipboard he was

carrying. He seemed to spend as much time writing down the life surrounding him as he did participating in it. This, my friend, was Ort.

William Orten Carlton to the birth certificate people, Ort to you
and me. Loud, intelligent, hypoglycemic, erratic-tempered and a
one-man walking carnival. Ort measured radio-station signals for a
monitoring service six months out of the year; the rest of the time he
traveled the South scouring flea markets and thrift stores, the more
out-of-the-way the better. He was the type of guy who'd go thirty
miles down a state road to find a general store where the owner
makes his own liver cheese. He was thirty-six at the time, his I.Q.
stratospheric, as defiantly individual and determined to save the
world one person at a time as any long-haired genius with dangerously fluctuating blood-sugar ever has been.

One of his 1969 freshman classmates at UGA was Fred Schnei-
der, a part-time waiter who'd wind up singing lead for the B-52s. Ort
knew all the members of R.E.M. long before the band happened, and
he was in the audience at their debut. To me, at the time, R.E.M.-head
that I was, that bit of esoterica was reason enough for canonization.
Right after meeting him at the Pub, I had him in conversation about
Peter Buck, guitarist for said Remsters. Ort started in with some details of Peter's grandfather's life that he assumed I should find interesting, how he survived the famous San Fransisco earthquake or
something. Yeah, yeah. Thrilling. What about Peter? It didn't dawn
on me at the time that Ort was talking about Peter as a friend, not as a
rock star. I wanted to know about a personality, and Ort was trying to
talk about the real human being.

Ort was a cult figure in Athens. He semi-narrated the film *Athens
Georgia: Inside/Out.* He had an encyclopedic knowledge of records,
the labels, who played on them, and a fascinating ability to recall the
catalogue numbers. He was a recognized nationwide authority on—
of all things—obscure brands of potato chips. I didn't even know
there were more than five or six different brands. There are hundreds,
the best of which is available in only three counties in Iowa. Ort can
recall the name. I can't. His collection of beer cans and bottles was
the closest one got to comprehensive. He would always open a beer
can on the bottom, with the sharp end of a bottle opener so as not to
disturb the collectability.

From the minute Ort saw us, we were his new project. When Ort
got into something he *got into* it. He decided Government Cheese was

one of the greatest rock bands he'd ever seen, and he'd seen plenty. We were the perfect mixture of rock and humor for Ort's taste, and, according to the man, were only slightly worse that night in the Pub than R.E.M. were at their debut. We took that as a great, albeit conditional, compliment.

Ort was a semi-regular presence at Cheese gigs after that. He took the job as Cheese MC. He wasn't offered the job. He just took it. Fine by me, though Ort tended to complicate his surroundings as much as accent them. Like Skip, though, if he cared about you, you were in. He'd do anything for you. If he *didn't* care for you, watch out! And if his blood-sugar was out of whack, just pray nothing cataclysmic happened. If he'd eaten recently, he was fine. But when he hadn't, when his hypoglycemia would kick in, he became the devil in thrift chic. I've seen him chase a moving car down the street with a stick in a fit of anger when his body was jonesing for that special sucrose something.

Ort bought our EP by the boxful. He took to sending it to friends. The trunk of Ort's car was a record store in and of itself. You wanted a copy of the Swimming Pool Qs' first single on dB Records? You talked to Ort. You wanted each and every issue of Tasty World Magazine? Ort had back-issue stock in his trunk, right next to the two cases of seasonal bock beer he'd just scored, right next to the great cache of old postcards from the Wigwam Village in Cave City, right next to the Frank Sinatra and Hank Williams 78s he'd nabbed at Freeman Kitchens' grocery/post office in Drake. If Ort found out your particular taste in budget gifts, you'd wind up getting more than you'd ever dreamed of.

He crashed at my apartment and discovered a lack of coffee cups. The next time he came to visit, he came with a box of coffee cups. The theme was that they all had the logo-stamp of a radio or television station somewhere. Great, Ort! Thanks, man! I thought that's where it would end. The next time he visited, he had another box of coffee cups. And another box came after that. I thanked him heartfeltedly every time and said "that's all, Ort. Please, no more"; but he couldn't stop. It was Ort's new mission in life that people in that apartment would never AGAIN lack for a morning java vessel. It eventually peaked out at three boxes of coffee cups shoved in a closet and never used. They couldn't be. If I drank five pots a day, I couldn't go through all the cups in a year. There was no room in the shelves for any more cups. The door wouldn't close completely, there were already so many porcelain mugs in there. As I type this, I'm sipping coffee from a KET (Kentucky Educational Television) cup. I have my choice of two.

Going to an out-of-town gig—in those pre-van days—was done in the following fashion:

Two or three cars. Equipment strewn everywhere. Guitar cases across laps. Huge speaker cabinets filling up the backseats, taking up the rear-view mirror. Trunks crammed full. Entire gig monies eaten up by the petrol bill, etc. Going to gigs this way ranks right up with whacking yourself in the face with a two-by-four on a comprehensive list of fun things to do. A two-hour trip to Louisville with three guys in the front seat of a car, with two guitar cases across their laps, can make blood enemies of the nicest people. And for the entire first year, we did it this way.

I don't remember how much we shelled out for that first van, but it was a pittance, and we grievously overpaid.

It belonged to an old retired minister who had used the van to ferry churchgoers back and forth to various righteous functions. Judging from the looks and general condition, he'd also occasionally taken a sledgehammer to the body and motor just for the hell of it.

Billy Mack may have been the first to spot it, as he was always looking for another vehicle anyway. It had one big back seat with a giant rip in the naugahyde, all the yellowing foam rubber inside exposed like muscle tissue.

The godly curmudgeon explained to us "Now, young fellas, they's just like horses. Ye put enough food in 'em, don't run 'em no harder n' they oughta, last ye twenty years." Yes sir, thanks. We swallowed the bull, handed over the cabbage and, with some difficulty, started the damn thing up. Off we smoked and belched down Glen Lily Road.

We picked up Skot and tooled out onto Scottsville Road. The engine was overheating so bad that someone got a bright idea. Hey! Let's unclamp the console/motor hood and let all that heat out!

The motor hood was at knee level of both driver and shotgun rider, held in place by a pair of latches. We snapped it open and took the thing off.

Yaaahhh! Suddenly we had this great, coughing, sputtering beast of an engine right in our face, spitting, smoking, and offending every orifice in our heads. Yep, the heat could escape easier now. Of course, it went no further than the inside of the van. We were gagging and rubbing our stinging eyes all the way down Scottsville Road, convincing each other *how great the van was* and how we were going to *take it all over the country* and *play gigs!* And all the while it was getting harder to see inside the van. All the thick blue smoke was getting thicker and bluer. Skot! Is that you over there?

We never made it onto the interstate. Coming back towards the bypass intersection, I lost my nerve and hopped out. I walked home smelling like gasoline, oil and smoke all over, hoping the others got out of it before the whole thing blew.

I don't know who bought it from us, but some sucker did. Skot found some guy, sold it to him, and we spent a few sleepless nights wondering if the fellow was going to come back and kick our asses for siccing a useless hunk of junk on him. He never did. A few months later, we saw the old thing in the Houchens parking lot. It was still alive, and had found a good home, presumably.

And so much for us and a van. Back to the old way. Three in the front seat, feet covered in mikes and cords and beer cans. Naked, caseless guitars stabbing us in the necks. Wonderful. All the way to Louisville in the afternoon, and then back home again that at four that next morning. Beautiful. You must try it sometime.

We went back and played the KDF Riverboat again. This time, unbeknownst to us, there had been a drowning death on the previous weekend cruise. A beer-spitting contest had gone awry and a fellow had gone over the rail. You can call me crazy, but the minute I walked on that boat the next weekend, I felt bad. We played two nights, sucked both nights, and said gigs involved weird energy we'd never quite experience again. One amp made a funky, whiny noise it hadn't made before and would never repeat later when we tried to get it to. Brand-new guitar strings broke with little or no provocation. The PA blew. Lights failed or browned-out. At the end of both shows, the only people still watching us were our girlfriends and that bastard who drowned. I haven't gotten on that boat since.

It was too much to think our little playhouse would chug along as a business indefinitely. We were fooling ourselves if we thought the Briar Patch brass were just going to sit idly by week after week while Skip turned Michael's Pub into the Whiskey-a-Go-Go. When the squeeze came, though, it was a shock, if only for the cold-blooded sudden speed with which the axe fell. They crushed our little rock and roll dream with their size sixteen stormtrooper boots, with little warning and all deliberate speed.

The story we got was that the club would be closing its doors in three days and reopening in a few weeks as a pizza parlor, with *no bands!* That was it. No arguments. No chance to plead our case. We didn't even know who to bitch to. Some faceless conservative in the hierarchy made the decision to screw up all our lives.

And so we did the last gig in April, and Michael's Pub was an absolute seething throng for it. People were standing between bandmembers because there was nowhere else for them to be. It was a human jello mold, occasionally upsetting the speakers from their stands. Jeff Sweeney sang "Great Balls of Fire" with us.

My best memory is everyone, and I mean everyone, in the place, jumping up and down in time with "People Who Died". Skot exhorted them to jump up and down! Harder and harder! In unison! C'mon! Up and down! Up and down! The goal was to break through the floor to the wine-cellar/basement. Presumably there would be massive injuries, perhaps a little loss of life here and there, but at least we'd spite the closers, the slime stomping on our sacred, corrupted Yuppie Den Gone Bad. We'd take the damn ship down with us!

*"Fukkabunchapizza! Fukkabunchapizza!"* That's what we all kept shouting that heady, sweaty moment when the whole place jumped in unison, upwards of a hundred people all bobbing two feet up and down in the air for eight bars, sixteen bars, thirty-two bars. Every head, every single person, up and down, two feet in the air and to the ground again, in perfect sync. Up. Down. Up. Down. It was an incredible sight.

The whole old stone house palpably vibrated. There was no one not drenched, not basting in their own juice. It was intense, angry and celebratory, because for six months Skip had had his way. I'd had my way. *A scene had been born!* Things once impossible, unthinkable and undoable *had already been happening!*

They couldn't stop us now. It was like centurions knocking down a church building. The believers'll just move on. Poor bastards, they'd let the cancer spread too long. The beast is awakened. And the people will want more. *"Those are people who DIED! DIED! Those are people who DIED! DIED!"*

And the next day, once our heads cleared, we roadied out our gear, and dealt with that feeling—that you didn't realize you were in love until she left. There was no guarantee a night of rock and roll that good would ever happen again, to any of us, ever. What was Skip gonna do now? Hell, what were *we* gonna do?

It never did re-open as a pizza parlor. It was a sports bar called Player's for a while. I don't know what it is now. The Briar Patch next door has been knocked down. It's a vacant lot. Ward and June chew their animal flesh elsewhere.

The ex-Pub, that innocent old dwelling house, that old stone den of iniquity, squats in mute triumph next to its vanquished and vanished sire, which is little more than a patch of weeds now. The Pub's mortar and glass has outlasted its patron, with a little vague stench of dreams, young and lusty, still whipping up out of the basement occasionally, for any person who can smell it now, who knows what once went on there.

* * * *

# man and/or myth

The relationship between musician and businessman is a fractious, contrary one more often than not. It's the two sides of the brain coming together like separate air masses, setting off sheet lightning. Talk to the musician, and the businessman always comes off like a conniving villain. Talk to the businessman, and the musician gets painted as a fuzzy-thinking one-worlder. It's a classic story, as old as rock and roll itself. Good meets Evil. Yin meets Yang. Elvis, Colonel. Colonel, Elvis.

The fact that I am on the "musician" side of the fence, armed with a word processor, has given me pause here and there lately, because this whole story already sets itself up like a bad novel. I don't have to exaggerate a thing. Okay, you tell me: We're a rock and roll band, and this older guy with shifty eyes and a goatee descends on the scene. He's got an eastern-seaboard accent, obviously not from anywhere around here. He swears a lot and all our friends hate him on sight. And then he sets up a company called *Reptile* Records? Oh, please! And then we sign a big long contract with him? *Stop!*

Scott Tutt. Where should I start? With the nice things, I guess. And there are some.

First, I might not have ever been in the music business without him. I might well be, but it was his initial push that got me there, and let the record reflect that. Second, he spent a hell of a lot of money trying to make Government Cheese rich and famous, and while I can definitely call into question some of the ways he unloaded said cake, the fact remains that he spent the money. Third, he spends time nowadays coaching little league football. He has apparently even helped a couple of underprivileged kids on to sports scholarships, or so he says. That's a cool thing, deserving of a karmic brownie point or two.

He was thirty nine in '85 when I met him, having grown up the son of a cop in Doylestown, just outside Philadelphia, Pennsylvania. He had curly brown/black hair beginning to thin, frizzing on the sides like Avery Schreiber. To this day, I haven't seen a picture of him where he didn't have that goatee beard and moustache—that beard and a hard face, like a white Chuck Berry, only not as handsome as Chuck, framed by that tight-curly coif and deep-set black eyes. He probably had that goatee when he was ten.

November, 1985. The first EP was just out, and the Pub era hadn't even really begun yet, when we first met him. Jeff Sweeney had done an article on us for the *Metro,* a new music magazine in Nashville, and Tutt, having seen it, came up to Bowling Green.

He walked up to us on the Picasso's dance floor right after some Tuesday night type gig, wearing a black satin jacket with *Scott Tutt Music* emblazoned on the back. We were sweating, catching our breath, and suddenly here was this actual *music business guy* in front of us.

He was chewing gum. Nobody chews gum with more conviction than ex-cigarette smokers, as he was. Chomp, chomp, chomp. Chewing to work off that excess nervous energy. You could see his inner mouth off and on, like a strobe display of his uvula. Chomp chomp chomp.

He swung into his patter right away, told us how he'd heard some good songs, thought the band needed "direction", and he might have mentioned something about needing more rehearsal. I don't remember much beyond that as far as what he said specifically, but I remember how he looked—that goatee, the small, sunken eyes, the tight, curly hair.

He had two people with him, standing behind and to his sides like a pair of lieutenants. They both had the black satin jackets too. Like Tutt, they were Yankee transplants from outside Philly: Susan Marshall, all five-feet-barely of her, with a curly blonde mane; cute, only twenty or so, with "aspiring country singer" written all over her. I've seen early pictures of Barbara Mandrell that look surprisingly like Susan in the face. Jon "Mr. Big" D'Amelio stood on the other side and said not a single word, just giving us a handshake and a hello. He looked a bit younger than Tutt, less hard, with neatly trimmed short black hair and glasses. We shook hands all around and said goodbye for now. They turned around to leave, and it was three black satin *Scott Tutt Music*s bouncing next to one another on the way to the door.

We looked at each other quizzically, still wet, sweating from the gig. The whole thing had taken two minutes, maybe, if that long. So *that's* what a music business guy looks like. Oooookay.

The next Saturday, while Kiss played Municipal Auditorium across town, we played Cantrell's in Nashville, the place that had been such a revelatory learning ground. We were one of the last bands to ever play the place.

We had hit a point in our development where one gig would be righteous and the next night a ruptured pustule. This proved to be the latter variety, absolutely retchful. The place was freezing, and the guitars wouldn't tune even by our less-than-picky standards. Sweeney had managed to coax local hero (by then Nashville cat) Bill Lloyd out to hear us. Bill was horrified, an appropriate reaction.

Tutt, Susan, Big and a girl named Ellen McQueary were there. They bought copies of our EP and asked us to drop by their office on Music Row the following week to "talk business" with them. With a mingling of misgivings and excitement, we accepted. Those words were so strange to our ears. *Music Row. Business.* Nice words, though.

Billy Mack and I went to Tutt's office a few days later, and, for the first time, caught the full blast of his personality. We were courteously seated in his office, given coffee, and after that, found it completely impossible to get a word in edgewise for the next forty-five minutes. Tutt hit us square in the eyes with one of his principal weapons: a stupefying ability to talk incessantly for however long the situation demanded. He took over, and the only things Billy and I got to say for the rest of the meeting were "Yes, well . . . " and "Yes, but . . . " before he would start on a new tirade again, jumping from subject to subject, caroming off topics like a pinball.

To be fair, he said some good and educational things that afternoon, many of which I remember today and have tried to apply. He came out blasting with his *"Lecture for Young Bands #246"*. He explained how Billy Mack and Joe desperately needed to tighten up as a rhythm section immediately, and he painstakingly went over how Billy's bass had to lock in with Joe's kick drum, and explained how they could practice alone and work on that. You would have thought we'd have already realized the importance of that "tight-playing" thing, but we hadn't. Oven mitts and baby-powder, yes. "Tight rhythm section", funnily enough, no.

He went off about buying our own microphones, and demonstrated how you could drive a nail with a Shure SM 57 (or 58, whichever one's got the big metal ball for a mouthpiece. I never can remember), and that they would be great investments for a young band to make, assuming, I guess, that we'd ever consider buying a microphone just to drive nails with it.

He talked about PA systems, and how he'd been the king soundman of his hometown back in Pennsylvania. He analyzed our record and explained how he would have done this better and that better, and he was certain he could do it *all* better.

He cited this person he knows, and that person who thinks Scott Tutt knows the music business better than anyone else, and he dropped other names, and he explained at length how he was the BOSS of his organization and how anyone who climbs on board needs to understand that *Tutt is the THE FUKKIN' BOSS* and that what Tutt says goes, and if he says don't wear the fukkin' red pants onstage *then don't wear the fukkin' red pants onstage,* and by the time he'd finished there could be no mistaking who and what we were dealing with. We'd been given enough clues for any babe in any woods, no matter how thick and low the branches. Let's just start crossing adjectives off our Scott Tutt list. Easy-going? That one can go. Humble? Outta here. Confident? Yeah, he is that. Charming? No.

Still, I was amazed. The man was a work of art. Top to bottom, from one end of his ego to the other, every gesture of his body and every thought out of his mouth was full-force. If you're going to chew gum, then by God *chew gum!* If you're going to use profanity, use it like a sweeping scythe of verbal destruction! Scott Tutt chewed gum and said "motherfucker" better than anyone I'd ever met.

He just kept talking and, as I sat sinking in his couch, I began to daydream. I could see his mouth still moving, but the words didn't register any more. I was busy plotting his gum-chewing and "motherfuckers" into time signatures: Four-four time (*Motherfuckerchompchomp! Motherfuckerchompchomp!*), waltz time (*Chompmotherfucker! Chompmotherfucker!*), perhaps a brisk cha-cha (*Motherfuckerchompchompchomp! Motherfuckerchompchomp-chomp!*). Ah yes, we're swinging now.

Sitting there, we could see that he was master of his domain, such as that domain was, anyway. He had office space on Music Row, which, as you might guess, is the place to be in Nashville. Music Row is technically 16th Avenue, a gorgeous strip of studios and houses customized to be tony "this is the life"-type offices. 17th and 18th Avenues contain a lot of these offices too, and this is where country music (and a lot of other music these days) lives and breathes.

Perpendicular to these streets is the strip of souvenir shops that the visiting public initially *thinks* is Music Row: Hank Jr.'s Souvenir Shop, Alabama's T-shirt Heaven, Cars of the Stars, etc. These shops, and Gilley's, where the stars of tomorrow played, were what the citizens of the world would flock to, in those pre-Wildhorse days, to feel the authentic country experience down to their boots and up to their Stetsons. The real nuts and bolts of the industry, however, lay calmly, purring in Jaguars and pouring the Perrier, just down the street from this neon artifice.

We were sitting in Tutt's second floor walk-up, still listening to him go. We knew by now that he talked a good game and made himself out to be a big noise, and the fact he was on Music Row was nothing to sneeze at. We knew before we got there how he'd managed Alabama in their early days, that he had had a couple of tiny record companies form and fold out from under him, that he had managed Charlie Daniels' band after they'd left Charlie, or something like that, and we knew we were sitting on a real piece-of-crap couch that sunk down in a most uncomfortable way, the kind of worn-out couch you have to have help getting out of.

We saw how he decorated his office, with a big blanket nailed to the wall, festooned with every fan-fair button and souvenir he'd acquired out of twenty years in the *"Music Business!"* The desk was a mess. Add it all up, and it was apparent even to our virgin sensitivities that we were looking at a low-rent bullshit artist.

After an hour, Billy and I were just looking for a gracious opening to wrap things up and get out of there. Of course, there hadn't been a gracious opening in the conversation the entire time we'd been there. There hadn't been a pinhole. Nothing. We might just have to help each other out of the couch and make a run for it.

Then a miracle happened.

Jerry Dale McFadden walked in the office with a cassette mixdown of the previous evening's session. Tutt was managing and producing this guy, a young Oklahoman mixture of Jerry Lee Lewis and Joe Jackson. A very talented fellow with leanings toward Queen, Elton John and honky-tonk piano-pumping stuff all at the same time. He was Reptile Records' first signing (along with Susan, who had been blithely typing away at something in the outer office the whole time we'd been there).

They'd all been in the studio the night before with Duane Eddy, the twangy, seminal '50s guitar legend, and Warner Hodges of the hallowed Scorchers, my long-suffering target of adulation and guitar-interrogations.

So one minute Scott Tutt was this talkaholic, gum-popping, goateed guy with a mildly interesting past and a filthy mouth who was starting to scare us, or at least get on our nerves. The next minute, he was somebody who'd recorded Warner Hodges and Duane Eddy in the same evening for one of his artists' records.

In a heartbeat, my whole attitude changed. Scott Tutt went from profane to . . . *colorful.* Sleazy to *wily.* From no way to . . . *well, maybe.*

Scott Tutt came to Nashville from Philly in the early seventies. A true child of the sixties, he saw Dylan in '62, before I was even born, and shook his hand after the show as well. He had run a classic hippie record store, and, from what we know via his yarn-spinning and reminiscing, he must have had quite the free-loving hippie time. He got into promoting shows, and developed an affinity for the no-bullshit, hard rock popular in his hometown.

He promoted lots of early Ted Nugent and the Amboy Dukes shows, and told us marvelous stories of promoting the MC5. They would ride into town on Harleys. One of them wore a machine gun strapped across his back. A motorcycle gang followed them around, and scared off any civilians who might have wanted to see the show.

Along the way, Tutt played a little guitar. He wrote a few songs, and whether he intended to perform or not when he got to Music City, no one knows. If he did, the urge fell by the wayside soon enough.

Sometime in the early seventies, Tutt moved into a big house in Nashville with a young unknown singer named Earl Thomas Conley, Earl's wife, and some other communal types coming and going. One night Earl was sitting in the Gold Rush on Elliston Place. He overheard someone saying to his pal "I dunno, I guess *this time I hurt her more than she loves me . . .*"

Ding!

Earl rushed home and wrote the song. Conway Twitty took "I Hurt Her More Than She Loves Me" to the top of the charts, and Earl

Thomas Conley was on his way. For a while, Tutt performed some managerial duties for him.

Then Tutt hooked up as a radio promo man, his true talent when he was not being too belligerent. Tutt could sell brass knuckles to a priest.

He became a promoter in local markets, getting radio stations to play his clients' records. Perhaps his all-time achievement came in the summer of '76, breaking "Moonlight Feels Right" by Starbuck in the Atlanta market, and thereby catapulting the song onto the charts, resulting in a worldwide smash. Next time you hear that xylophone solo on an oldies station, you may thank Scott Tutt for making it possible.

In '77, when he came across a band called Wildcountry, Scott Tutt knew he'd found his Beatles.

The story goes that their instrumental prowess was nothing to write home about, but their harmony singing was incredible. Wildcountry consisted of three cousins from Fort Payne, Alabama: Randy, Teddy and Jeff, plus the drummer of the month. When Tutt met them, they were playing for tips in Myrtle Beach and going absolutely nowhere. He had them under contract quicker than you can sing "Tennessee River".

He got them a deal on GRT Records, a tiny independent country label, and changed the band's name to Alabama.

Things were going decently. They even cracked the Country Hot-Hundred charts for a brief period of time. Then Elvis had to go and die.

GRT Records then put all their teeny indie muscle behind a young Elvis soundalike named Ronnie McDowell, who had quickly written and recorded "The King is Gone" for the label. It became a monster smash. Alabama was virtually forgotten by the label heads, and Tutt couldn't do a thing about it.

As time went by, though, Alabama began to garner much interest in the upper reaches of the music industry. By late '78, RCA was getting hot for the band and wanting to sign them, just as the band was growing cold on Tutt for various reasons.

The deal for Tutt to fade into the mist gracefully was for him to get paid for a bunch of T-shirts, posters and 8x10s he'd had made, and—more importantly—be given the publishing rights on four Alabama songs of his choosing. Tutt knew their repertoire in and out, and he has never in his life made more astute decisions than he did on that day, when he picked those four songs.

Scott Tutt walked away with the publishing rights to two future #1 singles: "Tennessee River" and "Lady Down on Love". Both songs were, incidentally, written at the Red Carpet Inn in Bowling Green, Kentucky during the band's salad days. The two Alabama songs which essentially financed Reptile Records and Government Cheese were written in Bowling Green. So you see, class, economic chickens do come home to roost occasionally.

Alabama became the country success story of the decade. Their 1980 debut skyrocketed. Country music was irrevocably changed by their rock-level success. Radio loved 'em. Women loved 'em. Kids loved 'em. Mom loved 'em. Everybody loved Alabama. People don't realize now how different they were, that there had never ever been a country *band* before. Alabama started all that.

For a few years in Scott Tutt's life, checks with lots of zeroes flowed in steadily. When you own the publishing rights on a country #1, life is good.

Unfortunately, Tutt never found an artist to follow up with. He formed a label with some investors and got burned, either because said backers were dishonest, or Tutt pissed them off, or both. Tutt drifted from project to project, gave plenty of people a piece of his mind, and, as years went by, formed the coterie of folks, including Mr. Big, Susan and Ellen, who would hang around, listen to him talk, and become the nucleus for what would be Reptile Records.

Susan wanted to be a country star, so Tutt hired her to be his secretary, made up a label and signed her to it. They played their relationship so close to the vest that it would take us a year to figure out that Susan was Tutt's girlfriend, and basic slave, and that he had the fear of God efficiently fused into her innocent bones.

Big wanted to be a sound engineer, so Tutt said "stick with me, you run the cables, I'll make the decisions, we'll make millions", etc. We weren't exactly sure what Ellen wanted. We knew she wrote songs, and she had a nebulous position—"vice president"—in the record company chain of command, but that was it.

Tutt's personality was an enigmatic gumbo, a bundle of contradictions. He was vehemently chauvinist and despised women. We heard he'd had a bad marriage and a worse divorce. Yet, curiously, he hired women predominantly to work for him, and screamed at them regularly.

He dutifully went to Mass every single Sunday, though he kept quiet about it, and the effect on his behavior—at least his vocabulary—was minimal. The same manager who yelled not to wear the fukkin' red pants onstage was also the guy who wore the same three fringey country-western shirts every damn day, when he wasn't in green Philly Eagles sweats that came halfway up his legs.

He was by turns musically learned and completely out to lunch. On the plus side, he was an enthusiastic proponent of Joe Ely long before it became hip outside of Texas to be so. He loved Guadalcanal Diary as well. But he was also the same fellow who once told me the Who sucked, R.E.M. didn't have any songs, and that the flute ruins Marshall Tucker's "Heard It In A Love Song".

He was loud, coarse, well-intentioned, egotistical, funny, vulgar and charismatic all at once. Not a single friend of ours could stand him, either. I don't know anyone who didn't have him pegged for a sleazebag from day one.

What they couldn't see was how this guy, for all his faults, represented a leg up to the next realm. He talked a good game, and yeah, maybe it was all talk, but he was the only one talking to *us*, for damn sure. We were looking over the horizon, feeling out the terrain, seeing some big mountains. We knew we had no idea how to get across those mountains. Tutt claimed that he knew how to do it. He also intimated strongly that the only way he would drive us through was if we gave him the keys and title to the whole shebang.

Control. Complete artistic and business control. So that's how it's done? Yeah, he told us, that's how it's done.

\* \* \* \*

# 8

# calling all
# inner transients

When you are the morning man at a radio station, it's a bit rare to be five hours late for work and still keep your job. I did it, though.

In the summer of '86, Government Cheese was becoming something in our little corner of the world. After the Pub closed, Skip began renting out rooms and promoting his own shows, most of which starred us. Picasso's was, step-by-step, relinquishing key nights of the week to us and our ilk. We were road-tripping to Louisville, Nashville, Lexington, playing big outdoor festivals in fields on the backs of tractor-trailer beds. We even played Warren Central High School's midnight after-prom party. I wore my special tux pants for the occasion—the ones from high school with the crotch, by this point, completely ripped out. We plunged the whole gym into darkness with our first chord, having promptly blown every fuse in the building.

All this time, I was making it to the station at five AM (six on weekends), screaming around curves in my '74 Maverick, burning down the station driveway in mad, sleep-jonesing, dark-eyed rushes to get the station on the air in time. So often was I five or ten minutes late, the regular listeners came to take it for granted. It was just a part of the show.

When sign-on time came and Darth didn't have tapes cued up ready to play, the whole thing freaked out and started spitting out paper. I'd burst into the control room at 5:10 many mornings and the damn thing would have already flooded the room with cybervomit. I would scramble around the room, spilling coffee, cuing up a Reba McEntire single, taking transmitter readings, checking the temperature, doing the weather forecast, watching Darth freak out, and occasionally just throwing things around the room and screaming a lot.

We played Tewligan's one night in Louisville. We had played a fraternity party the night before and, prior to that, Picasso's. The last time I had slept at all was the afternoon before the Picasso's gig. All the way back in the van I dozed fitfully. We got back into Bowling Green from Louisville at around four AM. I had to have the station on at six.

It was coming up on Sunday morning, and that would mean live preachers in the studio. Never a dull moment there. One of the preachers was great. He'd come in with his wife and kick serious spiritual ass. The other guy was an idiot. He'd get on the air and just ramble, making up words, citing Bible verses out of books that didn't exist. *Y'all out thar in radioland turn to Second Jebadiah, chapter nine!* He was constantly trying to save me, talking about how women in these nightclubs were wearing halter tops with their belly-buttons showing. That was a big thing to him, belly buttons. Every week he'd come in and talk to me about evil women with bare belly buttons.

Coming home from Louisville, I was looking at the other guys in the van. They were turning into seagulls and flying around me. The van would stop at a light, and I'd see the scenery outside continue to move as if we hadn't stopped. I needed some serious sleep.

I got home and fell into bed, telling myself I'd nod for an hour, get up, and go to work. I needed some repose before I could face the preachers. The last thing I remember was looking at the digital alarm clock. It said 4:30. The sun wasn't quite making any presence known yet. I closed my eyes.

I reopened them. A bright sunny day. The clock said 11:40.

Mmmm, that's nice.

Shit.

Aaaaaarrhhhhhh! In the clothes I was wearing, I tore out the door.

I beat Maggard to the station by ten minutes. I'd just signed on the AM station and was loading tapes onto Darth. He walked in like he was about to put the sharp attachment on the Electrolux, shove it up my ass and suck out my brains with it.

I dropped the reel of tape I had in my hand and threw my upper limbs skyward. I threw my eyebrows so high they left my head like a comic strip. I don't remember exactly what I said, but it boiled down to "Hey, just fire me. Go ahead. I understand. *Do it, you sonofabitch! You want to! I want you to! C'mon! Do it!*"

He didn't fire me. He helped me fake the transmitter log and concoct a story for the preachers who had already come and gone, leaving their angry little righteous notes on the front door of the station. We'd had a transmitter failure and had to go to Nashville to get parts. Yeah, that's it. We didn't leave a note? Gosh, I'm sorry. And that was it. No chewing-out. No harangue. Nothing.

I think he was numb. I had struck him dumb. He didn't know what to do with me. I was the guy who had worked 60-hour weeks when Rich was away on emergency family leave and the news director had quit. I mowed the lawn without being told, which was nice. Of course, I ran the mower over the tower cables and cut the station off the air, which was not so nice. I was the guy who'd work when they needed me to and only occasionally bitched about the money, or the lack of it. I was also the crazy rock and roll guy who snorted helium to do the weather forecasts. And now, I was the only morning man in history to be five hours late and keep his job.

It was obvious I'd run out of cards, though. I'd also run out of steam for this double life. A couple of weeks later, with the sanction of the other guys, I became the first member of Government Cheese to quit his day job and go full-time on the band's salary.

One day, Billy left Sears for lunch and didn't go back. He lived in his basement apartment until the end of the month and then moved home for a while. For a couple of months, we'd go to Billy's house in Horse Cave to rehearse, and that's where we met Mammaw.

Flora Hill was Billy Mack's grandmother. She was both about as old and as cheerful as anyone has a right to be.

This is the God's honest truth. Mammaw thought we were a basketball team. For some reason, it just stuck in her head that that's what we were. She always did think that, and no amount of exposure to our music would get her thinking otherwise, at least not permanently. We were a basketball team and that was that. She would hear us playing the music in the back house behind the garage, and she'd stand in the driveway underneath the basketball goal, laughing her head off and clapping along. She knew music. After all, she'd taught half of Horse Cave's children to play piano. So she would love it when she saw us playing our noisy mess. And then, before we all left for the evening after practice, she would hug us best as she could, and wish us luck in the big game.

Billy wrote a song for her. A circular riff that's probably the most clever thing any of us ever came up with musically. I played this little repeating lick in G and the lyrics concerned a fantasy where we hit the road with Mammaw as our loose-cannon bus driver. "Mammaw Drives the Bus" was finished up behind Billy's garage, with Flora Hill laughing in the driveway, clapping her hands, slapping her thighs, waving her shaky hands, and waiting for one of us to hit a three-point jump shot and save the day.

Once I was awake long enough to enjoy it, I saw what was happening to Government Cheese's little kingdom and how I fit into it. We had something going on. It felt like we were so unorthodox, so unique. Of course, on a grand scale, we weren't, but that made no difference. Those were the days of jumping around, hitting myself in the face with my own guitar neck, wearing the same stage clothes for three days—that old tux shirt and pants, and the ripped vest with the Elvis button. It was the days of free beer and *Life's Rich Pageant.* *"I am! I am Superman! And I know what's happening."*

Like every young hip band in the US in '86, we were playing R.E.M. covers, like every other young band, we thought we were the only ones doing such a thing, and like most every other young American band at the time, we butchered the poor songs.

For those of you who came along later, a lot of the appeal of those early R.E.M. records was the diffuse, swirly nature of them. The bass was playing the guitar parts, and the guitar was playing accents, and the drums didn't care what the bass was doing, but it seemed to all work. And on top of all that was poured vocals like so much liquid smoke. One big difference between the band you know today and the one that stole our hearts back then was that the lyrics were completely impenetrable. Michael Stipe had nothing to say and a lovely way of not saying it.

I'd spend hours upon hours listening to "Sitting Still" and "Radio Free Europe," scribbling down theoretical suppositions of what the lyrics may or may not have been, or trying to get a handle on what the song was about. It would be hard to find a bigger waste of a young man's time, because, oftentimes, said R.E.M. lyrics then were certain phonemes used as touchstones along a path filled with, as a fellow once said, ethereal bleating. There *were no* words!

This was a main point of conversation whenever I'd run into

Steve Gorman, one of the three Gorman brothers from Hopkinsville, south of Madisonville. He played drums in a band called Lack of Interest, and they played a local party house called the Bat Cave.

We'd walk down the street trading what subversive information we'd gleaned as to what the words were to a number of tunes in the R.E.M. canon. Bootleg live records were useful in our own Stipe elocution analyses. It was from Steve that I found out the chorus verse in "Radio Free Europe" was "Calling all in transit". I thought it had been "Calling all inner transients". Another popular interpretation had it to be "calling all inner trenchcoats".

Steve moved to Atlanta the next year, met some folks and helped form a band called Mr. Crowe's Garden. You know them now as the Black Crowes.

I came home from WLBJ and went to bed for a week. Then I celebrated my liberation from the place with a decent-sized bender. My God, this is it. I have no other job. I'm a musician. This is it.

I looked at the calendar in the kitchen. It was loaded with dates. I noticed that last month had been loaded with dates as well. Next month already looked pretty good. I had missed a lot of fun doing this radio station thing. I wasn't going to miss any more, that was for damn certain. And did I have some fun? You bet your ass I had some fun.

\* \* \* \*

# part two

## the road

# 9

# vannage point

The first Cheese van had made it five miles, if that far. Joe got pretty I-told-you-so about that boondoggle, and enforced an edict that no more Cheese money was to go for garbage. The next van would have to be something solid and practical—preferably something that wouldn't fill the whole interior with smoke.

We found such a beauty behind Nat's Outdoor Sports. A blue Ford Econoline. Two captain's chairs. Good stereo, and a steering wheel that adjusted. It belonged to some Nat's employee. Skot and I took it out on the interstate, and when we reached eighty-five with no problem, we looked at each other and smiled in agreement. *This* was the one. Ort helped us out with some of the money, and we raised the rest ourselves. Thus, the official commencement of the van years. No more three-to a front-seat now, boy! Go ahead, spread out and stretch your legs.

For the next four years, a great deal of our lives took place within that metal shell. We came to know it as well as you know the house you grew up in. We grew to know the smells it could conjure. The way sour beer smells in carpet. The way meat-centered food gets when it's shoved behind chrome stripping for two weeks.

At first, given that there were only two seats in the van, folding chairs filled out the seating arrangement. A folding chair is not only uncomfortable over hours of high-speed travel, it's damn dangerous. The guy next to the sliding door had to be ever-vigilant that a chair leg didn't slip off the side onto the step platform and crash the door open. I learned the hard way that folding chairs do little to hold back stacks of amplifiers and drum cases. I remember trying to stretch out and nap on the floor behind the folding chairs and in front of the rattling stack of equipment. I didn't know which was going to kill me first.

Guys in folding chairs tend to be mobile. They pick up the seat

underneath their legs and shift around constantly, scooting this way
and that. They stab the guy lying behind them with chair legs. Ahhhh!
You're on my hand! Wha? Who's down there? *You're on my hand,
asshole!* I remember lying down there when whoever was driving at
the time stood up on the brakes. Everything shifted forward with two
G-forces. I could feel that agonizing crack right over my head like
tunnel-digging POWs recognize, that awful groan a split-second before the tunnel roof collapses.

Down came everything on me. Five guitar cases. One heavy bag
full of pedals with sharp corners. The bass drum. It's teetering. Down
it comes. I was semi-shielded, because the guitar cases had already
collected above me like cave breakdown rock.

As a general rule, Skot or Joe drove, because they were the best
drivers and they didn't trust the other two of us behind the wheel any
farther than they could have thrown us. Skot once gave me two dollars *not* to drive. He said that I tended to weave.

Billy never drove. I once saw Billy get lost in a parking lot; he
pulled in one end and couldn't find his way out again. He once
walked home from Picasso's, aiming for his apartment six blocks to
the west. Somehow, he wound up at the Barren River, nine blocks to
the east, looking confusedly at the water below him; and he'd *walked*
there, with an hour's time to question whether any landmarks looked
familiar or not. So Billy didn't drive much.

September, '86. What a month. Got the van. MY BAND! It was
happening. It was really happening! *"I am! I am Superman! And I
know what's happening!"*

Our first road misery story: We were in Sewanee, in the mountains of eastern Tennessee, playing a fraternity party at the University
of the South. It was a beautiful place, and the fraternity houses were
no exception—great century-old stone edifices looking like rural
churches in the English countryside. It was already fall in the mountains, the leaves blazing, the air chilled.

The fraternity members did not actually live in their houses, and
thus, didn't bother to heat them or leave any food around. No one
was actually meant to stay overnight there, least of all us. So what
did Skot do? After the gig, with none of the equipment even packed
up yet, he decided to take the van and go chase girls. Just like that.
He stuck in the key, pulled out and left us all there, without a thought
in the world. An hour went by. Two hours. He didn't come back.

I couldn't believe it. What's he thinking? Sewanee in September is not warm, especially in a hundred-year-old stone fraternity house with no heat and nowhere to sleep. Here we were, stranded, just walking around the place, waiting to see if he'd come back, punching fists into open palms to pass time. I remember breaking beer bottles repeatedly against the side of the house, screaming "He took the fucking van! He took the fucking van!"

I'd left him a note on all the boxed-up equipment onstage. "Asshole! Happy loading!" He showed up in the morning, none too apologetic. I was on a couch and he nudged me awake. I rolled over, told him I was going to kill him later, and went back to sleep.

Ort was with us on this trip. He hadn't eaten in a while, and he had become Satan. We started for home; his blood-sugar needle shook beneath E as he sat in the van, in one of those folding chairs, throwing body odor like tear gas. With little flecks flying off his lips, he spent fifteen straight miles screaming blistering epithets at Mr. Willis, who had made it worse on himself by carrying on as if he had no idea he'd done anything wrong.

Ort's voice was a guttural, flesh-tearing Hitlerian torrent. He raged a litany of terrors that awaited in the fires of hell for Skot! He screamed of how Skot would not be spared if he bathed in "the blood of the Dead Mary!" I remember thinking "Dead Mary? Hmmm." I'd never heard that particular religious colloquialism before. I suspected Ort was making it up as he went along, but it was appropriately terrifying, given his delivery.

Mile after mile, it went on. Ort tore Skot a new asshole up one end and down the other, pummelling him with a verbal tirade about respect and consideration for others. He stopped only when I asked him to, not because I felt Skot had had enough, but I was getting tinnitus from Ort's Boeing-level oratory. What followed were two hundred more miles of cold, withering hostility. In years to come, Skot would still occasionally split like that, without telling anyone, but he did it on foot when he did.

That next week, I typed up a nerdish list of van rules. For instance, number one, *don't just take it and split, man!* Don't do drugs in it, don't unscrew grenades, etc. I taped it to the front passenger dash. Then the other guys doodled phallic rocket ships all over it. It stayed posted about a week, as I recall.

Two more captain's chairs were secured at a flea market, and we were set. Miraculously, an old brown beer cooler with a hinged top just happened to fit neatly between them. Over the years, it was hauled in and out of position enough times to wear a protruding foam-rubber welt in one of the chairs. We wrenched the seat off a school desk chair and placed it on the cooler for the inevitable fifth guy. Whoever happened to be sitting there would get a good upper thigh workout, since he was constantly getting up and holding himself in a medium crouch, while guys went to work beneath him in the cooler, either retrieving or replenishing malt-pop stock.

The band took off, we had a van, we had gigs every weekend, and I got to go places in a van and go to parties and crash at peoples' houses in different towns and see how different people lived. I got to frolic. I thought I had already said goodbye to frolic for the rest of my life. I had no idea how much was yet ahead. There were big underground kim-chi pots full of frolic on the way.

There was the first time our name appeared on a stamped-out, Ticketron-type ticket, opening for Guadalcanal Diary in Knoxville. It's the little things.

There was meeting R.E.M. backstage at the Opry House. Ort engineered it. Bill Berry came up to me and said "Government Cheese, right?" He had to have have been prompted, but he did say it. He knew one of our songs, "Face in The Crowd", I think. David Ainsworth walked up to Michael Stipe barefoot, clutching a magic marker and shouting "Sign my FACE! *DUDE!*" Stipe wouldn't do it. I think they compromised on signing his pants leg.

We'd played Lexington without much success so far, having done the Bottom Line five or six times with limp results. We gave it one more try, expecting not much more, and this time the bartender told us the phone had been ringing about us all afternoon. From then, it just took off for some reason. Lexington became a bigger town than home was.

Then, Louisville followed suit. We played Tewligan's, Phoenix Hill, or the Red Barn on U of L's campus. The Barn was especially great because you got paid the amount agreed upon by check prior to the gig. No bitching. None of that. The catch was you had to put on this ridiculous plastic bracelet that allowed you four thimbles of beer and then you were done. Uh, uh. This is Government Cheese you're talking to here. We snuck in whole cases more and hid them behind the amps. The spotlights would occasionally catch the glint of an aluminum can.

Every six weeks or so, we'd try Nashville, at Elliston Square or the Exit/In or any of a dozen other places we played over time. We had all gone there for years to *see* bands. Now here we were, one of them. We were always considered a bit of a red-headed stepchild down there, owing both to a Kentucky address and to our tendency to come off as less than professional by their own media-savvy standards. There was nothing like a gig in Music City to leave you feeling slightly unloved.

In '86, there was still no one else in Nashville who reached up to Jason and the Scorchers' ankles. They were signed to a major label, winning critics' hearts, playing two hundred dates a year, and doing their best to live up to the hype around them. It was wearing them all out from the inside, but none of us knew that at the time. The record labels were wanting to make mince-meat of their original 50/50 country-meets-punk sound, trying at every turn to morph them into another hard rock band. Live, however, they still uniquely deserved most every impossibly inflated compliment ever thrown their way.

The Scorchers gave Nashville's underground rock and roll community an intense jolt of esteem, and a sense of the possibilities. The trouble was that it was still *the* Country Music Town that couldn't possibly be bothered with what the strange, patchouli-and-scowl denizens of Cantrell's and Rooster's were up to. When the Scorchers came along, though, and had the audacity to win a record deal *from the coast,* it was like taking a hill and running up a flag with an extended middle-finger emblazoned on it. It was a Declaration of Independence. They spawned a whole, lecherous wave of imitators, us included. We weren't a slavish copy like some, but we stole enough elements for it to be obvious. A reviewer once called us "Scorcher-Lite and derivative".

Then along came cutting edge Nashville, synth guys, moody young Morrisseys and a segment that hung out in the bars so much they couldn't possibly do much else. You didn't so much play gigs to them as run their gauntlet.

Everybody was looking for a record deal, enticed by that Scorchers coastal pot of gold. There were some local indie labels paying attention: Praxis, Carlyle, the aforementioned Reptile, Dread Beat, NEO, etc., but an attitude had set in. Everyone wanted the golden-egg from the coast—east coast, west coast, *any old coast will do.* Nobody wanted those low-budget local indie deals, and no one for a second stopped to wonder what made them ever think they would be treated any less abominably by a major label than the Scorchers were being treated.

This was the Reagan '80s, with plenty of money to be spent, acquired as it was by de-regged S & Ls and other short-sighted means of capital disbursement. What it meant at ground-level was that A & R guys from labels situated on either of the aforementioned coasts had ample budget for coming to Nashville and looking for bands, and there were plenty to be seen back then.

Walk the West signed with Capitol, the Royal Court of China with A & M, In Pursuit with MTM, Webb Wilder with a series of indies and then Island. There were so many bands: the Questionnaires, the Dusters, the Movement, Raging Fire, the Boilers, Shadow 15, the White Animals. That's just the tip of the iceberg. It was quite an era.

Looking back on our old lists of dates, I see now that we averaged a gig almost every other day. Now it is just that, a list—faceless and full of secrets. Every line is a date, place and time, a day out of our lives, and whatever happened then is now an onion of layers. Peel back one memory to reveal another underneath it. You'll swear something happened on the same night *this* happened because *this thing* happened to connect the two. But it didn't, because you will then remember that the first memory involved snow on the ground, and the second recollection concerned a barefoot girl in shorts dancing up front. Then you'll remember a third thing you thought happened on both nights at the same time, and it was in a whole other town.

The list of gigs for the first five years is anal. Details are written down and rewritten on three separate typewritten lists in my files. I was so into it—I wanted to remember it all.

We played virtually nonstop back then. There was no marketing strategy, usually no record to promote or sell. If we cleared a hundred apiece at the end of a weekend, that was an event. There was no rationale to any of it. All we knew was that we were young, and if we were ever to do this, now was the time to do it. We knew we were the envy of our friends, and we were envying *the idea of ourselves as they saw us.*

Was it fun? You bet your sweet ass it was fun. This was the dream! This was what I wanted and I was living it! It was really happening. *"We are! We are Supermen! And we can see everything!"*

We would usually leave Bowling Green on a Wednesday or a

Thursday and travel to wherever the first gig was. Then would come the weekend gigs in the better towns, and we'd be greased and ready. There'd always be a party somewhere Saturday night after the show.

Sunday evening, we'd roll back into Bowling Green, dirty and baggy-eyed, and generally fairly fatigued. Two or three days later, the cycle would start up again. While at home, we were expected to do whatever was needed, order T-shirts, make a new newsletter, update the mailing list, fix the broken guitar, fix the broken van, dodge the landlord and run the bar tab at Picasso's up as far as possible.

The amazing thing about all those years is we got along as well as we did. People were always remarking about how different we all four were. We knew it was a selling point, and that the music reflected all our differences, but after awhile we were so inside the situation that we no longer thought about it.

Skot had finished up his degree, and to this day, Government Cheese is the only completely college-graduate band I know of besides Queen.

We even managed to put our degrees to use somehow. Skot was a marketing major, Joe and I broadcasting, and Billy geology. Skot kept the ledger, sold the T-shirts and paid calls on record stores. Joe and I attacked radio stations, doing interviews, and Billy took soil samples everywhere we went. Okay, not really, but that was the joke we told everybody.

Money was a constant problem, even in the best of times. Billy had moved back to Bowling Green, into the apartment underneath Skot's, and the only thing that kept the two of them from being tossed out on the streets was that their landlord was a fan. Even he got tired of excuses occasionally, though.

There were all sorts of money-stretching schemes. Billy ran a spliced phone line precariously across the roof and into Skot's phone. It was understood that only those in Skot's apartment would answer when it rang. To answer down in Billy's apartment was to invite a torrent of abuse from above. If the call was for Billy, then Skot, or whoever was up there, would stomp on the kitchen floor as hard as possible. Eventually, the plaster started falling in on Billy's ceiling.

Both took in roommates when their apartments were barely large enough for a boy and his dog. Skot's apartment deserves an honor-roll of co-tenants throughout the ages. David "Purple" Hayes, Chris "Viva Las Vegas" Becker (who will figure largely in our story later), Chris Heric, Tim Brown (who used to amateur wrestle wearing a

Government Cheese T-shirt), and many others. Skot had a tiny alcove that you couldn't stand up in, above the kitchen. It was the Last Chance Crash Pad. Gus Moore lived there awhile. Jason Nuttle. I lived there awhile.

Billy took in Jason Harman, his own brother, Ned, me for a while and Dan Dilomarter, who was always driving them crazy upstairs because he would never fail to answer the phone on the first ring. He never learned the procedure.

Ken Smith was the idea man's idea man, but the little practicalities of club maintenance often escaped him. When he had a soundman to look after the stage, lights and equipment, things ran smoothly, but during bare patches when Ken either couldn't—or wouldn't—pay somebody full-time, he looked after the Picasso's gear himself. That was where the trouble would begin.

Not to disrespect Ken, who is, as I have said, a great man of the blues; but when he ran things alone, stuff got broken and never got fixed. The mike-stand population would dwindle. Patch cords would become increasingly valuable each gig. Things would either fall apart or vanish altogether.

The boiling point for Skot came before a gig one night, at soundcheck, when he discovered that not one of the stage lights worked. As it was, for weeks already, there had been only one light left, a red one we'd bloom out all the way so we would be bathed in its anemic scarlet vibe. We looked like a rock band in a photographer's dark room. And now, that light was gone too.

Fed up completely, Skot went back to his apartment and detached all his table lamps. He brought them back and set them around the stage in a rather affecting pattern. The look was automatically so striking that I wondered why no one had tried it before.

Suddenly, that trashy little stage was such a homey place. The lamps made furniture out of the amps. The whole stage now looked like a living room. It was as warm and inviting as the front window of a furniture store. I raced home for a lamp of my own. Thus, a short-lived, yet fondly remembered craze, was born.

We casually passed through the grapevine that bringing a lamp would suffice as cover charge. We got dozens of them. Classic wooden ones. Great, ornate, faux-glass mini-chandeliers, huge shades, tiny shades. We earnestly tried to be grateful and use them all until several gigs into the endeavor, when we found ourselves too often tripping over and bumping into what had become an ungodly number of table lamps. The lamps became combatants we fought for stage space.

Once or twice, when we were out of town, we sold lamps to people in the audience who'd expressed an interest. "Oh, I've just *got* to have that one for the foyer!" It's yours, baby. Twenty bucks. We became both a show and a showroom.

It was sad to see the lamps go, but they had to. Table lamps didn't travel well in a rock and roll road situation. They flailed around in the back on top of other gear. The shades got holes. The nice china ones shattered routinely. We tried taking all the shades off and stacking them. No good. We had to bid the lamps goodbye, and people were sad. We were sad. Too bad no one made a road case for table lamps. No one does yet, to my knowledge.

Jane Pearl carried her cannon of a voice from group to group around town. She was in the Ken Smith band for a while, sang with Clayton Payne occasionally. She stood tall and took no crap from anybody, with brown hair all the way down her back and usually wearing some loose, muu-muu dashiki-type thing. She used to say "We don't tell you what to drink. Don't tell us what to sing."

She was also handy with stitchery, and made us curtains for the side windows of the van. They gave the side windows a hip, fifties kitchenette feel.

Some fan who worked at a magnetic sign factory in Louisville made us three "Government Cheese" signs to slap on the side of the van. We used them, too, that is, until somebody finally took us aside and told us they looked a bit silly, frankly. We pulled them out of service and eventually misplaced them.

Weeks later, people started telling us they'd seen us driving in places where we hadn't been, at times we couldn't have been there. It confused us until we learned that a gray van in Murfreesboro, Tennessee was driving around with "Government Cheese" slapped on the side. Whoever that was, and why they were doing it, is anybody's guess.

I was the band's big reader, which isn't saying much. There were no reading lights in the van, either. When it got dark, it got dark. And then we listened to the tape deck, that is, until Lou Reed got stuck in there one day right in the middle of "I Love You Suzanne". It would doggedly stay that way for years, despite the best efforts of a squadron of butter-knife-wielding audiosurgeons. From then on, for years, all we had was the radio.

And then, sometime down the road, the left speaker went out in the van. To our dismay, this coincided almost to the day with the onset of classic-hits radio. I can't tell you how many times I've heard "Radar Love" with no guitar, since it was shunted off entirely in the one channel we could no longer receive. The first couple of times, it was interesting. Then it became an incredible irritant, and finally, it became strangely normal. To this day, there are classic rock tunes that don't sound right to me with both speakers, because I'm so used to they way they sounded when I heard them over and over again in the van. Now, it sounds like there are extra instruments on top of the version I'm used to.

Before you chastise us for not being hip and listening to the college radio at the left end of the dial, let me remind you we played most all our gigs in the American South. There was no such thing as the much-heralded, mythologized *college radio*, except perhaps within twenty miles of a large town. All we had that we could all four settle on was classic hits. I hate classic hits now. I despise "All Right Now" by Free, which is a tune I really used to love. I used to really like Creedence Clearwater Revival, and now I passionately wish none of them had ever been born. The worst thing you can do to me is strap me down, and put "Green River" on the stereo. *No! Stop! I'll tell you anything you want! Stop!* And as for Jim Morrison, don't even get me started.

That van was drafty. I remember putting duct tape across the gasket gaps in the side windows. When it was really cold, we had to put our feet up on the seats because they went numb at floor level. Thick hunting socks helped a bit.

There was one "bed", the bass-amp speakers laid on their sides behind the back chairs. We had two orange foam pads to put on top of that, and if you hopped in first thing in the morning and grabbed it, it was yours.

People are hypocrites about farts. They seem to privately enjoy their own whilst voicing indignity regarding neighborly gastric exhaust. One's own causes a swell of esteem, yet this same sulfurous air-mail offends when viewed as foreign intrusion. Why this is, no one knows. I think it's an evolutionary holdover, having something to do with the same reasons dogs and cats pee their initials on their property.

If one fellow was asleep, policy held that we blamed him and the matter was put to bed, so to speak. He was then the one who got things thrown at him and charley-horse punches to the ribs and legs until he woke up surly and retaliatory.

For a while, we played an intolerable game called "Slugs and Safeties". The rules were simple. If you cut a good one, it was up to you to shout out "Safety!" and that meant the other guys couldn't slug you. A slug was, technically, one sharp jab to the upper shoulder musculature, using the obnoxious fist perfected in adolescence, with the middle knuckle pushed forward as a missile. I'd been slugged about five times (at least three of them being convictions without a trial) before I fully lost my temper.

I remember thinking, here I am, twenty-four years old, and I'm in Tennessee with snow on the ground and my feet are numb and Willis just slugged me because I didn't say "Safety" and it wasn't even *my fart,* man! (Was too.) *Was not!* (Yes it was.) *It was not!* (Was too, man.) I can't believe I'm a grown man participating in this conversation. (Then you admit it was yours.) No! I don't!

Then again, if it was something truly heinous that could oxidize paint, it became something to claim rather than deny. Yeah motherfucker, that was me. Here, have another. Skot was generally pretty good about owning up to his own. Billy would offer commentary you didn't really want regarding them, analyzing and talking about "particulate matter", and how some air-current phenomenon called a "convection cell" allowed the shotgun-rider to get a full-force intestinal blast from the guy sleeping on the bass speakers, while leaving the middle-seat guys unmolested. (I never understood it, but damned if it didn't work.) I confessed about half the time. Joe was a big baby. He never ever owned up to his own farts.

\* \* \* \*

# 10

# mice do not read longfellow

*It's been ten years since Terry Cates' Gremlin and 8-tracks that go ka-chunk. It's the sound of Picasso's now, the sound of a dream, the sound of new freshmen who think we're God.*

*Spinning around on the little Picasso's stage, in my crotchless tuxedo, jacked to the innocent bejimmies on white-crosses, peppermint schnapps and Edmonson County homegrown, the stage is like the remnants of a hurricane—tipped-over bottles, guitar picks, broken drumsticks, broken strings, discarded shirts, ripped-up set lists, requests written on napkins, snaking mike and guitar cords, and little globs of spittle like North Sea whitecaps or Himalayas from space.*

*The crowd is like a bunch of agitated ferns clustered and reaching. We're bashing through "White Light/White Heat" by the Velvet Underground because everybody plays Velvets covers now. Don't ask silly questions. Our version sounds more like "Wipeout" than the original, but fuck it. There are no critics down front, just youth as ferns. Skot tears from one end of the stage to the other. "White Light! Oh white light a bustin' up my mind! White light, oh wha huh huh make meh go blind!" Bless him. A monster performer, but he never learns words for shit.*

*The energy. THE ENERGY! I'm jumping around. Billy's hunched over his bass like a condor and swinging it like an axe. Joe's bashing the shit out of his crash cymbal into my ear. I climb up on my amp, I rip off my shirt and the amp wobbles underneath me, about to fall forward. I throw my shirt aside and, while my guitar feeds back, beat on my chest, "Ahhhhhhhhhh!" I jump into the air and hit a wild A-chord just as Skot slides underneath me on the stage, like Pete*

*Townshend at the end of that movie. I land square on his ankle. It must be painful, but the moment is too intense. The only way we know Skot's in pain is the change in the lyrics he never knows anyway.*

*"White Light! Oh white light a bussin up my miaaahhnd! White Heat, uh . . . (I land on him) GAAHHDDAMMITT!!! GAHHHD-DAMMITT!! WHITE HEAT! WHITE HEAT!" Skot gets to his feet, looks at the youth ferns and screams like I just did: "AAHHHHHHHHH!!!" He dives into them, they swallow him whole, chew him, glaze him with youth fern spit, love him, and vomit him back. Oh, the kinetic sodden blarney of it all.*

It was the fall of '86. We bore no resemblance to the ramshackle outfit that had driven them away in that cold frat basement and perplexed them at the Alibi. We were loud, fresh, fast, popular, and never again to be this young. It was a great time to be the four fellows we were.

The show was tight—not the most musically impeccable thing in town, but nobody touched our energy level. We hopped onstage, slugged a beer or two, and went nonstop for two hours. We were at Picasso's at least twice a week, and got to watch while a lot of Western students got wrecked. A lot of others used us as their aerobic workout. Whatever the reason, a night we played meant a lot of people were late for work or missed classes the next day.

Numerous were the nights I stumbled in way past dawn. I was young and could take it, I suppose. There was no such thing any more as a gig at home without a post-gig party. It was a given, and we were made to feel like the licentious guests of honor. Having not been used to being the guest of anything before, I tended to party my skinny little irrepressible ass off, and then spend my mornings in post-party introspection, worrying and wondering about what I might have done THIS time. More and more, as the mornings passed and added up, I was giving myself plenty to worry about.

September, 1986: we played at 12th and Porter in Nashville. The Dusters, a ZZ Toppish blues trio starting to work with Tutt and featuring Ken McMahan on guitar, opened up for us that night. A fellow showed up by the name of Tom Sturges. He was the son of legendary Hollywood writer/director Preston Sturges, and worked in Los Angeles for Chrysalis Music, the publishing division of Chrysalis Records. He'd flown in to Nashville to see some act, seen them, been there, done that, and then had come over here to check the Dusters out.

A bit boozy, he and a friend tumbled out at 12th and Porter just in time to see us, missing the Dusters completely. Tom stayed for our entire set, though, and fell in love.

That evening, Tom Sturges, of Chrysalis Music, located in Los Angeles By God California, determined that Government Cheese not only had the look and the attitude, but the songs as well. They needed a little tweaking, polishing, etc, but not to worry, fellas. He was *in* publishing. He *knew* songs. This was a *song* kind of *guy*.

He had just engineered the putting-together of George Michael and Aretha Franklin for that one song they sang together. We cared nothing at all for George Michael, but were impressed that Tom Sturges talked to him on the phone. That was a hell of a lot more than we did in an average day.

We met him and exchanged small talk, then assumed he was out of our lives forever once he walked out the 12th & Porter door. It was nice and a little exciting that someone from L.A. would be interested in us; but we didn't expect it to continue. It was like the beautiful girl in high school who kissed you one night when she was drunk. It's not smart to dwell on it, 'cause she ain't comin' back.

But Tom Sturges *did* come back. He came back the next week, and he called us! And then he called *ME* from *L.A.* Me! Then he called me again while driving down the Santa Monica Freeway. I had never talked to someone who was phoning from their car. That was pretty cool.

During that last conversation, he told me straight out that he wanted Government Cheese on Chrysalis Music and would see what he could do about getting us on Chrysalis Records.

He said that. Exactly what I just told you. He said it from his car on one of those freeways I'd seen on television, that Squad 51 Rampart freeway. He wanted us on Chrysalis Music and would see what he could do about Chrysalis Records.

Rockinassmutherfucking A. Yes. Dream a little dream, sing yer little song, make a little record and the man from Cali with the phone in the car calls yer ass. Yes. Mutherfukkin kiss my ass in Kentucky! It's happening! It's really happening! *"I am! I am Superman! And I Am What's Happening!!"*

Yes!

Scott Tutt smelled another dog in his backyard.

He had offered us a management and recording deal and we hadn't signed it yet, though he was hot for us to do so. He was sure that we wouldn't be savvy or confident enough to shunt him aside and make a deal with Tom directly. No, he figured, that would have been *way* too smart of us. He was right.

Sturges and Tutt were a study in contrasts. Tom Sturges never raised his voice up to what was Tutt's standard decibel level to begin with. Tom wore T-shirts and leather jackets, but you could bet your ass they were always the right T-shirts for the right jackets. Tom Sturges was L.A. all the way, could probably order wine and mix with anyone without offending any sensibilities. Tutt, on the other hand, chewed gum open-mouthed, and at any moment might pull out his "dancing pussy", a two-inch-tall vagina replica that hopped across a table top when wound up. I remember that at the time, we in the band were just hoping the two could work together somehow. I don't know how we figured they could, but we hoped. Tutt was just banking we didn't realize that we didn't need him at all now. We didn't figure that out. Tutt already had us in his grip a little bit, drawing us into his cult of personality.

We were learning from Tutt about the recording industry. We thought we already knew something, but he assured us—not entirely without merit—that we knew nothing.

Tutt loved to sit in his office and pontificate, telling us all the ins and outs of the music business, sharing his knowledge of twenty-something years. We would sit there late into the night listening to him, while he sat in his chair with one leg pulled up underneath the other one. He always sat like that.

One thing about that guy, he told a great story. He would jump up and run around the room, acting scenes out, waving his arms, laughing and screaming, profanity billowing like sails at the front and back of every sentence. In such a manner, he put us through the Scott Tutt School of Music Business. We would listen like little kids, all but taking notes, expecting a test. Here are some of my mental crib notes from those nights of indoctrination:

The first term we must learn is *major label.*

Most all the records you can buy in stores, most all the bands you can go see playing your town, virtually all the video artists and an overwhelming majority of the hits come to you courtesy of acts signed to major labels. You might look in a store and see all the different labels on the back of CD jackets. It looks like there's hundreds of them, all different logos, different genres, etc. With that many labels, it would seem that the odds are in one's favor of eventually snaring a deal with the right one. Yes, it would seem.

But there aren't hundreds of major labels.

Look on the fine print at the bottom of the package, where it says "Dist. By." It'll say another record label's name, hidden under the other's bigger logo. THAT is the major label. And there aren't hundreds of those.

A paltry handful of major labels actually exist, and they're becoming, essentially, distribution houses for all types of sub-labels who have slugged their way through the industry jungle to a resting spot under a major's umbrella. The major provides the clout to get the record in the stores, the money for making the video, the promoters who get the record and video played, the connections with booking agents to get the act on the road with other bigger artists, yadda yadda yadda. Whole books could be written about this set-up. Whole books already have been.

Suffice it to say that money talks and bullshit walks. Without a major label, a band has such an uphill climb that you can pretty much go ahead and say that, so far as dreams of riches and fame go, the band is screwed before they've started. They keep their honor and little else.

Thankfully, in the noble causes of art and beauty for its own sake, hundreds of independent record labels fight on, doggedly making records on shoestring budgets and struggling to get the product in the stores. It's an amazing trial just getting a record into your local outlet without major label clout at the distribution warehouse, as we'll point out later.

For an artist, as we learned at Tutt's knee, the main advantage to an indie label is artistic control. An indie label artist can, in most cases, still have a serious input on how the record sounds, what the songs say, etc. The only hope for non-commercial or fringe artists, those with less than mainstream messages, are the indies.

The majors are run by accountants now. Time was when rock was young, and the fellows with cigars sat upstairs and (wisely) let "the kids" make their music the way they wanted. It is a truism that virtually all the great rock records were made by artists given complete rein in the stuido, to create sounds and styles, to venture into territory untested. The honchos got out of Jimi Hendrix's way, for instance. They stood back and said "I don't get it, Herb, but he knows what the kids like. So long as he doesn't say anything dirty on the record . . . "

It's a fact today that the likelihood of Jimi Hendrix being even *signed* to a major is nil. Today it seems like a fantasy that Elvis Presley was allowed to run all his own sessions in the fifties and trust his own instincts, or that a 21-year-old Brian Wilson was given complete control of Beach Boys' sessions in '62. Nowadays, that would be unthinkable. The only instinct trusted today is the bottom line.

Today, majors assign an act to a producer who makes the act sound like everyone else who has sold records recently. And, as with all things mass-appeal-oriented, the edges are filed down. All intriguing facets are smoothed over like a steamroller on a hot new road.

Hence, the battle. The major's the only game in town. The band makes the music, but the major makes the rules, and guess who makes all the money?

We would listen to Tutt talk about these things incessantly and over time, we assimilated what he wanted to do. He wanted Reptile Records to someday be one of those many indies with a "Dist. by" under its name on the jacket. He conjured this infectious vision of that wonderful day when that would happen. There would be wine, women and dancing in the streets.

And he persistently reiterated how he would have to have all our legal rights signed over to him in order to someday negotiate this dream deal. All of 'em. The right to manage. The right to be producer. The rights to the song publishing. All the rights. Everything we could give him. *Everything.*

The deal Tutt offered us was one he kept calling "the standard deal for any new artist". This was code for "a deal so bad only a naive and desperate new artist would ever consider signing it".

There was nothing terribly sneaky about the deal, no fine print involving our first-borns or anything. It was just incredibly one-sided and preposterously long, that's all. A five-year slavery deal. The contracts gave Tutt final say on everything and a hand in every pie — record producing, publishing royalties, management. He would get

the rights to run the whole show and disregard our opinions whenever
he cared to. An incredibly onerous package. We wouldn't be able to
go to the bathroom without his permission. It went totally over our
heads, too. It was so bad, we thought it was good.

We weren't *complete* idiots. We knew what lawyers were for, and
we went to several. Joel Stoner looked over the deal first. He worked
at Cumberland Trace Legal Services in Bowling Green. Yes, the contract was onerous, he said. And yes, from what he knew, so many
music contracts *were* onerous. The guy offering you the deal holds
every card, he said. All you hold is your guitar. It was, he surmised, a
legal deal — better than some, worse than others. We were giving him
everything. His advice? Sign it if you want to. It's your life.

Then we took it to Richard Frank, an honest to God old guy attor-
ney in a *big office building* in Nashville. He had done lots of music-
biz contracts. He told us basically the same thing Joel Stoner had —
that the contract was onerous and one-sided, but aren't they all? His
advice? You're giving him everything: management, recording, publishing. He's got the whole pie for five years. It's legal. Sign it if you
want to.

At our next meeting with Tutt, we sat down in his office and told
him there were several clauses we wanted changed. He got nasty with
us, and immediately so. All these years later, I can quote him.

Holding the contract aloft by its stapled corner, he leaned across
the table and snapped "Listen! The more you guys wanna fuck
around with this piece of paper, the less excited I am about working
with you! You guys don't know shit about the music business! You
have never sold a single record before! Not a single record!

"I've sold *millions . . . !*"

He let a moment of silence linger, as we sat there quiet and
cowed. Then he repeated that bold little word.

"*Millions . . . !*"

Tutt may have promoted a million-seller or two, and he did own a
couple of them, and he may have said "motherfucker" a million
times, but he hadn't *sold* jack shit. It was an incredible lie, a big, bold,
juicy show-biz lie he told looking directly into everyones' eyes at the
table, and it worked perfectly. We clammed right up.

He did, however, eventually change most of the clauses we
wanted changed, and he did another thing that worked out very well
for the band, by agreeing to a clause that we not pay management

commissions until we were making two hundred dollars per man per week. We never ever paid Scott Tutt a penny in management commission because of that very clause.

One morning, perhaps afternoon to most people, I was sitting in the living room chair, smoking the cigarette butts left in the wastebasket. I was strumming my guitar watching CNN with the volume turned down. This was the typical depressive beginning to my day. Then, I got an idea for a chorus. "Fish Stick Day! Fish Stick Day! We can't wait for Fish Stick Day! Run-run-run to the cafeteri-AY. Fish Stick Day! Fish Stick Day! F-I-S-H-S-T-I-C-K! Fish Stick Day!''

It was the stupidest idea I had ever had in my life, and I was thusly compelled to finish it.

The band learned the "song", such as there ever was one, on-stage, during actual gigs, changing it as we went along. It was a drum beat with words chanted over the top of it. "The teacher lines up the whole third grade, OOH AAHH YUMM YUMM! It's Fish Stick Day", etc. We never ever rehearsed it. It just came to life one night in the middle of a Picasso's gig, when Billy started screaming "F-I-S-H-S-T-I-C-K", spitting out each letter in a voice that let you know it was all caps. I held my guitar up in the air to show when to change chords from A to C to D to E. And we didn't have to change chords much.

Immediately, it was a huge hit with our crowd. I guess I can see why. Everybody had a fish stick day growing up. The lunch room invariably served fish sticks every Friday, because of the Catholics who have rules about that sort of thing.

Everywhere we played, "Fish Stick Day" was a hit. It wasn't a "song", per se. You didn't get a spiritual lift out of playing it. There was no melody at all. It was, at best, a drum-based chant.

None of us considered it an integral part of the act until one night about a month later when we didn't do it all night, and the howls of protest rang in.

"Where's 'Fish Stick Day', you bastards!?"

"Man, sorry, the club's closing. We gotta stop now."

*"NO MAN! NO! 'FISH STICK DAY'! 'FISH STICK DAY'"*!

We were dumbfounded. People wanted to hear it *that badly*? What gave? From then on, though, we made sure to always do "Fish

Stick Day''. Some nights it was still funny to me, some nights not so, but you give the people what they want.

Skot conjured up what he called his ''Flying Fish'' dance, which he did during the number. He hopped up and down on both feet as if there was an invisible pogo stick between his legs, folding his arms up and out at the elbows but keeping his upper arms tight to his ribs. Then he flapped his hands wildly, like flippers, bopping from one end of the stage to the other.

This was Skot Willis, Mr. Cool, flapping his flipper hands all over the stage, bouncing up and down, and occasionally flopping to the ground to do the ''Flying Fish Out of Water'' variation.

We discovered that the couch backs on Billy's sectional furniture—long rectangles of foam rubber with a rough, brown, cloth zip-up covering—looked sort of like fish sticks. Billy started bringing them to the gigs.

They were huge. They barely stood up straight on Picasso's stage because they were so long. While we played ''Fish Stick Day'', Billy would haplessly try to wave them around or gesture with them somehow, or give them to someone to do what they chose with.

I vividly remember Tutt telling us, ''Okay guys, Tom Sturges is coming in from L.A. with a publicist. *Don't let Billy forget to bring his fish sticks.*''

It was that important. One day we were a punk band with a mission, and then the next day we were doing flying fish dances and waving Billy's furniture around because they looked like fish sticks. Ooooookay.

In October, 1986, we all signed our names to a long management contract with Scott Tutt. A month later, we signed an exclusive recording contract. We gave him everything we could legally give him in the music business. He got the exclusive management rights. He got exclusive recording rights. He got all the publishing. He got everything.

They were five year deals, running concurrently, actually, one year deals with four one-year options to each of them. This meant the contracts could be renewed over and over for up to five years *by Tutt, not us*. It was his choice. We just plopped our lives in his lap, and from then on, he owned us completely.

Speaking only for myself, I signed out of naive enthusiasm, along with a healthy dose of underconfidence and gullibility. Tutt was the smartest guy around, or so he kept telling us over and over. So what the hell. Here goes nothing.

The main thrust of both contracts was that Reptile would release a full-length Government Cheese album every twelve months. That was the deal. It was in writing. One album a year for five years.

It would take only a short time into the deal to realize how few records we were going to actually wind up getting to make, and to what extent we'd altered our futures—together and separately—with a few adult strokes of a pen. But, let's not get ahead of ourselves.

You hear whining crap from dullard rockers all the time: "Oh, our old manager was a dick, man. He screwed us over. He did this wrong. He didn't do this at all. Etc. . etc."

In many cases I'm sure this is true, but, in fairness, I must contend it's extremely rare for a manager-type to sit behind his desk and greedily rub his hands together, saying "Oh boy! Who can I *SCREW OVER* today?" Malice does not seedbed these affairs, generally.

I am quite sure that Tutt unshakably believed we would release five albums, just as I was completely convinced of it when I signed my name on the last line, on the last page—and came back a month later, and signed my name on the last line, of the last page, at the bottom, right over where my name was typed. At the time it was all beautiful. Somebody cared. Somebody believed. We were going to make records and tour and get famous.

Meanwhile, the road show continued and grew wilder. Lexington was nuts. It wasn't the most polite crowd we would come to know. It was an unholy mixture. Button-down-shirted slam-dancers is a social cocktail that never quite rings true. But there were lots of great people. Afghan Whigs used to open for us, and I recall Ashley Judd being a regular presence, as she was a UK student at the time. In the next few years, it seemed I'd spend as much time in Lexington as I did at home. There are many Lexington faux-colonial walk-ups I woke up in wondering where the hell I was. We stayed in at least half the rooms at the Congress Inn just past New Circle Road. Twenty-five bucks a night. The "n"s on the bedspreads were backwards. They must have been stitched in Russia.

We took a trip to Memphis to open for Jerry Dale McFadden, whose record was now out. Reptile's debut product. Ort came with us. Tutt tried to put up with Ort as best he could, because he knew how we seemed to feel about our errant manchild genius. Ort did not return the sentiment. He despised Tutt.

That night, the problem was not between the two of them, but between Ort and the doorman at the Antenna Club. The doorman, whose name was Dirk, or something of that manly nature, was tough as nails. His hair was already graying and he had a couple of places on his face that could have been laugh lines or, just as easily, knife scars. He was past forty, maybe. His sleeveless, age-spotted arms were still hard as coconuts, though. Dirk lounged in the front door and took the gate money, keeping an eye on his bike. It would not have been a good idea to touch his bike.

Ort was trying to talk to some young bowhead chicklet who couldn't hope to understand or care about what he was trying to say. He was trying to tell her about Freeman Kitchens' general store/post office in Drake, and how it was a repository for all things wonderful in this corrupted and cynical world. This young sorority lovely couldn't care less. She assumed the long-haired, bespectacled fellow with cracker-crumbs in his beard was trying to hit on her. These girls always assume that people are trying to hit on them. "Eaumuhgawd!" She complained to Dirk, who approached Ort, who hadn't eaten recently enough, judging by how he thundered into Dirk, calling him a "White Trash Nazi Motherfucker".

When Ort thundered out "White Trash Nazi Motherfucker!", he didn't say it like you or I would have. Ort said it with a forefinger thrust high in the air, like Patrick Henry saying "Give Me Liberty, or Give Me Death." All Dirk heard was the "Give me death" part, though. *"Please kick my ass, biker-man, sir".*

He was very gracious, I think, in letting Ort live. The two were split in opposite corners and Ort accepted that his words for the bowhead were pearls before swine.

Meanwhile, Jerry Dale was winding up on stage. Things had already gone awry between Tutt and Jerry Dale. Jerry Dale was a quiet guy offstage, and as much Tutt's opposite as anyone. Jerry Dale didn't like the way his album had turned out. The basic tracks were great, but the final mix was ultra-dry and low-fi in a way that perhaps no one but Tutt had envisioned. Jerry Dale, for one, didn't like it at all. He was in a rough position. At least with Government Cheese, there were four of us against only one Tutt, but Jerry Dale was all alone. He found he couldn't get Tutt on the phone; he'd have to talk to Susan or Ellen, whom he couldn't stand. He was spooked by their whole scene, and over time, had started acting more and more agitated.

Jerry Dale's main song was a rollicking S & M sendup called "Country Beats the Hell Out Of Me." The punch line was "I like to listen to *Hank* while I'm being *spanked.*" He immediately found himself in the same boat that we had with "Fish Stick Day." It took over his act, and suddenly Jerry Dale, pumpin' pianist with one foot in Jerry Lee and one in Elton John, found himself labelled and promoted as the "S & M Cowboy." This wasn't at all what he had intended for himself, and, being only 22, he hadn't had the hindsight yet to know it would have happened. All he knew was that his image and career were out of his control, and he wasn't happy about it.

Jerry Dale finished his show with a leap and a flourish. He was a white-hot showman, turning flips on his piano, telling jokes and diffidently tossing off honky tonk piano with no small amount of major-scale polish thrown in at just the right moments to let everyone know how much he could really play.

At the very end of the show, he took a flying leap off the piano and banged the hell out of his leg. Blood and bruises were involved. Clamors for an encore would have to go unheeded, as he had really knocked himself good.

As we were all backstage checking on Jerry Dale's injuries, we suddenly heard a voice from onstage. Ort.

"Ladies and Gentlemen, it comes to my attention that Jerry Dale McFadden has hurt his leg. An encore, sadly, must be reasoned a nonpossibility. As impossible as my executing Limbo District in 9/13 time. I shall now entertain you with my rendition of the Dennis laugh . . . "

And then we heard this distinctive "Nyyyaaiigghhhh!" shriek, which is how Dennis (a fellow from Athens who drove his car into a wall and came out somewhat the worse for it) laughs.

Ort's oratory then took off on a Zen master plane of utter Dadaist nonsense that cried out for a tape recorder. It was beautiful, hilarious, and I can't remember any of it, except at the end, where he paused for effect and said, in conclusion, "But you know . . . mice do not read Longfellow . . . "

Tutt blew his top, "Mice don't fukkin read *WHAT?*", and forever banned Ort from the Government Cheese stage, apparently certain that he had the authority now to even say who we could allow on our own stage with us. And so Ort was banned from the stage. Every now and then after that, Tutt would yell when he heard Ort had been on-stage talking. Honestly, Scott, I don't know what you're talking about. Ort onstage? Not that I remember recently. You said no more Ort, and *you're the boss.*

Yes, he was the boss, all right. He called all the shots from this point forward. Ort blew his top the night he found out Tutt was going to produce our records from now on. It broke his heart. He was going to try to get Peter Buck of R.E.M. to produce us.

Whether that would have really happened or not was now immaterial, because we had now signed a five-year deal that said it *couldn't happen for damn sure.* Whether or not there was really a chance in hell of Peter Buck producing us was not so important as the fact that the door was now closed to the possibility forever, or at least for five years, which was pretty much forever.

It didn't take long to see how, since we'd signed the deal, people like Ort, Sweeney, Schkip, Byron and Marc—all of our friends and associates who didn't trust Scott Tutt any farther than they could throw him—were fading back a bit from our swirling center, like we were on the back end of a train, with the lantern swinging back and forth, waving goodbye. Their world, an obviously cooler one, was giving us up to Tutt's insular, spooky one. See ya when we make it big, we said waving.

Yeah, right, they said, waving.

One night, perhaps the night we opened for Rob Jungklas, we found Joe behind Tewligan's cursing his car engine. He had driven himself to the gig and, for whatever reason, his car was refusing to start. No one could figure out why. It was dead as Caesar.

Ort approached the vehicle and inquired as to the nature of the problem. Well, Ort, the car won't start. What is it you're not clear on?

Ort genially pushed Joe out of the way and did all those things you do to an engine when you have no idea what you're doing. You know, jiggle the spark plug connectors, knock the white stuff off the battery terminal, etc. Eventually, Ort stood up, pulled his filthy handkerchief out of his pocket and wiped his brow, leaving streaks of grease on his forehead.

"Well, Joe, buddy," he said. "I think that, at this point, all we can do . . . is pray."

Ort bowed his head with his hands folded in front of him and proceeded to do just that.

Silence. Sshhh. He's praying!

He finished his prayer. "Try it now," he said.

Joe did. The car started up, and Joe drove home.

\* \* \* \*

# 11

# who's in charge here?

(Author's Note: In the process of writing this book—which I hope you're enjoying—I've tried to keep forever in mind that none, or very few, of you ever heard Government Cheese's music and, therefore, don't give a damn about self-referential song analyses. Nor do you probably care for inside gossip, or any kind of detail that implies you picked up the book with any previous interest in the band. That said, however, considering that there *are* about an even five dozen people scattered over several states who do want that type of detail, and have various questions they want answered, and that they paid for their books too, there is hence a little bit of historical tidbitry—regarding musical and aesthetic matters, and just the occasional spleen drainage—here and there for their enjoyment only. I try to keep this esoterica to a tolerable modicum, and thanks to the rest of you for your indulgence. Now back to the story. T.W.)

Chelsea Studio is in Brentwood, Tennessee. It was built, I understand, by Tom T. Hall.

Tutt wanted to record us 32-track digital. In 1986, that was about as good as it got. You still used a reel of tape, but the information encoded on it was all binary numbers. No tape noise, no distortion— extremely *clean*-sounding. We'd heard that many jazz and classical records were being made this way.

We were to discover that, for rock and roll, a medium that actually *benefits* from aural distortion, the switch to the digital age has been a bit problematic. I'll spare you the tech-head explanation. Suffice to say it takes a crafty knob-twiddler to record a rock band digitally and not have them come out cold and bloodless-sounding. Not that we knew, nor cared, about the technical aspects at the time. We were thinking "hey, great! 32-track digital! That's really expensive and cool, isn't it?"

Chelsea didn't have a 32-track machine in-house—few folks did—but Tutt managed to get one for two weeks exactly, not a day more. The plan was for us to go in and record our album and mix it, or at least get rough mixes, in that fortnight period. It didn't happen that way. It didn't happen any way *near* that. The way it turned out, you couldn't tell that was the original goal at all.

The only way to have captured Government Cheese at the time would have been to hang microphones up in the room and get a real shitty, in-the-moment, documentation of what was, frankly, a real shitty in-the-moment band. It was ludicrous to drag out a 32 track Mitsubishi digital recording machine at ungodly expense to try to capture what we were about. You mean you're going to use every expensive '80s recording trick to capture a band that *can't get in tune?* Whoa!

But that was precisely what happened, and, at the time, it sounded to us like a really neat idea. We knew all the expenses were recoupable, meaning we wouldn't see any royalties until the whole thing was paid off. We *did* realize that. But we were young. What the hell, let the Yankee spend his money. For that matter, can we write off the beer as a recording expense? Really? *Hot damn!*

We set up in Chelsea's carpeted big room. It was breathtaking. This was no basement in Bowling Green, for damn sure. There was a beautiful grand piano in the back of the room, lovely wood designs on the walls, lights that dimmed, and a great big window in the wall affording the classic view: from the producer, godlike, behind the mixing board, to *his boys* in the room.

One thing that room *did not* have was ambience. I guess that's a compliment to the designers. Country record producers in the eighties didn't want sounds bouncing off the walls like a big-room Phil Spector record or anything. You could clap your hands in that room until they fell off and not hear a whiff of slapback. No reverberation. No nothing. A microphone in that room would just record pure sound, dead and dry. You could, presumably, add all the excitement you wanted later with the avalanche of cool expensive gear they had in the control room, where Tutt and Mr. Big already sat, like Mission Control engineers in Houston.

Joe was in one tiny room with his drums. Billy and I were in the big room, and Skot was in yet another, singing temporary "guide" vocals. We couldn't all see each other at the same time. I had to bend over and look through a little pane of glass to make faces at Joe. Tutt was across the big window from us all, and only Billy and I, standing out in the big room, could see him.

We did several takes of something. I forget what. Then we went in the control room to check it out like we always had. We listened and picked the take we liked.

Tutt spun around in his chair, and, with a wry smile, said "Guys, *I* pick the takes."

What!?

Yeah, yeah! We know what we signed, but we didn't really think he was going to *enforce* the damn thing, did we?! Up until then, *"Manager/Producer gets final say"* was just an abstract concept. Now it was reality square in the face. The bastard! He was serious!

He was in there. We were out here. We could think what we wanted, have whatever opinions we cared to. It mattered not. It was Tutt's money, this was his studio, and *we were to do what we were told!* I didn't like that feeling. I didn't like it at all.

We did our best to rock our usual charming ne'er-do-well way through a couple more tracks, looking in through the glass for approval from our lord and master, and it was apparently all too charming and ne'er-do-well, as we soon enough got our introduction to a most vile piece of studio moderne trickery.

A click track is a modern-age metronome, a computer-generated cybernazi tempo-god fed into the drummer's headphones, and any other band member's who wants it, though God knows why anyone ever would.

For us, the click "sound" was a cowbell. You got four of them as your count-off and started playing. And it kept clicking. It sounded like this: BOINK BOINK BOINK BOINK BOINK!

This was the '80s, and tempo was everything. The groove had to be perfect. Not soulful, not reckless. Perfect! Click tracks do not ebb and flow. They do not make the bridge drive fast and then let the verse relax. They do not swing. All they do is blast in your headphone and go BOINK BOINK BOINK BOINK BOINK BOINK BOINK BOINK!

We started working with it, and by eight measures into any tune, the click track would be completely out-of-sync with the band, a contrary beast blasting to its own beat, while we were trying to lay down a permanent lifetime version of our tune. It was a bit like being a painter working on a masterpiece while some guy behind you taps on your shoulder, screaming "hey hey hey hey hey hey hey!"

And then, I got yanked. Even with the click track BOINK BOINK-ing us into rigid submission, there was still something rushing the beat. That something was me. I got to sit in the control room while Billy and Joe laid the framework down, and I was expected to keep my mouth shut. I was getting the impression I was expected to keep my mouth shut from here on out.

In an attempt to put something special on the tracks in place of the chemistry that was rapidly getting lost, I became an embarrassing attempt at Brian May. Overdubs! Overdubs! Overdubs!

I was terrible at them. I didn't know what I was doing. I'd put down one guitar just jacking off, and then I'd put a second guitar down just jacking off, with some hoary notion I'd get something Stonesy and magical out of blending the two. I got a lot of jacking off.

We had worked up a version of Grand Funk's "American Band" as a joke, a punked-up take-off on the old seventies chestnut. We had no objection to recording it, so long as the fundamental jokeness of our rendition remained intact. But the way we were doing things, with big-league recording gear and 32 tracks and overdubs and endless re takes of vocals and BOINK BOINK BOINK BOINK, no tongue-in-cheek vibe was cutting through. Tutt was listening to the playback with the notion that this was the next big nationwide cover version revival hit. The idea that anyone would think we were *seriously* doing "American Band" with *no ironic intent* made us shiver, and here was our manager telling us how it was going to be the lead-off track and it would be the tune that got us the big ("Dist. by") record deal, and we were left just waving our hands, lifting our eyebrows and shaking our heads. No! No! That's not it at all!

Just when we thought things couldn't possibly get worse, we had to do final vocals. Billy could warble pretty well, but otherwise, our singing was catch-as-catch-can. Screaming and shouting were common devices. We didn't know what we were doing. We only knew that sometimes it was right and sometimes it wasn't. It was rock and roll. Asking us to sing backing parts one at a time in a booth and do it over and over until it was "right" totally lost whatever it was we would do live. It got frustrating and more and more embarrassing, and grotesque vocals began to be "kept as finished takes" because time was just running out. They got more painful to listen to each time we had to hear them.

Billy practically dropped out of matters, sleeping on a couch in the snack room as much as humanly possible, exiling himself. We joked that he was resting up for his next illness.

Skot and I tried to vent our frustrations to Tutt one night in the control room, just before we left for the night. Nothing against him, we said, we just didn't feel right about the way things were going. That stuff on tape doesn't sound like us, we said. Not that it's bad (we said politely), it's just not us, either.

He told us, and I quote, that we had never before heard ourselves, so how would we know? He said we had always been the guys playing onstage. *He* had been in the crowd. *He* had heard us before. We had not. *We had never before heard ourselves.* And that, as far as Scott Tutt was concerned, was that.

Two weeks later, our time was up. We weren't done. We weren't anywhere near done. We took home rough-mix cassettes and were horrified. Our friends hated it. Jeff Sweeney listened to fifteen seconds, looked me in the eye, twisted the cap off a beer bottle and said "Sounds like shit." Tom Sturges *really* hated it. And the 32-track machine was bye-bye. It had been shipped out to record Barbara Mandrell somewhere. We didn't know when we could get it back, and we couldn't do anything without it. It might be months.

And we couldn't just choke back the whole mistake and go make another record in Marc Owens' basement. We didn't have the legal right to make our own records any more. Until Tutt said so, we couldn't even make a jam-box demo with the reverb from my bathroom tile. It was galling. We had no say-so whatsoever, and our recording career ground to an indefinite standstill.

The rage of impotence is hard to describe now. I was furious. It wasn't MY BAND any more, it would never be again, and I'd been the dumbass who'd taken a pen and signed it over. The one thing I'd cared about, truly cared about, in my whole morose, television-fried little life, MY BAND, and I'd given it up to a megalomaniac misogynist Yankee who wasn't exactly filling me with optimism now. I kept telling myself I should feel grateful somehow. This guy had just spent a shitload of money on me, and I should have been sending him a thank-you note. But I didn't feel too much like doing that, really.

New Year's Eve, '86-'87, was a blur. We played Picasso's and then went to several parties for days on end, most of which I don't remember. You could hypnotize me to pull up those files and they would be blank, wiped clean with alcohol and panic. It had happened very quickly. We had signed away everything and the vibe was just *wrong*, now. Maybe I was jumping to conclusions. Yeah, that's it. It'll be all right. Whatcha drinkin', Tommy? I dunno, whatcha got?

In the first couple of weeks of '87, we played our take-home cassettes endlessly, trying to tell ourselves that they were all right, that they rocked, that they were cool. We tried to convince ourselves that we would listen to them if they were made by someone else we didn't know. Anyone who heard the tapes and agreed were our friends. Anyone who didn't was a dick.

We went to see Jerry Dale play at Picasso's. By now, there was but a flimsy, tenuous veneer over the relationship between him and Tutt. Open warfare was a shot away. By now, Jerry Dale despised his own album so vehemently that he would not even allow a copy in his own house. He was getting frantic.

That past fall had marked his first tour up North. The album had actually done quite well for an indie label debut. Tutt's skills as a promoter had borne fruit. *Stand and Cast a Shadow* had crashed the college Top 40 nationwide. Jerry and his band played fifteen-odd dates up and down the East Coast, with Tutt as their guide for every last long mile of it.

Reptile booked the entire tour and, to hear Tutt tell about it, it had all been a tremendous success. The boys in the band, however, had different tales to tell, of money being quite scarce and Tutt having a temper of titanic proportions. If Jerry Dale had been unhappy with his deal before, he was now ready to go to whatever extreme it took to get out of it.

Skot and I left Picasso's that night and drove around. It was freezing. Kentucky in January is barenaked trees and snowless desolation. It sucks. The air is bitter cold and so dry you shock yourself touching your car door. We talked about everything, and concluded we were a damn good band and no one was going to stop us. How exactly we were going to carry out these simple-minded decrees was up in the air. We only had to drag out our contracts and read through them to be reminded we couldn't make records on our own any more, or take certain gigs, or get certain people on the phone any more. It all seemed so different now.

Two weeks later, Jerry Dale filed suit to get out of his contract. We were stuck in the middle, whether we liked it or not. We had nothing against Jerry Dale. We didn't want to take sides, and for the most part, we didn't. We just felt toilets flushing in our heads. If it wasn't AWOL recording gear, it was legal bullshit wrapping up our manager's life.

Right about that time, someone bought the house Tutt had office space in. He found himself unable to get another space on Music Row for the rent he'd been paying. Suddenly, our manager was no longer on Music Row. He was on a suburban street three turns and a mile off Nolensville Road. It wasn't nearly the same.

And only four years and ten months to go.

On April 1, four nail-biting months later, the 32-track machine came back into our clammy grip. These would be the last sessions when we were allowed to leave with cassettes. Tutt never let it happen after that. He was out to quell disarray and stem the tide of Cheesehead gossip regarding the sessions. We were never again able to listen to our own sessions on our own stereos and make any of our own decisions about our playing, our tones, anything.

Before we left on the last day, Tutt gathered us in the control room and told us what our first Reptile release was going to be.

In consort with Tom Sturges (maybe), it was decided we should test the waters with another four-song EP. It would be entitled *C'mon Back to Bowling Green* (after one of the songs), and would contain four songs Tutt selected, in the order he determined. Every creative decision had already been made for us. We were dismissed.

Whatever frustrations were infiltrating our rock and roll dream recording-wise, the lifestyle itself was still washing over us in a low-budget but very enjoyable manner. If we weren't in a hotel room throwing beer cans at a television, we were onstage, or slumped in a van, one guy stuck with the driving and the rest of us watching the cows go by. There's worse lives.

In the summer of 1987, we played Phoenix Hill Tavern in Louisville. It was a live broadcast on WLRS. The tape of that night was a bit of a bootleg prize for years amongst our faithful. Midway through the first set, both Skot and I had become fixated on one particular fellow in the crowd. From the back we could almost place him. He was devilishly familiar. At the end of the first set, which he had danced through, he turned around and approached the stage.

"I like you guys, you have a lot of energy," he said, shaking Skot's hand. "I'm Graham Nash," he added, as if he had to.

For the next hour, we got to hang with Graham. He was a regular gentleman, and danced with a steady stream of pretty girls.

Then one of the disc jockeys from WLRS, beaming from the stage, announced to our radio audience that Graham Nash was honoring us with his presence that evening. Needless to say, that was the last we saw of Graham. He sang in Louisville the next night with his long-time buddies Steve and Dave, and then I presume he went somewhere else, to appear Christ-like to other disciples.

*C'mon on Back to Bowling Green* made its debut in August 1987. Given how it came together, I must say it is at least nowhere nearly as bad as it could have been.

The recording and production are actually quite sparkling and spacious in spots—without a doubt, a light-year's improvement over our first effort. We gave Mr. Big some good tones and some rotten ones, and he recorded them all perfectly without prejudice. It doesn't sound like us, but it sounds good, technically.

The songs were more put-together on this outing. The title track is a decent song, with some great piano work from Jerry Dale. Billy's "Inside of You" is one of my Cheese favorites. "Underneath the Water Tower" is a disastrous mangling of what started out as a good song and veered way off course. "Face to Face" is a damn rocking, well recorded piece of tripe.

I knew this record had a chance to be heard. Whether or not I would choose to play it at home for my own pleasure (and I was fairly sure I wasn't ever going to), it would certainly get further around than our little first record had. I knew there could be a lot of exciting stuff around the corner. I knew that some dreams were coming true. I also knew that, compared to our friends in the real world who had to get up every morning and go to work, we had a damn nice life. I knew I should be damn grateful. I'd just had ten thousand dollars spent on my grubby ass. So why am I . . . *extremely unhappy?*

OK, I remember saying to myself, so it's not the first Clash album all over again. No big deal in the grand scheme of things, right? Chill out. Blow it off. There will be other records, maybe, other chances.

Yeah, right. This is *all I'd cared about for years!* Ever since that Kiss commercial, ever since Terry Cates' Gremlin, I've wanted to make records—and they had to be *cool as shit! Almost cool as shit* didn't count! And making an *un*cool record was tantamount to suicide. It was the worst thing you could ever do. My God, why get out of bed if you've made an *uncool record?*

\* \* \* \*

# 12

# affairs of the heart, liver and regional zeitgeist

At the beginning of Government Cheese, my love life could be neatly divided into three separate periods.

The first was high school, when I had a succession of crushes on girls who wouldn't touch me with a barge pole. I have no fond memories of any of it. My high-school crushes are the type of recollections that cause people to be viciously assaulted in bus stations by people who stand by the candy machines for hours and just seem angry for no reason.

Then came college, when I routinely felt sorry for myself because of romance phase one. I had several chances at meaningful relationships, and fucked every single one of them up. There was a moderate amount of quick sex, and the only one I ever truly screwed was myself, because once it was over, it was over. See ya.

Then came post-college, adulthood (theoretically) and Beth, and one last chance to get something going without making a giant mess of it.

Post-college wound up lasting only a few months before it dovetailed into Government Cheese, however, and a second chance at childhood, and being able to screw up in ways I'd only dreamed of before.

Beth Tucker was from Horse Cave, Kentucky, just like Billy Mack. Mammaw gave her piano lessons when she was a little girl. She was a cute redhead with freckles. We'd met in the broadcasting classes and parties of years gone by.

Beth was everything I wasn't. She had common sense. I didn't. She was naturally optimistic, cheerful, and uncomplicated. I was relishing being "complex and intense", counting on people to misread it as intelligence. She liked to cook. I didn't. She played the flute and could read music. I could do neither.

We started dating in September of 1984. She used to come over during rehearsals and fall asleep on my bed while Toby bashed his drums four feet away. She worked at WLBJ before I did, reading news in the mornings, and, owing to the insane hours she kept, could sleep through anything if she had to, even Toby.

By the spring of '85, we were living together in an apartment on Chestnut Street, across from the First Baptist Church, which had my car towed out of their lot every Sunday morning when I didn't think to do it myself in time. I came to think of my tow-bills as a sort of latent tithing after a while, in lieu of actually going to church any time recently.

Beth and I were both twenty-two. I was out of school. She almost was. We went through all the hijinks to try and fool our parents. Oh, we're not living together. He's just around a lot, Mom. The answering machine became our deflector shield. We put on some message that involved neither party's voice and irritated both sets of parents equally.

One day, Beth's mom popped in out of the blue. Beth wasn't home. I was playing my guitar extremely loud, standing in my shorts and a T-shirt, sporting three day's worth of stubble, two day's worth of body odor, a cigarette dangling from my lips, and my stringy hair everywhere. I was Neil Young at Red Rocks, jumping off the couch, going crazy, making all the faces. I was right in the middle of the "Hey, Hey, My, My" solo when I turned around, and there was Beth's mom, who carries an Olympia Dukakis vibe, with a smile that says "Hello" and "What in the hell are you doing?" at the same time.

I took a quick glance around the room, quickly assessing if any stuff strewn around would give the whole cohabitation thing away. Mmmmm, let's see. Two pairs of men's underwear. Three *CREEM* magazines. Two guitars out of their cases. Two hundred extra record albums on the shelf. (Is their daughter into *Husker Du?*) Cigarette butts everywhere.

There was no way out of this one.

I talked a mile a minute about how it was so hot at my place since I didn't have an air-conditioner nor cable television and it was just so much more comfortable over here so Beth was good enough to loan me her key for the afternoon so I could come over here and play my guitar(s) through this (big heavy) amp and relax and blah blah blah.

She acted like she swallowed it all, and never made an issue of it, but, she *had* to know. Parents usually do know about such things. At least, when you confess later, they put on this well-rehearsed facial expression that says "Oh, try and tell us something we don't know".

Parents love to pull that face. They practice it in the mirror when you're five, so they'll have it down when you're twenty and you walk into the family room and tell them something that scares the shit out of them. "Okay, we've been practicing the stone face for years. Activate!" That way they can act like they knew all along about what you're confessing, when they're actually having a stroke at the realization of what you've been doing. "No! Not my child!" Yes, your child. With me, no less.

My progression into becoming a mature life-partner for Beth would have definitely gone along a great deal less molested were it not for the increasing success of the band, and for the times we lived in. Bowling Green, after being my sleepy college hamlet for five years, seemed to just wake up one day, and I was there, along with a lot of other people, to say hello.

Bowling Green was a mildly engaging place to be, but also stubbornly Southern and covert about the whole thing. There were good things going on, provocative opinions, and some cool people, but all those things were under three layers of sod and heavy window curtains.

In 1986, Government Cheese and other bands were peeling back the lid on that inner Bowling Green self. Suddenly, after years of bitching about "not having a scene," we . . . *had a scene!*

The first local band in our wake was James Jauplyn and the Park Avenue Dregs. They were younger, hipper and worse than us. The leader, James Jauplyn (real last name Hall) would go on to a successful career in bands such as Mary My Hope and a recent solo deal with Geffen.

Then there was Herman Nelson, who would scatter flickering televisions all over the stage. They added a Talking Heads-ish, provocative, arty flourish to our local scene. I remember one of their songs being titled "Bottles of Milk" and another involving one of them squawking like a chicken.

And then there was the festering pustule to our little enclave, the ones who reminded us that, no matter what, our shit stank.

The Toxic Shocks were a Replacements album come to life in front of you. They were *Stink!* on eleven. It was genuine, too. They weren't faking. They were the real thing. If there was any band Government Cheese can be said to have been the big brother to—taking them with us out of town, paying for whatever they broke, etc.—it was these guys.

When I met them, they were holed up all together in one unholy sump heap of a house off Clay Street. It was the sort of place where the landlord kept explaining how it was somehow *their* fault that the rats were inside. All the band equipment was set up in the living room, and everyone had bed space to call their own. Hanoi Rocks and Sex Pistols posters on the walls, New York Dolls and Black Sabbath on the stereo. Garbage piled up in the kitchen corner. Cat and/or dog turds everywhere. Black Label in the fridge, the door of which was a cellophane-ridden, magnet-studded leftist newsstand.

Books were scattered about, from Malcolm X to Marx to Vonnegut, and any textbooks from whatever member of the band happened to be serious enough about classes that semester to actually go out and buy them.

I saw them play at Picasso's for the first time in '87. They looked like such kids then. Pat, Chris, Jack and John. They came to Bowling Green, where little happened (even with our new little precious scene), from Elizabethtown, where absolutely nothing has happened since the Civil War briefly rolled through a long-ass while back.

They could have hung out a shingle: *"Shockboys! Jaundiced View Here."* I had seen them around town for a couple of weeks before I first saw them play. Chris was all sullen and slumping around, with cratered skin and curly dark hair, rumpled old jeans jacket and a worn-out policeman's hat. I didn't know he had eyes.

In the middle of their first tune at Picasso's, Chris bashing a Les Paul, John pummeling a cheap bass, Pat banging every drum at once, and Jack grabbing his balls and screaming (he always grabbed his balls when he sang and no one told him about it because we didn't want him to get embarrassed and stop), the band train-wrecked. The song stalled out and they all looked at each other, and Chris burst into a star-quality grin. Jack looked around from his mike stand and smiled just as big, and I got the Shocks' charm. They weren't disappointed they had train-wrecked. The mayhem was half the fun. Then they picked up the pieces and started another tune.

Pat and John were more of a small riot than a rhythm section, and tuning for the whole group was a joke. When they were perfectly in tune, it still somehow didn't sound like they were. But, let me tell you, once you've seen about eight hundred bands that don't ever smile, not even a bit, the first one that does turns away all wrath.

I started hanging around at their house. I was intrigued. They were barely into their twenties when I was uncomfortably close to the end of my own. Pat and I hung out in his room after that first gig at the inevitable post-gig Shocks party. It came right after the pre-gig Shocks party, which was interrupted only by the mid-gig party.

Every night was a blast at the Toxic Shocks' house. You didn't come to their parties to get drunk, you came to get out-of-your-skull, balls-to-the-wall blind drunk. I've never before or since been to a place where getting looped before sundown qualified as a political statement as much as it did there. When you were at their house, smelling the anarchy and the cat turds, being with them, getting polluted, it was all a solid statement of some purpose. You could get flipping blotto anywhere in Bowling Green—God knows I found plenty of places to do it—but heaving at the Shocks house somehow *meant* something. I whiffed that punk dream that eluded me the first time around. *Gabba Gabba we accept you! One of us!*

Like any great rock and roll band, they were all too often their own worst enemies. No band gets drunk every single night of the week and keeps it together. But occasionally, the whole fuck-all of that way of living flames out in a blinding flash. If we're lucky in these days of miracle technology, that moment is preserved when and wherever it happens, and the world has one more great rock and roll record. The Toxic Shocks got there, for sure, at least once.

The song was called "I Really Don't Care," a terrific send-up of compassion fatigue. (One great couplet: "How can I help Mandela? I don't even *know* that fella!") Everything about the song was great, from it's two-string "I Will Follow"-ish guitar figure to the innocent fifties chord changes against a backbeat that made the Dolls sound restrained.

The Shocks were the two Becker brothers, Chris and Pat, Jack Tapp and John Boland. All four had been like me, I figured: young, fairly bright, semi-literate kids from a small Kentucky nowhere town, who'd been subverted by Kiss and cheap beer.

You could size them up and figure that Jack and John would eventually straighten up a little—at least nix the appearance of delinquency—and finish college. John's quiet intelligence hid behind a face halfway between boyishly undeveloped and slyly blank. He looked pretty All-American, given that his parents were fresh from Ireland and still spoke with a brogue. Jack was a babyface then, with sandy blonde hair. In years to come, he would grow a great long mane and a beard that turned him into, frankly, the Cowardly Lion from *Wizard of Oz.* Those two at least kept up an occasional appearance "on the Hill", which was Westernese for "going to college." They occasionally went to Western Civ class between parties.

Chris and Pat, however, were lost causes. Any notion that they might finish up school and take positions in the straight world was laughable.

Pat was walking around all over town barefoot, with giant hoop earrings in each ear, a floppy straw Huck Finn hat, thick half-Italian nineteen-year-old's whiskers, wide open eyes and boyish lips. Chris was the older, quieter one, with his shock of black hair and a taciturn grimace. In a punk rock world full of junior Paul Westerbergs, Chris was pulling off the look without a trace of effort. It was just *him.*

Bowling Green had its own Keith Moon in Pat. He didn't play backbeats, he ate drums alive. Depending on how well he was behaving on any given gig night, Jack might hand him his vocal mic over the drums for a moment of dissertation. At that point, Pat would generally piss off everyone in the bar.

One night, he read Bible passages between songs, with unmistakable surl. In our neck of the woods, you just didn't do that. He could also scream note-perfect, syllable-for-syllable Paul Stanley monologues from *Kiss Alive!* And if Pat did Paul, Chris did Gene just as well, if not better. "ChrisTEEN! ChrisTEEN! Yeahuheahuheah!"

Chris became our roadie, the first we'd ever had who never got regularly spotted dancing with a girl in the middle of a show, or venturing completely outside the club jabbering to someone while I had a broken string dangling on every guitar and Billy's bass amp was about to fall over backwards. Underneath all the Keith Richards swagger and Westerberg aura, and aside from passing out before the whole show even began once or twice, Chris was a responsible guy, to a certain passable extent.

The Shocks went places with us. It was damn near the only way they could get work, since we kept taking their guitarist around to be our roadie, and also since they had an innate ability to piss off every club owner and half of every audience they ever had to deal with. The Shocks embraced pissing people off as a religion. Assuming you weren't the target of their current gust of ballbusting whimsy and didn't have a financial stake in the matter, it was great fun to watch.

We brought them with us to Lexington one night, trusting that they'd not do anything too grotesque. They did marvelously, as a matter of fact. A smooth gig. No train wrecks. Yes, even *they* got tired of train wrecks now and then. Even anarchy loses its zip after a while. So this was a good show.

After the show, John saw a condom dispenser on the wall in the men's room. His senses overloaded.

The machine was approximately two-and-a-half feet tall by two feet wide and four inches deep. It was bolted securely to the Bottom Line's stone walls by appropriately heavy-duty fasteners. John was wearing an overcoat that, with the wind on his side, *might* have concealed a shoplifted toaster. There was no way he was going to walk out of the Bottom Line, past the club owner and the bartenders, with this massive prophylactic dispensary. Ahhh, don't bother me with logic, he scoffed; this is going to look *perfect* above the mantelpiece!

With gut-wrenching fervor, John wrestled the prophylactics' home from its address on the wall behind the men's room door. Haphazardly grappling the great long thing, he tucked it underneath his flimsy overcoat and, as God is my witness, attempted to walk blithely out of the Bottom Line with a condom, tasty-lickable-flavor-oils and French-tickler dispensary nestled inside the garment, underneath his arm, for all the world like he was carrying a newspaper.

I don't know how far he got outside the restroom door, exactly. Ten feet? Twenty feet, maybe? It wasn't much farther than that. I mean, the guy had a huge chrome rubber rack under his coat! The kind with the big chrome mirror you're supposed to lift up to see the seventies-era naked girl photo advertisement underneath. Why don't you just shove a fridge down your shorts? Mike, the big guy who took the door money when Gavin wasn't around to do it, busted John in a big way.

I remember that I was standing just outside the Bottom Line door, out on the sidewalk on Short Street. I saw John hurtle towards me from inside the darkness of the club. He was about a foot too high in the air to actually be touching the ground. He seemed to be floating as he gained in size, like a locomotive hurtling down a tunnel. Mike was carrying John in front of him, having relieved him of his ill-gotten cargo. The glass doors flew open. FLAM! Mike spun around and slammed John against the wall hard enough to dislodge phlegm.

John picked himself up from the ground. He'd hit the wall hard enough to have a brickface imprint. Mike was gone. He'd thrown John out, and that was the end of it. There had been an impersonal angle to his hostility, like a legbreaker who works for a loan shark and is jus' doin' his job.

"You okay?" I asked John.

"Sure!" he replied, and bounded up to join Jack down the street, who'd been observing the whole thing bemusedly. John said "Sure!" like he couldn't believe for a second that I'd wonder why he *wasn't* okay! You lift something. You get busted. You break somebody's balls. They break back. The scoreboard shifts around. It happens. What's the problem? Nihilist nonchalance. Gotta love it.

Beth became the morning anchor at Channel 13, the local ABC affiliate. Good morning, Bowling Green, the current temperature is *not as warm as it will be later.* December corn is trading at such-and-such a bushel. Back to Good Morning America now, and why are you people up at this hour of the day, anyway?

She went to work at 4:30 AM. That wasn't when she got up, that's when she *left*, with her hair done, looking like a million bucks. Tough gig.

Sometimes, I wasn't even in bed yet. Maybe I was in manic phase, and there were still cigarettes to smoke and records to listen to, and blithering rants to type at the Smith-Corona. Sometimes I would crawl into the warm space she had just vacated in bed. We were on opposite ends of the clock, living totally different lives.

She was (and still is) exceptionally good at what she does. Her ratings routinely secured her position. While I was cultivating an image as Tommy Womack, wacko rock and roll animal, she was becoming Beth Tucker, esteemed journalist and keeper of the public good. The invitations poured in, addressed very specifically to *her.* Prominent weddings. Ribbon cuttings. Parades. Everybody wants to meet the anchorwoman.

Meanwhile, I was occasionally disrobing onstage and playing whole sets in my underwear, singing songs about taking acid in the woods, duct-taping paper-towel pasties to my nipples, wearing tux pants with no crotch, and generally carrying on at home exactly as I did when I was away on the road.

As scumbags go, I at least tried to be a nice one. But there was no way. I was too young to be married, common-law or otherwise. And when you move in together, dear reader, make no mistake, you are getting married.

Marriage is the grand skin condition of the soul. Some folks go from courtship to marriage, just like the preacher says to do. Congratulations. For the rest of us, it's like one day you're checking out your back in the mirror before you shower, before the mirror steams up. You see a couple of spots there, and you say, hmmm. What's that? And then you put it out of mind. A few weeks later you take a second notice and see the spots have spread. Hmmmm. And then a few months later you notice that those grotesque spots have spread *all over your body! Oh my God! Oh my God! I'm <u>married!</u>* That's how it happens.

I found myself resenting Beth. Why did she have to come around *now*? I could be having a real good time, and as long as she was going to be Little Miss Get-Up-Before-God-Does, I guessed I had no choice but to go out and have a real good time anyway.

And so, with the care and conviction of the earnest potter, throwing the clay, spinning the wheel and shaping the flying brown mud, I cultivated my own distinct and musicianly brand of marital strife.

It's all part of the myth: Sex, Drugs, and Rock and Roll. The amorality. The debauchery. The shooting up, the slugging of Jack Daniel's and the bedding of strange women. Unfortunately, in 1986-87, AIDS was tearing that grand sketch of licentiousness into shreds and leaving it on the floor for us all to sweep up, rationalize, or deny there was anything risky or wrong—and I did plenty of both— rationalizing and denying.

One night of indiscretion was now enough to ruin the next three months, nursing scenarios of what might *now* be coursing through my bloodstream, on top of the usual "I'm an asshole"-type musings. I remember when herpes was the scariest thing I could consider. That was like a common cold compared to this shit. This was the heavy weather. HIV. Death in a neat little package. Thanks a lot, baby-boomers. Screw yourselves blind, make me listen to your godawful disco music, and then stick my generation with the bill. Fuck and die, wotta bargain. Thank yew very much. Great new age our *little scene* has to coexist with now.

But still, we were strapping young men, weren't we? Young bucks leaping centaur-like through poppy fields of nubile surrender. On a manly bastard scale of one to ten, I cruised at about a five, with occasional surges to seventeen or more. I'm not proud, but it happened. That was mainly during the first couple of years when everything was so new and seductive. Then I imploded mentally about the way I was comporting myself, and came down with an attack of guilty conscience that still grips me on occasion to this day.

It manifested itself in vehement attacks of paranoia. I could be onstage in Bowling Green and be utterly convinced that everyone in the room knew every nasty thing there was to know about me. (There would, from time to time, be some truth in that.)

It had somehow escaped my master plan that when you did nasty shit, *other people talked about you!* The nerve! I would be onstage, terrified. It affected how I did my work. It affected the songs I was writing. It affected my self-image incredibly.

The rock fan rumor mill beat fiber optics for speed of transmission, but the accuracy was never very good. I considered it my due to be busted for stuff I'd done. Fair is only fair. But it was the *alternate versions* of stories that would dog us all, and endlessly perplex me for some anal-retentive reason.

For instance, I remember a semi-annual group-sex rumor that always cropped up like Old Faithful. Once every two fiscal quarters or so, some vivid story would come back to home base about an orgy somewhere that we'd all been at, and for the purposes of discussion I'll consider an orgy anything with three or more people directly involved, and the rest of us either acting as referees, serving hors d'oeuvres or whatever. I've never been to an orgy yet in my life, but I've heard convincingly detailed accounts about my performances at at least three. Nonsense. There might have been some occasional *watching of others,* if that constitutes group activity, but no serious twister decathlons, thank you. That's a small thing to be self-righteous about, but I have to do a bit of straw-grasping when reflecting upon that era.

I was amazed to realize how much I had actually liked myself before I became a lousy husband. I had always been the semi-meek, crazy guy that everybody kind of liked even if it was because I portrayed myself as slightly lonely and pitiful at times. I was certainly no one's role model, but at least I held some moral high ground, if only because I rarely ventured into iniquity's waters.

The way I was raised—righteously, hand in hand with Jesus—kept me pure, sure, but my character development was infantile. Once I took one step into the Jungle of Id, I became a lecherous fool, as if I were compensating for all those lonely teenage times watching television and "practicing" my guitar. Everybody loses their innocence eventually. But I don't think most people lose it with the velocity I did, with the volume cranked and the throttle open. I went from zero to sixty like a tweaked Corvette, and then spun out, with my karma bouncing and twisting down the road behind me.

Tom Sturges sent two letters, one to Tutt and one to us.

His letter to Tutt said that it was obvious no business could be done between the two of them and that it was, in Tom Sturges' opinion, entirely Tutt's doing. What it boiled down to was that Tutt owned our publishing, and Tom couldn't have it.

Our letter from Tom said we couldn't work together and that, regardless of whoever's fault that was, it was regrettable. He said he believed we had all it took to become superstars. That was the word he used, superstars. It was the last we heard from Tom Sturges.

Tutt explained that we couldn't give up any publishing without getting a record deal, 'cause what if Tom then couldn't swing a deal with Chrysalis records? Then we'd have given our publishing away. To record companies, he explained to us, a band with no publishing was a bride with no dowry.

This was a sound argument and all very true, but geez, we'd let the guy from Cali with the car phone go and kept the dude with the sweats and the gyrating, windup table-top genitalia.

You can trace the uncanny early luck of Government Cheese—

all the things that just didn't happen to other bands, all those good breaks. The record, the Pub, the opportunities, everything. You can also pinpoint exactly when it all stopped in the fall of '86. Two things happened. We signed with Reptile Records, and I quit coming home at night. And the Lord looked upon Israel, and He prepared to Smite in a Big Way.

\* \* \* \*

# 13

# karmic vapor-lock

We celebrated the release of *C'mon Back to Bowling Green* with a gala affair at Picasso's. It was quite the evening. A bunch of our friends sprung for a limo to squire us about town. We took it to Airport Liquors and bought a six-pack of Cook's. The damn limo kept breaking down, and we were late getting back to Picasso's for the gig and the party.

Everyone was there: the local newspaper, television cameras, everyone I had ever met in my life, it seemed. Lately, I had been able to put my problems with the record aside, if only because I was routinely creating interpersonal crises that superseded career worries. And hey, it was far from the worst record in the world. Everybody seemed happy for us. It was a night to live a little.

I was onstage playing, but I felt as much a spectator to someone else's triumph as I did anything. That first record, the one we'd done ourselves, as shitty as it was, I'd felt connected to. I got fulfillment out of that one. This one, I was just an extra in my own film.

Beth and I had had a terrific fight before the party. We had another afterwards, and then another the next day. Get up, shower, fight, have some coffee, fight. We went out to celebrate together, but we barely spoke to one another. We were both trying to be nice people who didn't want to hurt each other, but at the same time, the big picture was very shaky. So we were nice and shaky to each other all the time, painfully and delicately polite, bouncing between affection and distance.

Another major blowup came the night after the record was released. I resolved to move out of the apartment at four in the morning, just as she was leaving for work. Her car wouldn't start, so I wound up having to give her a ride to work, then go back home to pack and move out for what she tells me now was a week. I can't remember. Weird. Life was getting very weird. Thanks for the ride, now *go home and finish packing!*

The Reptile Records promotional machine swung into magnum force, with three people calling one radio station after another, sending out records, pressuring music directors, begging those in charge at stations to add us to their respective playlists.

This was the one thing in the entire music business that Tutt was inarguably talented at. Whatever his faults elsewhere, Tutt had a feel for record promotion, even though his human relations skills were now and then heavy-handed to say the least, and Pre-Cambrian to say more.

He would browbeat people, insult them and holler into the phone with it a foot in front of his face—but it did seem to make a difference for us. Government Cheese was a completely unknown band nationally, and Tutt was going to get us on the college charts if he had to sell the farm. He did it, too.

Radio stations complained about him to the survey journals. The University of Kentucky sent him a two-page letter accusing him of "terroristic threatening." But it worked. It certainly wasn't a long-term way of thinking—to antagonize the entire college music industry from a small suburban house off Nolensville Road—but over a short while, the good vibes began to outweigh the bad, at least where it counted, on paper, in the CMJ (College Music Journal) charts.

Week after week, the Reptile staff worked the phones. The radio adds began piling up. By October, we had the bemused pleasure of knowing our record was top-ten in places we had never seen before: San Francisco, Chester, Pennsylvania, Albuquerque, New Mexico. It was working! It appeared that as long as I kept my mouth shut and played ball, some nice things might actually happen.

Radio promotion was going great guns, but the fine art of getting the damn thing in stores was mired and sinking. It's all about the "relationship with the distributors".

Indie labels had a terrible time getting their product into the stores, because the major labels had a lock on the distributing warehouses. Record companies didn't send product directly to the stores, but to whatever distributor the store contracted through.

This distributor had its warehouses—cavernous concrete and metal buildings full of cardboard boxes, all sporting label names and serial numbers on their sides. At this stage of the game, the music did not exist. The records didn't have covers or titles, all they had was a serial number. A store that got one digit wrong might get shipped eight boxes of Julio Iglesias instead of the Bryan Adams they thought they were ordering.

In those warehouses, RCA would have a thousand or more boxes stacked up, all of them big chart-hit records. Reptile would have one little box misplaced in the corner while a bored clerk talking on the phone and carrying a clipboard didn't know who the hell Reptile Records was and didn't give a rat's ass.

Tutt used to go on and on about developing the "relationship with the distributors." One of us once sold a box of our new record to a store in Lexington, because the store had people asking for it and the distributor didn't have it. We figured it was far better for the store to be selling records however they could get them, but Tutt hit the roof. *"No! They gotta go through their distributor! That bored motherfucker with the clipboard! He's gotta learn who Reptile Records is! You think we're gonna spend the rest of our lives truckin' a box of records each to every fukkin' store in the world?"* He had a point there. He had a point, and nobody had records.

Now that radio stations in faraway places were playing us, it made things a bit easier to get clubs in those towns to return phone calls, to get them to give us at least a 100-dollar guarantee to come play, which would in turn, presumably, make it a bit easier to get the local hip store to order ten frigging copies of the record, and thus get "the relationship with the distributors" rolling.

This is where it got fun again.

The chance had come — our first reasonable shot at playing somewhere north of Lexington, somewhere bigger than Louisville, somewhere more meaningful to our career than Elliston Square on a Wednesday night, which had seemed so cool only a year before and now had long lost its newness and luster. It was time to actually go where I used to dream of five years before, standing on back porches, listening to the first Clash album duet with crickets.

We used to come into the Reptile basement and see the gig dates in grease pencil on a great big calendar. We had seen the words "Lexington", "Louisville", "Knoxville", and "Nashville" many, many times.

One day, we walked in and saw "Pittsburgh". *Pittsburgh.* Is this confirmed? Yes, it is. "Philadelphia"? *Philadelphia.* We're going to Philadelphia? Why, yes, you are.

"New York City?" Is that what that says? Yep, that's what it says. Guys, you're going to New York City.

\* \* \* \*

# 14

# new york, new york

The prospect of our first trip North was thrilling. For a Southerner, the Eastern seaboard was a mythical bedlam. As much as Yankees viewed us as closeted freakish imbeciles, boffing our own cousins and boiling the meat off hog jowls, we looked upon them with equal morbid fascination.

It was more than a road trip. It was The New Land—where people said "youse guys" instead of "y'all," where bagels were on menus, where mobsters got gunned down and Buffy and Jody were safe, where Johnny Thunders hung out on the corner and Iggy hailed cabs. It was that dirty-brick Eden I used to dream about while standing on back porches in my new-wave finery, staring at the moon. I was finally going there.

We hit the road in two vehicles, the van and a car belonging to Carl Middlesten, a high school friend of Skot's who was taking his vacation to go to New York with us. There were six of us, counting our soundman Broma, whose real name was Scott Davis. His nickname was a corruption of Brahman Bull, derived from the way he bulged in the stretch-knit short pants he always wore.

We packed enough supplies for a Himalayan expedition. We had an ice chest loaded down with cold cuts, milk, an avalanche of single-serving Frosted Flakes pilfered from somewhere, two loaves of Bunny bread with heavily smashed-in flanks, a full two cases of beer in one cooler by itself, peanut butter, chips, and salsa. We had all the current periodical reading, from *Rolling Stone* to *Spin* and *Time*. We brought notebooks to record the experience and enough covert radar and CB equipment to know the whereabouts of every officer on the New Jersey Turnpike.

It was odd to drive to Lexington and keep going. Seeing Eastern Kentucky at nightfall for the first time confirmed every mystical and forbidding tale told of it. The hard, dark mountains slatted against a sky with just a trace of blue left. I conjured fanciful ideas of who lived in that darkness. Being fellow Commonwealth Paisans didn't curtail speculation on our Eastern Kentucky brethren, like they were some distant relatives of the homosapien. Whiskey stills, perverted toothless mountain folk, creekbed casualties of five-generation family feuds, shotgun weddings between uncle and niece and the rest of the cliche gamut—just and unjust—ran through our heads. We were judgmental tourists in our own land.

The van whooshed on and off a short bridge that afforded a glimpse into the valley between two Appalachian mountains. There was a river and, suddenly, lots of lights on phone poles, dozens of clapboard houses and mobile homes all clumped together as tight as the big city. No road ran in or out that we could see, and very likely, no economy. It was just a bunch of folks crowded close together on a riverbed. No way in, no way out. And somehow they kept the lights turned on.

We came up to Ashland and the Kentucky-West Virginia border. Everyone needs to see Ashland once and come away pondering the spectacle.

There is a town named Ashland, I presume. I have never seen it, but I have seen the industrial nightmare that surrounds the interstate and borders the river there. I had never seen an oil refinery before, much less at night.

My God! It looked like a hundred smokestacks on either side of us. Jets of burn-off flame shot out of some of them. The whole monstrosity was beautifully lit in amber, and as horrifying and immense as it was, there was something wonderful about it. Joe almost ran off the road looking at it, as we dove for the windows to take in this majestic horror. For a hundred, maybe two or three hundred yards on either side of the interstate bridge, all below and beside us, were girders and miles and miles of pipes. Some were small, others were huge. Some pointed up, some went across. Some fed into huge white pillbox hats, big as office buildings, that all said ASHLAND OIL on them. The amber light made it all look like it was already its own time-washed sepia print. Smokestacks, pipes, jets of flame, strings of lights ringing the chimneys and running from the ground to the top like ship rigging. It was the devil.

That docile river next to it snaked its way through the mountains, doing what rivers do, the rustic, lapping border of Hell. Somewhere down the line it joined another river and found its way to the ocean, I suspect carrying a bit of Ashland Oil's loving touch with it.

Ashland fell in the distance, and then we were in West Virginia. We pulled into a truck stop and I bought the new *Playboy*, featuring Jessica Hahn's new chest. We ate beanie-weenies out of the cans, and passed Jessica around with the dome light on.

At Charleston, we bent north, heading for Harrisburg, Pennsylvania. The roads turned to two-lane. Houses passed us on either side.

After a while in a van, you always felt like the outside world was moving and you just stayed where you were. The seats and the steering wheel became more real than what was out there. It was a natural choice between what didn't change and what did. The scenery was an endless mural, peeling off the window and streaking away. And once it grew too dark outside, there would be no more world than the dashboard, guys' twisted, denim limbs trying to sleep in seats, magazines thrown to the floor like sleeping tents next to the Frito graveyard, rolling dead Budweiser soldiers and thrown-off shoes lying like open-mouthed fish wherever they were dropped.

We'd always had a rule that there would be no sleeping in shotgun. Shotgun Guy has to keep Driver Guy awake. I slacked and felt a drizzle of verbal abuse from Joe. I awoke with a start. We were in Maryland, it seemed, for no more than five minutes, crossing the panhandle. Now, even by antiquated Civil War standards, I was across the line in Pennsylvania. I was up North.

We entered the Pennsylvania Turnpike the same way you would enter Disney World, through great automotive turnstiles, eight-abreast. We didn't pay right then. They *assumed* we had the money. In the South, it was simpler and more benevolent. You paid as you went, and if you didn't have it, you got off. But on the Pennsylvania Turnpike, each toll was a dollar, and all they did was punch your ticket. It began to add up. The New Land ran a tab.

I hopped out for a cup of coffee so Joe couldn't cuss me out for nodding off any more. In my fifty-cent sports jacket, I gasped in the brittle air. It was Pennsylvania, 4:30 AM, and a good deal chillier than any October 1st I'd ever enjoyed before.

While we may brag of a better toll road philosophy, the Pennsylvanians could tell us what was what in regard to mountains. The Alleghenies, such as we could see them in those wee hours, were in no way like the claustrophobic Appalachians, which were peaks packed together like the end of a fistful of pencils, while the Alleghenies were long, like frozen waves coming to shore. The valleys swept across and up to those grades as if they had all the space in the world. To the east, the first little teases of purple were streaking peripherally. If you looked directly at the sky, it went coal black again, but sidelong glances told the eye more.

The last decent radio we had heard had been Double Q in Lexington. Eastern Kentucky and West Virginia radio had been a veritable wasteland. Stations came and went in the mountains like random conversation. Styx became George Jones on the other side of a crest, and then became a preacher around the next bend, all of it bathed in gushy freckles of static.

Around 5 AM, the whole dial woke up. Songs we hardly ever heard in the South came gushing out—songs like "Do You Love Me?" by the Contours, "Leader of the Pack," old girl groups. It was Philadelphia.

It was the first time I'd ever heard Howard Stern, and my first time to be disappointed by him. I'm half and half with Howard. Sometimes he's funny. Sometimes he blows. That morning, he blew hard.

"Ahhh jeeze . . . what time is it? It's uh . . . it's six-fifteen right now . . . what? Your headphones don't work? Hey, somebody, Robin's headphones don't work . . . Well, what do you expect me to do about it? . . . Somebody get her some damn headphones . . . "

A few seconds of silence went by.

"Naahhh, I don't wanna do that commercial yet . . . "

More silence . . .

"What?"

Silence . . .

"No, I said I don't want to do that commercial . . . I don't know . . . it bores me . . . Hey, does Robin have headphones yet? What kind of station is this . . .

"Well . . . are there any recorded commercials we can play? . . . I don't wanna read that commercial . . . jeeze, what the hell time is it? It's uh . . . uhhh . . . uhhhhhh six-eighteen and, uh . . . "

I could have sworn people had told me this guy was funny. I was never this boring in eighteen months on WLBJ.

I gazed out the window at the Allegheny ridge, the frosty valley between me and those gray bumps, which were miles away, and the lack of anything between them and me made it seem like I could reach out and touch one of them. The sky had long since come full blue, and farmhouses, two-story red homes with wood fences and silos Grant Wood could have painted, sudddenly exploded orange on one side, throwing hard dark shadows the other way. I looked eastward. The sun was up, and Howard Stern was still bitching about headphones and refusing to do whatever commercial it was he didn't want to read.

Most of us were awake now. Sleep had come fitfully at best, anyway.

Time went by, the mountains receded, we paid our bill and got off the Pennsylvania Turnpike. We headed south toward Philadelphia. The radio signal got stronger, and at last Howard's show developed some verve. Funnily enough, he got Jessica Hahn on the phone, which we took at the time to be some kinetic event, and not the all-too-common occurrence it actually was. Just as Howard mentioned his penis for the twenty-fifth time in ten minutes, the Philly skyline came into view. We were *there.*

No one was thinking about sleeping now. We went straight to the club, just to see it. We found it on South Street. For miles, Philadelphia spread out as three-story brownstones and townhouses. South Street carried a carnival atmosphere at 7:30 in the morning. Colorful stores, delis, early-morning short bald guys pushing fruit carts, cabdrivers. I could almost believe Rocky was going to come jogging around the corner any second. I could finally see why all those television shows depict life the way they do. Here were wildly different people all around, waking up in close quarters, living without front yards, never driving cars, going their whole lives next to and on top of each other, and they all looked immediately different, wondrous. The old bald guy with the cigar and the fruit cart was exotic to me, like a rare tropical bird. And, I thought, *this* is the big bad city? *This* is the urban nightmare? This is *gorgeous.*

We loaded back up after walking around a bit, and found a hotel way outside of town. We ate in a Denny's. A party of four sat down next to us. The man was a Frank Stallone lookalike. When they were joined by some friends, Frank said, ''Where yeh been? We've been waitin' on yiz!'' Yiz! Yiz! I got such joy out of that.

We slept most of the day, then killed the early evening doing Philly things. The cheesesteak is a Philly thing. God knows why it is indigenous to Philly, though. The ingredients are fairly standard stuff.

You take a deli-sandwich piece of hero bread, put a slab of beefsteak on it, drop a load of onions and peppers and melt a lot of cheese (swiss, generally) on it and heat the whole thing in an oven.

J.C. Dobbs is one of George Thorogood's former homes away from home. Postcards from George were tucked into all the corners of the mirror behind the bar. Framed portraits of him adorned the walls. It was said that he used to play three-night-stands and sleep on the stage.

The stage was in one corner of the back, and a square column of brick rose from one side of the front of the stage. Billy wound up standing behind it when we played, playing and singing all night long with no one ever seeing him.

I honestly don't remember much about the gig, except that the place was almost empty and our best audience was an old drunk black man. I think he bought a record. (We sold them to people directly at every opportunity, just steering clear of actual stores and Tutt's wrath about distributors.) We were old pros at whoring our merchandise by this point. The whole bit, mailing lists, t-shirt and record sales from the stage, we were great at all of it. I don't know what that old drunk black man bought, but he walked away with something. He liked "Yellow Cling Peaches", which was a song about a fellow who is fed peaches so much as a child that he eventually connects to them sexually.

The next night we talked our way into the Chestnut Cabaret to see the Beat Farmers, whom we had opened for not quite a week before in Louisville. We got along great with most of them, but I think Country Dick Montana got put out with us selling our records at *their* gig. We sold about thirty dollars worth, if I remember correctly.

We wound up heaving hearty beverages with a couple of Puerto Rican guys atop the marble steps Rocky bounded up in the first movie and several sequels. The view of Philly there is worth the jog.

We crossed the river and put Philadelphia behind us. All along it had been the mere dress rehearsal for the true insurgency, New Yawk Citay. We hit the New Jersey Turnpike and heard a cut on the radio from the Boss's new album immediately— "Spare Parts" from *Tunnel Of Love*—like it was a greeting. Welcome to Jersey. Bruce says hello, and enjoy your stay. As soon as we hit the highway, the weather turned nasty for the first time. The rain whipped across the windshield all the way to Linden, which was not far from the city but looked like Louisville. Trees. Suburban houses. The only hints of the

near proximity to urban meltdown were subtle ones: no space between houses, minimal yards, the deli on the corner and the train
platforms.

In Linden that early evening, Billy opted to stay in the hotel
room, and the rest of us hot-footed it to the train station. We ascended
a dreary platform with a spartan overhang that offered only the slightest protection from the elements. One talkative young fellow, a chef
in the city, was there already, thankfully. Otherwise, we might have
wondered if this whole train station was a decoy, some sham set up
for *Candid Camera*. We had ascended the platform on good faith that
some train would indeed show up. The young fellow assured us of the
train's imminent arrival. He sported a faint wisp of a moustache that
had apparently taken him the better part of a month to coax along,
and he made his full-blown contempt for New York City evident
quickly enough.

He told us all about Linden, and how it was close enough and far
away enough from the city for his tastes, how he hoped this chef gig
worked out because otherwise his old man was going to make a cop
out of him like all his brothers and his uncles.

Just minutes before the train arrived, a woman stormed up in a
Honda Civic, screamed to a stop and rocketed up the stairs, taking a
place perfectly in front of where the train's last door would stop. And
within bare seconds of her assuming this spot, the light winked into
view down the south end of the track. She'd obviously done this
about five hundred times before.

The train pulled up to a stop, and there in the back door, in his
transit authority uniform, looking no older than our chef friend, was
the ticket taker. The train had barely stopped when Ms. Honda Civic
went into her act. *"Gaahhhd-Deemmmm! Open da gahhhhd-
deemmmmm do-ah!"* She threw her arms sideways and dropped her
jaw in mimed exasperation.

Utterly nonplussed, the ticket-taker threw his own arms out and
mime-huffed right back in her face, effectively shutting her up. All us
in the Kentucky contingent smiled. Rudeness, just like the catalog
promised. Southerners would never behave this way. We might blow
your head off and bury you in seven separate graves, but we'd be
seamlessly polite about the whole matter. This was great. I was a tourist from my head to my toes. We would play at CBGB in a couple of
days, and for that hour I would have a purpose. Other than that, I was
here to see what I'd dreamed of for so long.

We took our spot on the train. It was half full of preppy teens all dolled up. Beautiful WASP kids taking Daddy's credit cards to the city for the night, or maybe Dad didn't even know this is what they were doing. Maybe Dad was in Europe for a month and couldn't have cared less.

It was an instant lesson in one big difference between the big city and home. At home, the rich had their end of town, and everybody else had theirs. New York City, I would soon learn, was way different.

One glance always showed a man sleeping on the street *and* a limousine. Here in the train car were beautiful kids, ten years my junior, whose neckties were worth more than I made in three weeks of gigs. They took the same train I took, the same one taken by the old, shaky lady with her three paper bags holding the odds and ends of her life.

We got no glimpse of New York City on the way in. It was dark, and the train dipped so far into the tunnel that we would have had a better chance of spotting dumped mob-hit bodies in the swamp than the skyline. Besides, in full daylight, the windows would have still been so mucky you could barely see the trains passing on the adjoining tracks, much less the city that never sleeps.

We came into Penn Station, and were impressed by the bassy rock and roll rumble that seemed to permeate the air we breathed. It was coming from up the escalators. We walked down New York's familiar tile-walled subway bulkheads and rose up one level. It was a . . . *mall.*

Here was a shoe store, and next to it was a pizza joint, where we went immediately. New York pizza is the best in the world, we soon found out. It was $1.25 all over the city, as if price-set by some pizza committee. Then we then encountered our first bit of low-intensity New York trauma.

Two short, pretty-damn-tough-looking fellows, their eyes wide and hard and their hair razor-short, approached Carl. Hygienically tough to be around, they twitched, grabbed their balls and tapped Carl on the shoulder, hard.

We all had been secretly afraid that Carl would wind up getting us all killed. Not that he was walking trouble, but Carl just knew less about road life. It doesn't take too many rock and roll road shows to be able to sniff the people who might be smiling at you one second and waving a knife at you the next. These two fellows, crew-cut, graying t-shirts and jackets wafting of dumpster, pinhole eyes and three-day shadows, basically our ages, were Central Casting ideals of walking urban trouble, and of course they went straight to Carl.

"Excuse me, could I buy a cigarette from you, man?" one of them said to Carl, who was lighting up.

He rebuffed them somehow. The guy doubled his offer, from a nickel to a dime, for one cigarette. Carl said, "You don't understand. They're not for sale."

I saw the guy's eyes light up like they do when the scent of fresh meat is wafting in the wind. "Hey!" he said, tapping Carl again on the shoulder hard enough to almost make a noise (Carl had gone so far as to turn his back on the guy). "You're not from New York, are you?" (He said "are you?" as "*ahhyah?*") Yep, damn straight. Got us on that one, pal.

I zoomed between the two with my pack of Marlboros at the ready. "Here, guys. Happy birthday. One for each of you. No, no! Keep your dime."

"Hey, thanks, man." The transaction was done and we shuffled on our way. Oh, Carl, by the way, from now on, when anybody in this town who could crush your skull with one hand wants a cigarette, *give it to 'em!*

It was a mall, all right, and it kept going around in a circle. It was crowded, like the day after Thanksgiving. The bassy rock and roll rumble kept throbbing from somewhere. It came from the walls and from down the long store-lined corridor. It sounded like dynamite rumbling, but it was definitely rock and roll.

We found the main lobby of Penn Station and the escalators that led up to street level. We stood for a minute, eating our pizza, uncertain about the New York up there. There it was. New York City. Right up those stairs. There was probably somebody wanting to buy my pizza crust for fifteen cents if I haggled.

A cop had us pegged incorrectly because of our hair lengths. "Concert's that way, fellas." He pointed up the escalators. Thus was the mystery solved.

Penn Station is directly underneath Madison Square Garden, and Twisted Sister was onstage upstairs. Some leather-jacketed guys and girls I'd seen on the train were bolting up the escalator steps three at a time, drawn to the throb.

There wasn't any doubt as to our first stop. Flowers had to be laid on the altar of Punk, post haste. The place where it started. CBGB.

Way back when, sometime after the bloom was off the hippie rose, a fellow named Hilly Crystal had a dream. He was a club-owner, and all club-owners have the same dream: *their* new nightclub will be *the* new nightclub.

Hilly's dream was rather focused in regard to the music. When asked, he had a ready answer: "Country, Bluegrass, Blues and Other Music For Uplifting Gourmandizers". (A gourmandizer is, I'm told, one who can find enjoyment in most anything.) Of course, that whole slew of words is a bit long to fit on the marquee out front, so Hilly just used the first letters. *C.B.G.B. and O.M.F.U.G.* Needless to say, folks quickly shortened *that* name, calling the club "CBGB", or, even simpler, "CB's", which was how the bartender answered the phone.

So, Hilly pursued his nightclub dream. Business was okay. New York isn't Nashville, though, and such music as Hilly offered at C.B.G.B. and O.M.F.U.G. was never regarded as more than quaint by most New Yorkers. But he paid the rent, best as he could, given the fact that his club wasn't in the nicest of locations. 315 Bowery Street is not Central Park West. Classic Bowery bums lounged in wine stupors right outside the front door. Many New Yorkers wouldn't go into that part of lower Manhattan.

One day, a band from Queens who could get no work elsewhere came into CBGB, four twenty-somethings with acne, leather jackets, torn and faded blue jeans and long hair. They explained their style to Hilly. They played rock and roll music so simply that the term "minimalist" was a bit busy.

They had tried to learn other people's songs and couldn't, so they wrote their own and played them through apocalyptically distorted, battery-operated amps. Their lyrics were about sniffing glue, chainsaw massacres and scary basements. The whole effect was great, deeply hilarious, and better still, no one could tell if the band got their own joke or not. Rock musicians had long played dumber than they were, but these guys were playing super quantum dumb. They had invented a fictional surname and posed as four brothers. Tommy, Joey, Dee Dee and Johnny — The Ramones.

With their buzzsaw guitar and frantic beat, the Ramones were about as wrong for Hilly's club as a band gets, but he hired them anyway. Nobody liked them. They drove people away in significant numbers, but Hilly kept hiring them. And it caught on. The sun set on Hilly's country music dream, and a full punk moon filled the sky.

This was 1974, and in the next two years CBGB became the birth-place of punk rock.

The bands who called the club home made CBGB one of the most revered club names in the history of rock and roll: Blondie, Television, Talking Heads, The Dictators, The Dead Boys, The Patti Smith Group, Johnny Thunders, Mink DeVille, Richard Hell, Wayne County, and, of course, The Ramones. By 1976, Hilly had more business than he could have ever conceived. He was the epicenter of Punk, and hip New York crowded in seven nights a week.

The Police got right off the plane and played their first-ever U.S. date there. XTC played there. Every punk band across the country, and plenty that weren't punk, once the term "New Wave" came about, played there. By the turn of the decade, CBGB was past its peak as any scene's epicenter. But what a peak.

It chugged on in 1987, with Hilly taking the door money and graffiti from a million bands in spots so high on the wall you wondered how the writer got there without a scaffold. Wobbly chairs and filthy tables, horrifying toilets, unidentifiable smells and—impossibly—amidst all the squalor of this dump-of-dumps, one of the finest sound systems of any club in the world. CB's became a recording studio from 4 AM to 4 PM. The band would set up on the stage.

From 10 'til 3 it was still a Legendary Rock Club, with four bands playing every damn night of the week. You got on, forgot about any kind of sound check, plugged in, wailed and got the hell off. You didn't even think about taking more than an hour if you ever wanted to play there again.

In two days, we would get our hour on that stage. We harbored no illusions that it was going to do much for our careers. That wasn't even the point, really. The place would be empty if it depended on anyone we knew to be there. But we were going to CBGB's, to bring burnt offerings to the Ramones' manger.

With horrendous rain outside, we rose out of Penn Station's safety into New York Saturday Night. You know how *Saturday Night Live* starts out, with the monochrome footage of a cab racing by and steam coming out of a manhole? New York really does look *exactly like that.*

The others tore across the street in the blinding rain. I had time only to look up and be frightened out of my wits.

Gahhhhh! It was the *BIGGEST BUILDING I'D EVER SEEN IN MY LIFE!!!* It just kept on going, higher and higher. I couldn't see the top of it in the rain. I was running across the street, following the other guys by ear, and looking up in horror at this huge fucking *THING!!*

My God! It was just a straight, concrete and metal Tower of Babel. Already bigger *across* than most any building I'd ever seen. And it kept rising and rising. And rising. Rain was splatting in my eyes. The guys were yelling for me to keep up. I almost got run over by a cab. I assume it was a cab. Most vehicles in New York City are cabs.

All we did was run across the street and back down into another subway station. Immediate problem. No one had the slightest idea where CBGB was.

A charming old lady who worked for the transit authority was very nice in showing us how to get to the Bowery, all the time wondering why the hell we wanted to go there. *"You boys be keh-ful. Det's a beehhhd paht o'town!"*

We got on our first subway, completely tourist paranoid, fully expecting to be knifed or something. Nothing traumatic happened, and we got out where she told us to. The street sign marking our subway stop in the tile walls meant nothing to us. 23rd Street might as well have been 88th as far as we knew. A yellow, rectangular street sign looked like any other. Broadway-Nassau? What's that?

All we knew was that when we ascended into the pissing rain again we were in Peking's party district.

Whoah! Everything's in Chinese! All the signs! Banners across the street! Everything was in Chinese. At least I assumed it was Chinese. *I* sure as hell couldn't read it. We tore off running. Block after block. Broma was in front, and we just assumed he knew the proper direction to run. It's a little unnerving to submerge in America and resurface in China, as if you'd been placed in one of those transfer tubes at the drive-in bank and whooshed through the earth's crust to downtown Hong Kong.

We dove into a Chinese McDonald's and asked directions. We were to discover that English language skills are not a given in New York City, not even in a McDonald's. I wish now I'd checked the menu to see if they had McPeking Duck Nuggets, or something exotic like that.

We found our way out of Chinatown in short order and, several wet blocks later, our sopping selves made it to Mecca. There it was, a little half-umbrella awning over the door: *C.B.G.B. and O.M.F.U.G.*

The buildings all up and down the street on both sides, some five and six stories tall, some less, weren't exactly falling down, but they probably looked a damn sight better eighty years ago. The rusted iron fire escapes looked simply glued on arbitrarily. Some windows were up. Some were down. Some had lights on. Some didn't. Cabs raced by and the manhole covers steamed. I looked down the street. It was those six-story buildings with their fire escape tentacles for what looked like miles.

For great distances, the street went on and these buildings bordered them, basically, as the walls to this urban ditch we walked through. In the days to come, I'd come to think of it as a mouse maze. People lived in the walls while we walked the trenches, and all around us they were either living decent lives or doing unspeakable things. Even when you couldn't see the atrocities committed, you could sense them.

The sounds of the sirens were a constant hint.

At no moment in New York City could we not hear a siren echoing off those canyon walls. Somewhere, always, reverberating back and forth down those long six-story corridors, was agony. The sirens never stopped completely, and often you could hear three or more at once. They were always there. They never quite went away. It was a constant cry for help in New York City.

We stepped inside.

To call an East Coast club claustrophobic by Southern standards was an understatement. CBGB went from the front of the building to the back, but it was barely wider than a living room. The first thing we encountered was the ticket-taking spot, which blended into a crammed little office where, presumably, all those great bands had been booked over time. We walked down a narrow path with tables on our left and the bar on our right. Way back there, in the right-hand corner, was the stage. Have to go to the bathroom? Go past the stage and entirely past the dressing rooms (no star trips here), double back to the left and down the stairs. Look for names of friends in other bands as you go. Graffiti *was* the decor.

I grabbed a Heineken for a serious price and went up front to check out the band, but not before running into Penn of the comedy/magic duo Penn and Teller. We exchanged a brief pleasantry such as the nobody does with the celebrity, and I moved on.

The band rocked. Their name was Blue Movie. I think they were a trio, and blonde, but that's as far as Police comparisons went. They were good, especially the drummer, and they had fans there that night. Where they are now, you tell me. I later saw their 8 x 10 on the wall of fame at Mississippi Nights in St. Louis.

As catchy as they were, I couldn't sit still for a band when the real show was outside. I went back to the front door and stood under the awning. No one in New York ever seemed terribly concerned with whether we took our beer bottles outside. In the South, it was a big no-no. Here, nobody gave a damn.

For that matter, my nostrils were tickled by the unmistakable skunky olfaction of a good rasta fatty being toked right there inside the club. I smelled it as I hit the door. That's another no-no in the South, in or out of the club, even though we grow most of the stuff.

I stood outside and looked down the canyon walls on either side. The cabs, the sirens. The Empire State Building rising up out of fog and mist, eerily lit.

Two people were out there with me, an old woman was one of them, and a big man with a malt-liquor bottle. They were black. I was white. She was very friendly. He was very not so.

She noticed me smoking and asked for one. I was the world's worst cigarette bum and always considered it my karmic debt to freely give when I had them. I handed her a Marlboro and she held it to her lips, shaking while I cricket-lit it for her. All the time she kept her other hand on the shopping cart behind her. There was a ratty red blanket pulled over whatever was inside. The blanket was splatting with what little spitty rain was still coming down.

"Thank you for the cigarette. I didn't really expect you to give me one."

"Why not?" I asked smiling.

She looked down at the sidewalk and her ratty leather shoes, obviously not her size. "Because I'm a Negro," she replied.

Damn, I thought. Been a long time since I've even heard that word. It sounded so archaic. *Negro*. Racism. Here was this nice old lady just assuming I wouldn't have anything to do with her, and I could feel the nasty stares of this other guy who's as suspicious of me as I am of him. He assumed I was against him from the get-go, and I must admit I was, because he was obviously geared and primed to kick my ass at the drop of a hat. That tends to make me nervous. I'm funny that way. Someone wanting to mash my brains puts me a little on edge. If he would have just assumed there was no need for tension,

and I'd have just assumed such, there would have been—guess what-
—*no tension*. But there was. Boatloads of it. For absolutely no reason
at all.

We stood there smoking, the big black guy taking great draughts
off his sack bottle and glaring at me. The nice old black woman smoking and smiling. That's when I first started noticing our neighbors.

Down on the corner were two guys slumped against the wall,
their wet legs sticking out into the sidewalk. Another fellow, also
with a shopping cart, was hunched over it a block the other way,
pushing his possessions elsewhere. On the block past that was a
young fellow with a white styrofoam cup in his hand, shaking it at
passersby. Every so often someone would drop a coin in. The white
styrofoam cup guys got more plentiful uptown, and we'd see literally
hundreds of them while we were in New York.

I guess they'd disappeared during the heavy rain, or maybe we'd
been running so fast and were so awestruck by the Chinese writing or
whatever, but I hadn't noticed them until this moment. I could look up
and down the street and count maybe ten people who obviously had
no home. You don't spread a blanket on a soaking-wet sidewalk if
you have someplace else to go.

I looked back at my smoking companion and noticed we'd been
joined, magically, by two others. I don't know where the hell they'd
come from, but suddenly, here they were. Noticing I had only a few
cigarettes left anyway, I exercised an option these folks apparently
didn't have. I went back in the club.

The last train to Jersey was earlier than we'd have liked, one-
thirty or something like that. We retraced our steps and subwayed
back to Penn Station, where we hopped back on the train to Linden
and vanned it to the hotel. I'll always regret we didn't figure some
way to stay. I only noticed looking at the newspaper ad later who the
headliner was that night at CBGB—Moe Tucker, the Velvet Underground's drummer. Who knows who might have been there. Lou
Reed might have told me to fuck off had I stuck around. Maybe not.
We'll never know now.

Billy'd had a lovely time back in Jersey. He'd gone down to eat in
the hotel restaurant, and there had been a floor show in the lounge.
He'd wound up dancing with an old lady to Broadway show tunes.

The next day was an exercise in how New York turns you into
one of their own, that cliche of folks turning a blind eye to every

bizarre sideshow New York's capable of throwing at you. After a while, it's simply impossible to be amazed any more. You just start walking by it all, jaded and blase'.

We walked all over midtown Manhattan, the six of us, from morning 'til midnight. We saw every type of person, every type of behavior. We learned to not look people in the eye but not to look away either. We walked down Broadway and saw the Ed Sullivan Theater. We took a tentative stroll into the fringes of Central Park. We learned how anytime you stared at a subway map more than fifteen seconds, somebody'd magically be there to give you directions anywhere you cared to go. *Then* came the bill. "Hey, man, ya got any spare change on you? Can ya help me out, man?"

We found the Dakota on 72nd Street and Central Park West. The guard told us all about it. *"Yeh, folks come from awwl ovuh de woild tuh see dis place."* We all got quiet and reverent, being in the place where John Lennon got taken away. It was a strange thing for us guys, all smart-assed as a rule, getting quiet and worshipful about anything. Then our attention was drawn to the ruckus across the street.

One angry fellow was kicking another fellow's ass up the street. Literally. One kick and the hunched-over target travelled five feet, cowering, covering his head with his hands. Halfway up the block, the poor guy couldn't stand any more. He was in pretty bad shape. Another kick. The dominant guy was howling vicious curses at his vanquished foe. The victim managed to get up and run about fifty feet before he fell in pain. His captor casually sauntered up and planted a few more kicks in his side, along with a few more curses. The poor target got up and ran ten more feet to the front door of a pizza parlor. The owner had run up and locked the door not two seconds in advance of the guy's arrival.

We looked at the Dakota guard as if to get some advice on how to react to this situation. Apparently, the true New York choice is to NOT react. Somebody's getting their ass kicked. It ain't yer problem. Welcome to New York. Stick around and the day will come when you feel that shoe on the other foot. And we would, too.

New York is simply too many sources of aural and visual stimuli, too many people walking by you, shouting things at you, trying to rattle you, and they're like dogs; if they smell fear, you're done for.

Cabs, big buildings, tons of people at all hours of the day and night, always a siren somewhere, people walking by you very fast in expensive trench coats, limousines, gangs, noise. The input valve on your brain simply shuts down or, shall we say, gets very discriminating. If it's not a *direct threat to your life*, it isn't relevant. And within a day of wandering around New York City, I came to understand that. You overload, and then you plane on stimulus' endless wave.

We found the Chelsea Hotel in the lower twenties, which was how they described the numbered streets. The Chelsea is where Sid Vicious allegedly killed Nancy Spungen, in Room 100. We stood outside for a bit and wondered how we'd get upstairs, since there seemed to be some sort of screening process inside the lobby.

I used to work in a hospital. I knew how this worked. All you have to do, I explained to the others, was walk in as if you knew exactly where you were going, and have this expression like you had business there and weren't to be trifled with. I'd gotten into every part of the hospital that way. I'd seen bodies in the morgue by doing this, so follow me.

So, assuming the other guys were behind me, I strutted boldly through the Chelsea lobby, which didn't look too shabby, actually. I walked straight past the clerk and up the stairs, through a set of double doors that shut with an echo behind me. Then I looked around. I was all alone on the floor where Sid (allegedly) killed Nancy. I waited for the other guys to come through the double doors. It appeared, though, I'd just half-explained my strategy to them, and then taken off. They weren't behind me.

The upstairs more than made up for the lobby in shabbiness and eeriness. The black and white tile floors led me down several hallways before I came to the cul-de-sac I was looking for.

There was no longer a Room 100, but it was fairly obvious how to narrow the choices down to the two rooms with the ancient brass number plates removed from the overhead door facings. One had 101 written in magic marker above it. One had 102 written in similar fashion. This meant there'd have to be two 101s or 102s and I don't get how they did that without moving a lot of brass plates around.

But here is where it happened, I knew. On the other side of one of those doors, John Simon "Sid Vicious" Ritchie drove a hunting knife (allegedly) into Nancy Spungen. Perhaps because she wanted him to, perhaps just to shut her up. No one knows exactly what happened.

One door down the hall kept opening slightly and then slamming shut. Before I could spin around, it would always slam shut again. Creeeak open. Slam! Creeeak open. Slam! And—before you could say "Jeffrey Dahmer is an unknown chocolate-factory worker and part-time cannibal living in Wisconsin"—I got the hell out of there.

We stopped at a Greenwich Village cafe, where I had my first espresso. I had to load it with its weight in sugar to get it down. I sped like a rocket the rest of the night. We got back to the hotel in Jersey and I stayed in the bathroom all night, writing post cards, reading and speeding my teeth loose.

We took the Staten Island Ferry at sunset the next day. I remember looking at the Statue of Liberty for the first time and telling myself that, for once, I wasn't looking at a television screen or a photo in a book. That was the real thing. There was nothing but air between my eyes and the statue. It had stood there for so many immigrants who saw it for the first time, America's first wave hello to the millions who built the place. It's an awfully funky shade of green now, but that does little to diminish its grandeur. Pictures and coin-bank models don't convey what must be seen from the sea. That's where it's meant to be seen. The lamp, the whole message, made so much more sense on that ferry. *Gabba gabba we accept you! One of us!*

Monday night, we were all in the city having a large time. We'd split into camps. I went northward for another gaze at the Dakota. This time the guard was nowhere to be found.

I looked up the street and then down. I looked past the ajar gate into the archway, to the place Lennon was actually standing when Mark David Chapman shot him.

I could see no guard. And I stood an eternity, unsure of what to do. Dare I? Is this a sign from God? One of those moments when one takes the initiative? . . . Damn right it is.

I slipped my skinny self through the cracked-open gate without creaking it. I walked in about five or ten feet and looked up at the arched stone ceiling. I looked down at the stone floor beneath me. I could almost see around the perpendicular stairway into the security office/lobby, and I knew. I knew. I was standing *right where* John Lennon was standing when it all happened.

For a moment it was John Lennon And Me, all alone. I think I'd have to rock a while in Abe's chair at Ford's Theater to get the same sensation from head to toe. It wasn't morbid. It was warm, a communion. For a moment there, a priceless moment, it was just John Lennon and Me.

And then it was John Lennon, Me and the Guard. I could just see around the corner into the doorway now, having inched a little further inward, and the guard behind the desk could just see me a little, too.

I beat him out the gate and down around the corner by about four seconds. I heard the gate slam shut with authority. I scratched a notch on my brainstem. I'd trod holy ground. A few minutes later, I came back around and sat on the sidewalk, rocking in the fall chill on my butt and my heels, my arms locked around my knees, just looking at that gate.

By the time we regrouped, it was dangerously close to Jersey train time. If we didn't catch the 1:30 am, we were stuck in Manhattan 'til 4:30, or something undoable like that. Broma had us walking an old friend of his back uptown to her walk-up, and then we broke into a run for the nearest subway station. We knew we were way late and shouldn't have taken this girl home. Put her in a cab, Broma! No go. We walked her back and made it to Penn Station about ten minutes too late. We were stuck in the city.

No cab driver takes more than four people in New York, much less goes to Jersey without a massive tip in advance. We were stuck, exhausted, and quite, quite pissed off. What the hell were we going to do besides sit awake in Penn Station and feel our hangovers hit us?

That's all we *could* do. We even discovered that cat-napping was not a consideration. Sitting in a little irritable row in Penn Station's main lobby, we were indoctrinated into homelessness for neophytes.

There is no sleeping in Penn Station. A sleeper is trying to live there, isn't he? A legitimate passenger stays awake. And those crusty New York cops were sauntering around, kicking feet, pushing drunk derelicts out with take-no-shit shoulder shoves, prodding old ladies in the ribs while they dozed, their sleep-sluggish hands keeping a grip on shopping bags full of trinkets, clothing and bits of memories.

A full, amazing half of Penn Station were homeless, all putting on valiant method-acting performances. No, officer! We're passengers, too. Don't gimme that crap. Wake up or get out of here!

The cops knew who was who. C'mon, how couldn't they? The homeless were the homeless, and looked a damn sight different from the rest of the world. It was a game, a big, bitter, brutal game. If you could keep awake and act like you were waiting for a train and didn't appear drunk, you could stay. The cops were walking around like they were saying "hey, work with us on this one".

The minute a drunk old guy gave himself away as soused, he was out of there. The cop would get him on his feet and push him one shoulder at a time, straight up an eighty-foot staircase. And the cop did it with a look on his face like he was shoving a side of beef down a ceiling-mounted hookrail towards the refrigerator truck. We popped what white-crosses we could come up with among the six of us and sat there, wide-eyed.

Skot had been so angry about missing the train that he had taken off, literally just torn off and gone down the street to the Empire State Building, touched it and turned back. By the time he reappeared, we were inventing all sorts of gruesome scenarios to explain his demise. He hadn't died, but we nearly killed him when he showed back up just for pulling that disappearing shit again.

A few at a time, we'd go upstairs and hang out on the street corner outside Madison Square Garden. It was an insane thing to do. At least downstairs there was order, some sort of government. On that street corner at two in the morning, there was nothing short of ugly anarchy. It wasn't lonely. No one lacked for company out there, that's for sure. But should any harm befall your sorry ass, there was no help coming. You shoulda been downstairs if you were concerned about the shape of your face, pal. You asked for it, hanging around on that corner in Manhattan at that hour of the day.

It couldn't be helped, though. Having to sit on a bench feigning wakefulness made us sleepier than we'd have been in any ordinary circumstance. And watching the whole homeless agony graphically played out before us made for intense emotions and feelings of claustrophobia. We all wound up hanging out on the corner in the (comparative) open air at one time or another, staring up at that huge, huge Tower of Babel building.

Outside, or topside perhaps, we met a guy named Reggie. He was about 29, with a ready smile and a quick wit. He'd been a medical intern on Staten Island, a middle-class black man with a young wife and baby daughter—until he took up freebasing. He lost everything to the pipe. He'd been on the street six months now, trying to get straight. His family'd disowned him, and his young daughter didn't know him at all. Reggie was bound and determined to beat freebase this time. This had been his longest stretch off the pipe, four weeks, living on the street, hugging onto a sack bottle of Colt 45 to numb the cravings.

He was an amazing guy. We talked almost an hour, and we found him quite useful in keeping a menacing couple of guys at bay. If the guy outside CBGB acted like he didn't like me, then these two cats next to me now were visually skinning me alive and boiling me in oil.

I don't think I was imagining it. When it's four in the morning and a six-foot four fellow walks up to a foot from your face and asks in his best James Earl Jones voice *"Did you know that people DIE in New York City everyDAY? They die and nobody knows what happened. They FUCKIN' DISAPPEAR! Did you know that, motherfucker?"* I take that as a definite hint. I did my best to keep these fellows on one side of Reggie with me on his other, just rocking on my heels as the Manhattan night inched along. Reggie's implied endorsement of us was all that kept the streetcorner situation tranquil by 3 AM Manhattan standards.

Reggie never seemed drunk, and he was putting away an ass-kicking amount of Colt 45. Freebase craving must make nicotine fits look fairly lame in comparison. He didn't know what he was going to do, he told us, but he was going to do something. He knew there was hope as long as he could get off and stay off freebase. That was his whole life. Stay off freebase. Stay off freebase. Go to sleep. Wake up. Stay off freebase. All day long. Stay off freebase.

Billy would write one of his best songs about that night. It's called "No Sleeping In Penn Station". Should you ever get to hear it, it will pretty much describe our night. Everyone should have to spend one night underneath Madison Square Garden. It's an incredibly uncomfortable and exhausting experience, and the homeless do it every day. Once you've seen and felt how they live, close up, it changes everything; and maybe if everybody had to do it once, nobody'd have to do it soon enough thereafter.

We made it back to Jersey in the harsh, cold pre-dawn. There was a tremendous argument between Broma and Skot about making us late, and for a minute it looked like Broma was going to pull out and fly home.

"This is going great, just great," I thought. "Here we are in New York, and our soundman's leaving and we play CBGB tonight, and nobody's slept. This is wonderful." If there was a blessing, it was that everybody was too bushed to argue with any gusto. Broma and Skot agreed to get mad at each other all over again after some sleep, when they had more energy for it.

We awoke far too early. Skot and Broma resumed their argument. We split them into opposite camps, and Joe and I worked on Broma. We convinced them to patch up their differences, and the day began, albeit precariously. We got to Broma with some cockamamie variation of the *"You'll miss out on the millions later if you bail out now!"* speech. It reeked of bullshit, and it worked.

We took the van for the first experience of actually taking a vehicle we loved into the wilds of Manhattan. The streets of that town are best left to the cantankerous cab-drivers who know its ways.

It never ceased to amaze me how anything they can charge money for up there, they do. Just like Disney World, just like the Pennsylvania Turnpike, there were eight lanes of turnstiles to back up traffic and take your money before you hit either the tunnel or the bridge. It wasn't so much a toll as it was an admission charge, a fee for the right to hunt on the property, a basic shakedown.

The second compulsory cash-flow came on the first street corners in the city, the windshield-washer brigade. Some were cool. Others weren't. It's not up to you to ask for the work to be done. Your windshield *will be cleaned*, and you'd better have some coinage ready for the guy. If not, well, you'd be well served to be larger than the guy with the squeegee. I can understand the windshield washer's take on the issue. "Hey! I could be selling crack, motherfucker! I'm making an honest living cleaning windshields. There's dignity in this work, and there's 75 cents in your ashtray. Give it here! Now!"

We'd told Rob of Freedom of Expression, "Guess what, man! We're playing CBGB next month." "Great," he said, "make sure to take everything out of the van you ever want to see again."

"Don't worry, man," we said, "we've got an alarm installed that starts chirping if you even jostle the outside of the van." He laughed and said "That's great. They *look* for alarms on vehicles up there. It livens things up, adds twenty seconds of spice in their day while they bypass it and take all your stuff."

We completely stripped the van, taking tied-up bedsheets of stuff inside with us. We actually got a soundcheck, which was a rarity there. The sun was still up; we had quite a bit of time to kill. Tutt had flown up.

We were the second of four bands that night, and it ran the ridiculous gamut. The first act was based around one egotistical guy. He played his black Telecaster with his hoariest-of-cliches power-pop stage look. Black stovepipe trousers, black sports jacket, and white shirt buttoned to the top. He had the whole band, pro session-types backing him up, backup girl singers. It was his moment, and no less than five record companies were there to see him.

I tell you, they've got it down to a science up there. Those record company types came in literally minutes before this guy started. They grabbed a Heineken each and sat down the minute the band counted off their first number, like it was a movie, with no reason for downtime, like *Gilligan's Island* when the relevant news story would always air the very second one of them turned on the radio.

Two friends from Lexington, Greg and Larry, showed up out of the blue. They were goosed on X and Jack Daniels, and had flown up from UK just to see little old us. Whaddya know. We had friends there after all. Larry had the greatest laugh of anyone I've ever met. High and piercing, like a hyena. And he liked to laugh a lot.

Just before we went on, one of them passed out. I can't remember which one. We hauled him out to the van, to sleep in the back and, if not guard it, at least ride with it placidly wherever thieves might take it.

The Long Island No-Future Power Popster finished up his meticulously planned, expertly paced set, and his band tore down. We set up in a matter of minutes because the record company guys were still out there. Gee, maybe they'll hate him and sign *US*, we thought. We still believed in miracles in those days.

Tutt was in the back with Hilly Crystal, who was holed up in his office, snarling at folks. When we did "Fish Stick Day", Hilly came around the door and looked at us. He laughed and pointed out to no one in particular. "I like that shit!" he said, and went back into his office.

Oh my God! Look who's here! *Schkip!*

Skip and his girlfriend Cathy had shown up. Cathy was from New York, and I believe it was a couple of her old friends who came with them to the club that night. It was good to know that Skip was there to see his boys play the big time. And yes, to us at the moment, CBGB was the big time.

Skip had left Bowling Green to tour the country with Cathy, buying, trading and selling comic books. Cathy spent her time that night buying me beers and telling me how Scott Tutt was going to screw us someday. She could see it in his eyes, she said.

A trash-metal band with a husband and wife front-duo went on after us. A booking agent from New Jersey, a lady from Polygram and a radio lady from Pennsylvania all came backstage and we all talked exciting business, about great Government Cheese deals that never went any further than that night.

It hadn't been a sellout night to say the least, and when Tutt went to get paid, Hilly handed him 27 dollars. Tutt was dumbfounded. We had a contract. 27 dollars??? He looked through it to make sure it was all at least American money.

"Hilly, man, come on." Tutt said, trying his best to be charming and pulling the contract out of his back pocket. "We have a signed contract for a hundred-dollar guarantee. Come on, a hundred lousy dollars for guys who came from Kentuck. . . ."

"Listen," Hilly said, cutting Tutt off. "This is one of the biggest clubs in the world. You wanna play here again?"

"Well, sure, but . . . "

"Good." pronounced Hilly. "Take the money and shut the fuck up." He turned and went back in his office. That was the end of that. We loaded out and went back to New Jersey.

We played the Underground Railroad in Morgantown, West Virginia on the 8th, two days after CBGB. I have a static, one-camera videotape of the whole gig. It was freezing in the West Virginia mountains, and the fact that the club had a huge hole in the wall behind us, emptying out into the alley, didn't help matters any.

All I remember about Morgantown is that all the streets were steep. It's a mountain college town. I think experiencing West Virginia in direct contrast to New York is why I can't remember much about it. All I recall is that Skot and Broma patched things up fully there, I had a nice walk down a mountain road next to the fleabag motel we stayed in, and that I could see my breath onstage while we played.

We'd been warned about the Electric Banana in Pittsburgh. "Get paid before you play," people told us. "The owner keeps an automatic pistol behind the bar," we'd heard, "and if he decides you suck, then the pistol comes out and you leave empty-handed."

Pittsburgh visually explodes on you when you come out of a mountain tunnel. One minute you're on the highway on one side of rural Pennsylvania, then you enter a tunnel in the face of the mountain. You come out the other side straight onto a bridge over one of those three rivers, and on the other side of the bridge is PITTSBURGH! All big as life, all the buildings. The trick is to come in at night. The lights make it.

We killed a night in a Pittsburgh club with a first for all of us, a Yankee cover band. I was in heaven.

All my life, I'd dealt with Southern cover bands. If I never hear

"Free Bird" again, I'll be happy. I'd never seen a Northern cover band, the sound of the steelworks copied and recopied.

The lead singer played a Telecaster just like Bruce Springsteen's. He looked just like Bruce, except a little fatter. He sang all of Bruce's repertoire. He did "Thunder Road" solo with piano accompaniment, just like Bruce. It was a good band if you could get past this guy's slightly disturbing identification with Bruce. He *was* Bruce. The band did lots of Chuck Berry, and rather properly too, I might add. Most people jack off the Chuck Berry covers. Oh, it's just three chords and some words. These guys understood the swing of it. They did "Nadine" and "Around and Around". They even did Stray Cats covers like "Look at that Cadillac".

And then they did "Jungleland" from top to bottom, with no editing. And the guy *WAS BRUCE.* It wasn't billed as a tribute band, like Strutter or the Back Doors. It was just another Northerner with a Bruce Springsteen fixation. Then I noticed that all the people in this bar on a Friday night in Pittsburgh, all of us drinking Rolling Rocks, were just taking it in. He wasn't bizarre to them like he was to me. He was just another of many bar band singers who *thought he was Bruce.* It was a regular thing.

And that made me think, is Bruce *himself* even real? Or does he simply do THE GUY better than anybody, the prototype rock and roll greaser guy. Is Bruce even genuine? Or does he know that this is the look, and this is the stance, and this is the way you wear your hair? Did he one day say hey, this is what people want, this is the amalgam?

Did he figure out that the people don't want Bruce, they want Bruce-*ness? Everyrocker?*

It's true. He's not really Bruce any more than someone's really Lou Reed or Bob Dylan. They're just famous folks who got the idea down and turned a nickel from it. They transcended, came into the Christ, the Buddha, the Everyrocker. By this thinking, then, the guy in the bar onstage who thought he was Bruce was, perhaps, just as important as the real Bruce, that is, if he was just as good a Bruce as Bruce was a Bruce.

Elvis impersonators are, then, perhaps, as truly important as Elvis. The priest is as important as God. It's the acting out of the archetype, the taking on of a more exalted being. *That's* what's important, not the person him or her*self!* Yes, it's the losing of self! That's what's important! Of course!

Up North, women in bars walk away from you when you start talking like this just as fast as they do in the South. Some things are probably the same the world over.

The next night, we went to the Electric Banana for our gig. Skin Yard from Seattle were soundchecking. They were the first band. The headliners were some local geeks; the lead singer spoke in a British accent onstage when everybody in the club knew he was from Harrisburg, or somewhere like that.

Speaking in fake English accents seemed to be a disease among local club rockers in the '80s. We had several in the Nashville market who used to pull that stunt all the time. Why people do that when everyone knows where they're from mystifies me. Tina Turner is only the most famous example.

We did our set as the middle act and went over okay, for the few people who were there. There were two older couples who'd grown up together, apparently. They'd always been rocking couples, the two husbands and the two wives. They'd been rocking together since the early seventies, it looked like. Now, here they were at our show, listening to the words, laughing in all the right spots. They had nine-to-five hair now. Nice clothes. Being that they were from Pennsylvania, maybe they'd even really been to Woodstock.

But they weren't the principal focus of my attention. That honor went to the young blonde who kept exposing her chest.

She had this maniacal smile, eyes that went in two different directions at once, two front teeth that did the same. She was, I must say, reasonably attractive for a cross-eyed bucktoothed wench, with decent breasts she felt she must show.

All through the gig, she was showing me her left breast out of the top of her ill-fitting red cocktail dress. No one in the club seemed even slightly concerned with stopping her from doing this. Indeed, the staff seemed to be regarding her as some kind of regular. There she was, showing her tit and smiling from it to me, as if she were covertly trying to sell me a stolen watch.

After the show, she came up to me and shoved her hand in my crotch with no degree of subtlety. She stammered "Maybe we should go outside, huh huh?! Maybe, maybe we, maybe we should go outside, huh? Huh?" She was grabbing my balls like Farmer Joe grabs Bessie's udder. It wasn't pleasant. Damned painful, actually.

I kept my wits about me, carnally. It wasn't difficult. Dogbreath and track marks do quell the woody.

And so we partied with Skin Yard to a certain degree, partied with other people no one remembers now. Fixed a flat on the van, caught *The Godfather* on HBO in the room. Slept, woke and headed out of Pittsburgh, back south. Our virgin breach of Yankee ways and means was over. Four days after the Electric Banana, we were at The Nick in Birmingham. Five days after, we were at Picasso's. Six days later, we were opening for the Neighborhoods at the Red Barn in Louisville. Ten days after the Electric Banana, we were at Picasso's. Twelve days after, we played a sorority party at UK. Thirteen days after, we were at the Ivory Tusk in Tuscaloosa. Fourteen days after, we were at the KA House at UT-Knoxville. Seventeen days after, Picasso's again. Eighteen, the Red Barn again. Nineteen, the Hangar in Carbondale, Illinois. Twenty, the ATO House at UK. Twenty-one days after Pittsburgh, Picasso's again.

It was a way of life just continuing. Lots of beer. Hotel rooms. The constant pre- and/or post-cold sniffles that we hadn't anticipated would be as large a part of our lives as they were. Splitting eighty dollars four ways at the end of a weekend. Catching the middle part of the same movie on hotel Showtime fifteen nights in a row. Telling the Shoney's waitress that we didn't need to see a menu 'cause we had it memorized, thanks. Going over the fence and taking a dip in the hotel pool after hours. Eating cold ravioli out of the can. Waking up under a table, or in a bathtub, or in a car. After a while, you didn't ask why any more.

\* \* \* \*

# 15

# how's my rouge?

As a kid, did you ever stand in front of the mirror holding a hairbrush like a microphone with the record player going, mouthing the words along with whoever? Of course you did.

Did you ever get out the tennis racket and play along with "Stranglehold" or "Do You Feel Like We Do"? Of course you did.

*I* used to dress up in that old tuxedo when I did it. I remember my mom coming into my room with a fresh load of socks to put away while I was wearing the tux, with evening bow tie and Steve Martin arrow-through-the-head. "Surrender" by Cheap Trick was screaming through the speakers. Mom was in and out without saying a word. The poor woman could only take so much by that point.

I staged complete tennis racket and hairbrush concerts in my room, with imaginary roadies and backstage hospitality areas, hindered only by the fact that no one makes a microphone stand for a hairbrush.

Imagine yourself in front of the mirror lip-synching, and someone (other than Mom) enters the room right when you are really getting into it. You can't blush any more than when you're caught in mid-hairbrush vocal.

Now, picture being busted in such a way by a crew of fourteen people and a hundred extras. That is what it feels like to shoot a rock video.

We had already tried to do one, with questionable results—a soundstage performance piece of *C'mon Back To Bowling Green* shot on videotape. Tutt had hired a makeup lady who dabbed at our faces with a vast assortment of brushes and triangular squishy pads. Then she played with our hair endlessly, with us trusting that these are things you have to go through to wind up looking on videotape like you always do anyway to people seeing you live.

No. The end result had us looking like Motley Crue on the *Theater of Pain* tour. I remember seeing it at Tutt's house/office and laughing—because it was pretty funny—but I was also terrified somebody might actually *see* this piece o' shit. Thankfully, to this day, few have.

We tried again, and this next time was much better.

The "Face to Face" video was quite a big-budget achievement for Government Cheese. WKU footed half the bill, as Cory Lash made it a project for one of his classes. Half the town was in it, it seemed. Skot's girlfriend at the time, Annie, figured in it as some sort of love interest. The plotline apparently got left on the cutting-room floor, but it all *looked* great. We shot some "concert" sequences and other disjointed stuff, including Billy Mack blowing an ex-girlfriend's pinata away with a 12-gauge as it hung from a tree branch. It was all just put in there together. I liked it. I didn't have much to do with it, but I liked it.

Tutt knew the head guy at MTV. They had grown up together. He made a few calls and we got the thumbs-up. We were going to be on *120 Minutes* in a mere two Sundays. Giving credit where it's due, Tutt pulled this one off flawlessly. He got us on MTV and he can claim that accomplishment for himself.

Of course, we told everyone we were going to be on in two weeks, and of course, we weren't on that night. There were parties planned, VCRs set and all sorts of embarrassing shit. All bands have to learn never to believe any deadline. They are invariably wrong. The record will never come out the day they tell you it will, and your video will never premiere on the first night they say. It's a plot. The lines they feed you are never right, and if you pass on the info to your friends, it's a tacit hubris guarantee you're going to wind up with egg on your face.

So, with eggy faces, we watched for it the *next* week, and there it was.

I was sitting in the Cardinal Inn in Louisville watching it on a big screen, the kind that is three times the size of the screen at home, but everyone has to sit directly in front of it or else they can't see anything, so you have a roomful of people sitting, drinking beer, all in a long diamond shape stretching away from the screen to the back of the room. Government Cheese, the guys who were freezing in a frat basement three years before, who used to make unholy racket in the kitchen, were on by God MTV. Kevin Seal said our name. There we were, broadcast all over the world. I was sitting there with a Budweiser mug and a foamy upper lip, watching myself at the same time as did more people than I had ever talked to in my whole life.

The light our faces reflected had stamped itself on emulsion. That image was transferred to magnetic pulses on a strip of thin iron-coated plastic, and *then* transformed into long ridiculous coded combinations of ones and zeroes. Then some people played with that image until they had it like they liked it. Then it was all moved back to another long strip of magnetic pulses, packed away and shipped to New York, where somebody took it out of the box and stuck it into a machine. That machine transformed all this information into radio waves that shot out to a satellite hovering far above the planet. That satellite shot it right back to Louisville, where somebody with machines put the pulses and waves into a cable and sent it to me and my Budweiser at the Cardinal Inn, and there I was, looking just like I did the day the whole thing started, all embarrassed and busted with my hairbrush in the mirror.

For a brief while after that, we were in the stream, that big roaring current of electromagnetic data from which the whole world drinks. It's amazing how much life changes from even the veriest moistened toe, such as we had. The video aired precious few times and only on Sunday nights, but suddenly everyone in the country knew us. People coast-to-coast who wouldn't have known us or cared the week before suddenly started returning our calls. Our price went up.

For a few short weeks after that night at the Cardinal Inn, we were on a different plane. Government Cheese was *something*. We were *known*. Hi, I'm calling about Government Cheese. Perhaps you saw them on MTV last night. Damn straight, you did!

The last shot slow-motioned out with me throwing a copy of our record at the camera. We faded, slowed-down more, faded further and then we were gone. So cruelly how our moment in the sun was swept away, like Emmett Kelly mopping up a spotlight, and how unmistakably MTV restated what was really important. We had segued into a Michael Jackson commercial.

\* \* \* \*

# real men
# don't do soundchecks

In the wake of the MTV exposure, we stepped up the touring. We were now officially away from home more often than we were there. We'd brushed up against that threshold before, and now we were fully over it.

There were two types of days on the road: hotel days and crash-pad days. Both had advantages and disadvantages. In a hotel, the towels were clean and there was no behavior-constricting host. You could fart and spit and be impolite and didn't have to be in a good mood first thing the next day. Hotels charge a larcenous rate for this.

A crash pad is free, but no amenties are guaranteed. You might get a bed, you might get a corner with the hound. You might get to sleep 'til one in the afternoon, you might be stepped on at seven-thirty in the morning by a raving neo-hippie on the phone who charges through the room and doesn't see you sleeping on the floor 'til he knocks bongwater all over your face.

Why is it so odd to hotel maids that fellows who got to bed at four are a little punchy and slow-on-the-uptake at nine, a full five hours later? This was about the time they started knocking on the doors. "Housekeeping!" they'd shriek. Hanging out the "do not disturb" sign was a 50/50 waste of time. They'd knock anyway. Why do the zombies keep knocking, captain?! It's all they know, son. All they remember.

I was always known for my so-called "coffin-like demeanor" while sleeping. I got in bed with my arms folded across me and didn't move all night. Billy instinctively slept with one giant arm slung way up and behind his head, like Morrissey does in half his photos. He was apparently comfortable, but hardly looked it. He was also inter-changeable about it. Depending on which side of the double-bed Billy was on, the far arm was the one he threw behind his head, so his bedmate didn't have to worry about rolling over and getting a snout-ful of armpit.

Skot had precious few pair of underwear, and usually forgot to bring the ones he owned on the road with him. If they wound up in bed together, Billy would sleep between the comforter and the top sheet so as not to roll over and wind up with a handful of Skottie's fetching, bare ass.

We were a contact-lens band, all but Skot. The rest of us would assume four-eyed status the minute we hit the hotel room or crash pad. Joe would often fall asleep sitting up with his glasses on, watch-ing television. Chris impressed me as being able to sleep anywhere, anytime. I had to have the basics: a blanket, an improvised pillow of some sort, and at least some of the lights out. Chris needed none of these things. He could crash out in the middle of a freezing floor with everything on and nothing to pull over him.

In the mornings, I slept until the last possible moment. So did Billy. Joe had a wristwatch with an anemic chirp for an alarm. Some-how, in the leaden arms of too-brief repose, he would always hear that alarm when it went off, get up and take a shower. Then Skot would generally get one. Billy, Chris and I were noticeably less into the morning shower thing, and by then it was usually time to go anyway.

Billy used to "wash" his hair by shaking baby powder all over his head, letting it sit there for a second soaking up grease, then brushing it out. It would never come completely out either, leaving his hair salt-and-pepper gray from the experience. Billy would smell a bit from the neck down, but be quite nice and baby-ish on top. Slap-ping him on the back would cause a cloud of powder to flutter and dissipate. I am not making this up. All day long, he would have little white baby-powder speckles all over his shoulders and on his face, until someone told him to wipe them off.

So out we would tumble, into the hard light of day and the glare of a maid who was under the however erroneous impression that only two people were registered for this room. The inside usually looked like the remnants of a bachelor party. Sometimes, depending on friends, hangers-on, seasonal roadies and/or late-night party guests, there might be as many as three or four times the number of officially-registered people staggering out of the room, filing past a pissed-off maid who could not finish up and go home until we, the last people in the whole damn motel, had seen fit to leave.

Crashing somewhere was always better in the morning. No deadline. No bitch from hell banging on the door. But there was always the oppressive consciousness of being in someone else's home. No matter who they were, we felt like we should sit up straight and not stink up their bathroom, be smiling and politely conversational and make at least a token effort to clean up before we left. We made a lot of friends on the road and had some great times, but there wasn't any private time when you could turn off and be inward, so as not to grow surly. After a few days out, there was always somebody surly at any given time. Never was everybody hip-hooray-happy simultaneously.

Occasionally we crashed on someone's floor and, the next morning, the *other* roommate would awaken and discover the heathens who had come home with the the one who said "everything was cool." I remember waking up on a floor in Macon at 8-ish in the morning. It was way out in the country, far enough that no one would hear our screams. The girl, our host, had a beautiful face and body, a strong, Jay Leno-ish jawline, and she was one of the mellowest people I've ever had the privilege of meeting. She invited us to what turned out to be her family's home, a nice two-car garage ranch-style on a wooded plot — the type of place she would probably live in with her Camaro in the driveway until someone took her away from all this. Her parents were gone and everything was great, until her redneck brother discovered the five of us strewn all over the living room floor the next morning. *"WHO ARE THESE MUTHERFUCKERS!!??"* is a get-your-shoes-on-and-boogie-*now* kind of reveille.

Then there was Tupelo, where we awakened at seven to our lady host screaming into the phone *"We wasn't drinkin', Mawma! Ever'body had there CLOZON!"* Everybody *did* have their clothes on, but the "we wasn't drinin'" part was an outrageous lie. Skot had dropped into one bed and the afore-quoted lovely had fallen in next to him, collapsing into a sodden sleep and wetting her jeans, the bed and Skot. It was a baptism of which he would not be made aware until we awoke to her screaming. I can't remember what woke me first, the girl or the satanic little yippy dog that was using my beer-raped body and head as a jungle gym.

There was crashing with the hippies in Atlanta, one of whom kept us awake an extra hour searching around for an electric fan (in the dead of winter) because he liked to sleep to the sound of it . . . or the place in eastern Tennessee somewhere with candle wax everywhere and pentagrams on the walls and a live tarantula in an open coffee-table terrarium, where we slept in our parkas because the front window glass was broken out . . . or the riot house in Lexington . . . or one of my favorites: Skot's parents' home in Louisville.

Purple, Skot's roommate, came with us to a Tewligan's gig and we shared the Willises' guest-room bed afterwards. They kept an immaculate home with no smoking, no eating in the living room and no fingers on the front glass. Purple tended to sleepwalk. Sure enough, I awoke to the sound of a sprung fountain early in the morning. Purple was wedged upright between the Willises' guest-room bureau and the door, completely asleep and pissing all over the wall and the carpet. "Purple!" I barked. He stopped what he was doing, grunted something in his own little private sleep language and came back to bed. I'd like to think I got out of bed and fetched a towel but I don't remember. I certainly *hope* I didn't just roll over, see Purple fouling the Willises' wall, and go right back to sleep. All I know is that, the next morning, there was no evidence whatsoever. No stain. No smell. Amazing.

Whenever we left the places we crashed, the first item on the agenda was coffee, and lots of it. Shoney's was always good for coffee. It was usually already lunchtime, or beyond.

Tomato Florentine was always the Shoney's soup of the day. There would be two different soups du jour: Tomato Florentine or Clam Chowder. Tomato Florentine or Vegetable Beef. Tomato Florentine or Cabbage. Tomato Florentine or Cream of Broccoli.

Tomato Florentine was only good the first day it was made, while the pasta shells still had some *al dente* to them, before they became sludge. I learned to look in the pot for a quick visual appraisal before deciding whether or not to partake. To this day, I can spot a first-day pot of Tomato Florentine. I probably can't tell second from third-day any more, but I had the chops at one time.

Shoney's and Waffle House ruled all. You can live well off Shoney's and Waffle House. Denny's and Bob Evans were at the bottom of the list, with the worst service and worst food awards respectively. As for drive-throughs, Wendy's was always a good choice because there were few arguments about the place. Wendy's food was always so unremittingly bland that nobody *didn't* like it. There was nothing there to like or dislike, since it didn't taste like anything *at all.* Hence, we steadfastly patronized this paragon of non-taste, which just bolstered Dave's bottom line, encouraged the place to stay tasteless, and made us part of the fast-food problem and not the solution.

Then off we'd be in the van, on the way to the next town. There would be a gas stop, a convenience store generally, where we could buy a newspaper, aspirins, sunglasses for whoever'd lost theirs, vitamins, whatever. Russ Seveney roadied for us awhile. He was a Nordic mountain of a man, big into science-fiction and theater, a good actor. Russ always bought two pint cartons of chocolate milk, although we would have just eaten breakfast. Being six-foot plus, he would have just polished off a full meal, and, several miles down the road, would already be ready for his chocolate milk and Oreo cookies.

Russ sat on the beer cooler between the two back seats, part of him overlapping into both adjoining chairs, hunched over and knocking back that chocolate milk. Russ was a good guy, but we eventually had to let him go before we went to Texas once. He was chocolate-milking us to death, and we didn't know if we would have the budget that journey to withstand his consumption. Russ used to sing along with every Boston song on the radio, in full voice. He could hit all the notes and he knew every word.

We would sit there in the van with the special delights we had bought, provided we had recently split any money up to buy anything with.

Billy liked olives. He would sit and eat a whole jar as we rolled down the road. Later, he got into tuna and would insist while eating it that we call him "Tuna Man" like he was some sort of superhero. The tuna was okay so long as an open can of it didn't roll underneath a seat and get lost to all but our olfactories. This happened occasionally

Joe drank gallons of iced tea, the 7-11 Big Gulps or the great big ones from Wendy's. Skot ate those white Zero bars because he knew no one would ask him for one. My habits were the worst. I smoked cigarettes and drank coffee. When Chris was with us, I smoked *his* cigarettes and drank coffee.

The fields rolled by. Given as many cows as I saw, one might presume that I learned a great deal about them. I've never seen so much of and learned less about anything else. I still don't know why they lie down before it rains. I don't know if they are hip to the slaughterhouse. I don't know the complexity of their relationships with one another, nor their emotional makeup. And only once did I catch a couple of cows doing the nasty. We spun around and shot back down the interstate to watch some more, but they'd already finished. So I don't even know how long cows last when they do it, or if the lady cows get anything out of it, besides baby cows, that is. But I saw plenty of cows. That much is true. I'm sure there were different types: Black Angus, Simmental, Polled Herefords. Just cows to me.

So one of us would drive and the rest of us would ride along, listening to the one-speaker classic-hits radio, reading magazines, slugging and safety-ing. On top of that was the free entertainment only we were privy to. It was not the least funny bunch of people to ever ride down the road with. Billy Mack did a wonderful impersonation of Charles Nelson Reilly that for some reason never did get old. He pulled his glasses down funny and lowered his mandible, creating five chins to get the maximum effect out of the gag. And Skot Willis was one of the funniest human beings I've ever known. It's nothing I can quote now for illustration, unfortunately, since his skills were mostly in the realm of pantomimicry and scatological gross humor. Most people didn't know this side of Skot, as he had a tendency to cool out for the viewing public, and he was never very funny onstage, but he was quite the rubbery-faced genius in our little van theater. He was one of those people who knew exactly what his face looked like without a mirror, which is a devastatingly funny skill, provided the proper atmosphere and/or intoxicants.

Many miles and cows later, we would hit that exit. The next town. The next club. The next crap shoot. Would it be a packed house or a bomb? Would the equipment work? Would we be great and the crowd suck? Would there be any advance publicity? Would the club even know we were coming?

Over time, we played every type of place in every type of town, from big clubs with great sound systems, lights and big stages to the corners of restaurants with no mikes on the instruments and one speaker for the vocals. We played on terraced stages set up amongst balconies and staircases. We played horse barns, quonset huts and basements with low ceilings. We played on land and on water. You name it, we played it.

The two worst times of the day were always loading all that shit in and loading it back out. By this point, we were using big heavy tube amps and hefty Marshall cabinets with four speakers in each.

Billy had a monstrous SVT speaker cabinet that had the road case built around it already. It was five and a half feet tall on its own, and would maim any man it tipped over on.

We would have to bring the van around to the back of the club and load all our gear in the stage door amid the redolent charm of the dumpster. Either that, or we had to carry it all the way from the front door of the club to the stage in the back. Either way stunk, involving lots of lifting with the legs and getting your shins scuffed on the swinging corners of whatever speaker cabinet you were carrying.

Then, once it was all in, we could trudge amongst the darkness of the rock club in the afternoon, stumbling on the stage, hooking up amps, plugging in foot pedals and stringing them across the stage, pulling out guitars and cleaning or changing the strings, changing batteries.

Maybe the place was already open and people were milling about, having a good time. Maybe it wasn't open yet, it smelled like spilt beer and the only guy there was the one who had to be there to let us in. That guy already hated us. He could be home getting high to a Godzilla movie, but instead he has to be here to let *us* jerks in.

Once everything was set up, it was a matter of waiting for the soundman. He could be there any minute, he could be two hours late. We would never know. The bartender might have to call him at home and tell him we were there. He might be a really cool guy, he might be a meticulous techno-geezer who numbers all his microphones and watches us cord-thief musicians like a hawk. He might be a beer-bellied sad-sack with his ass crack hanging out of his jeans and a three-beer buzz on at five in the afternoon, he might be wanted in seventeen states. Soundmen are like high school teachers; they all start out fine but, later in life, have had to deal with way too many morons and dangerous types to have much good nature any more, or patience, or belief that people are basically good.

All rock musicians and soundmen are deaf in some form or fashion. No one can do these jobs for a living for many years without frying something out. The purpose of the soundcheck is to arrive at a convergence between band and soundman, to determine who is deaf, where and by how much, and make each other a little deafer.

He (or she) hooked up the microphones and went out to the soundboard, which was a control-panel-like device with lots of knobs, faders and meters, for mixing and balancing our sound that came off the stage, and sending a finished package to the PA speakers that straddled the high-intensity sonic blitz already coming from the stage between them.

The only thing actually worse than load-in was always drum check.

For an eternity, the soundman would have Joe whack his snare drum, bass drum and other drums, one drum at a time, over and over and over and over and over and over and over, while minute adjustments were made to the EQ and reverb. Whack the drums over and over and over again.

EQ stood for Equalizer, a device that took the bass and treble knob to a ridiculous extreme, a long box with a squadron of little faders on it that boosted and/or cut various frequencies all along the sonic spectrum. Soundmen loved to fiddle with EQs.

To an extent, this was necessary, as some frequencies, when bounced fiercely around the room at ungodly volume, would "feed back." That is, they would bounce back into the microphones that picked them up in the first place, making a loop that goes around and around, creating squeals that sliced your brain and unnatural, low rumbles that were fiercely unpleasant. You isolated those frequencies—which ones they were depended on the shape of the room and how *INCREDIBLY LOUD* the offending sounds were—on the EQ and removed them. Past that accomplishment, fiddling with the EQ amounted to expressions of taste preference and aesthetic masturbation.

Billy would get up with his bass and the rhythm section sound would be figured out. Then we would get up with our guitars, and the soundman would tell us to turn them down, and we would act like we were without really doing it, and sometimes it fooled the guy and sometimes it didn't.

Then came the nightly grudge-match vocal monitor battle. Monitor speakers are those wedge-looking black things that sit on the lip of the stage and face away from the audience back towards the singers. Their purpose is to allow the singers to hear themselves when the drums are going and the guitar amps are turned up to eleven.

The battle is a classic one. The singer always wants more monitor. The soundman always tells the singer that the thing is cranked all the way. The singer never believes this. The soundman gives the knob that extra crank and a blast of high-pitched feedback sends everybody screaming and covering their ears and everybody goes just a little more deaf than they were before.

Over years, we got used to the fact that we never sounded onstage like we did out in the crowd. It didn't happen. The guitars never sounded as loud onstage as they did ten feet away in the front row. The first bass wave was over fifteen feet away from the speaker before it was formed. It couldn't be heard on a small stage. We learned how an inexperienced musician always turns his amp up too loud, demands the vocal monitor be cranked all the way, until everything's louder than everything else, until the guitar rig is louder than the PA amplifying it, until there's no hope of sounding good at all. We got better about things over time, but Government Cheese was always a frighteningly loud band. Something just wasn't right about that band when it was quiet.

What we wanted to sound like often didn't even matter, because in the long run, provided our stage volumes were manageable (which they usually weren't), the soundman was going to make us sound exactly like he wanted us to anyway, and there was nothing we could do about it. If soundmen are bass-freaks, they will push the woofers 'til the windows rattle. If it's a treble freak who has fried his ears on the *White Album* with headphones on and can't tell how much is enough any more, then the audience gets a white-noise blizzard of high-end sawing their heads off while Mr. Soundman smiles contentedly from behind the board, deaf and happy.

We learned never to make them angry. *Never* piss off the soundman. If you do, the band will have trouble hearing vocals out front, maybe the guitar mike'll get fainter and fainter. Maybe the poor, smelly guy'll just decide he's got something better to do and he'll abandon the board, walk out the front door and not come back . . . until it's time to get paid, that is.

We hired soundmen to work with us on the road, and I think we were pretty lucky with whom we chose. The great John Drennan was one we stole from Picasso's, where he was staff guy. On road trips, after he fell asleep, we'd surround him in bed and mimic the voices of the Ken Smith Band. One of us would imitate Ken, one of us would do Byron, Jonell, etc. "I need more monitor, John, dammit!" He'd roll over and mumble "Bitch, bitch, bitch!" in his sleep. That used to break us up.

Broma replaced John at Picasso's, and when John took some other job, we stole Broma from the home club too. Marc was always around if we needed him. Each of them had a specialty. John got great drum sounds, Broma got great bottom-end in general and loved to play with echo settings and Marc got great, chiming guitars, which I think rubbed off from working with Bill Lloyd so much.

Real men transcended soundcheck. We heard how Rick Richards was once spotted soundchecking his guitar for the Georgia Satellites. He donned his guitar, walked up to his monitor wedge, blasted an A-chord and, satisfied he'd heard enough of his A-chord self, put the guitar down and walked away. The fifteen-second soundcheck. He never even took his sunglasses off.

We stopped using a hired soundman after we'd seen Webb Wilder for the third time in a month, in three different clubs, and he'd had a different local soundman every time, and he always sounded exactly the same. Hmmmm. Maybe it's us? That's when we learned what soundmen had been trying to tell us for years—that when you sound like shit, it's often because you *sound like shit*, and the soundman can only polish a turd so far.

Set lists were up to me to make, since their construction appealed to some anal-retentive germ. First, I had to find a large piece of paper and a magic marker, two things that were always surprisingly hard to come up with when I needed them. Buying my own supply would only work for a couple of days and then I'd be out again. I don't know why.

Once I acquired this paper and marker (Sharpies worked best), I would sit at the bar and figure the running list of songs for the evening. I would write it out once on a napkin, look at it, grumble, solicit other guys' opinions—getting dick for a response, generally—and then write it all out four times on the one large sheet of paper I had found (usually a poster ripped off the club's wall), which I would then fold and carefully tear, making four skinny little sheets of paper. The last sheet would be very faint of ink and bear the imprint of me pushing down hard on a dried out marker.

I would place those sheets—one near each guy—on the stage for us all to follow during the show, which we never really ever would. Skot, for one, never paid attention to a set list in seven years. I always had to shout the next song in his ear.

If all this list preparation sounds like a rather intense pain in the ass, it's because it's a rather intense pain in the ass, and over time I learned to blow it off occasionally, saving my energy for the "set list" gigs, the ones where we definitely didn't want to look like idiots between songs arguing over what to play next while the audience just looked at us blankly.

For instance, opening for They Might Be Giants in Cincinnati was a definite "set list" gig, while playing three sets on a Wednesday night in Carbondale, Illinois, wasn't one. On those latter occasions, we would just wing it. The biggest problem with winging it was having to always be thinking of the next song to play while still playing the one before it. Otherwise, we'd have down time, standing around like idiots.

The guys would get their heart set on certain "intro" songs, the big rockers that got everything off on the right foot, and those "intro" songs naturally led to stuff that sounded right in sequence with that song, and then we would have to do the same old "big finish" which, for a long time, was "Come On Back To Bowling Green/Fish Stick Day/People Who Died", seventeen frantic minutes in the key of A—and before we knew it, we were pretty much doing the same set night after night after night.

To a large extent—out of town—this was good, because it made us tight, but, when you're playing Picasso's for the fifth time in three weeks, you feel pretty silly opening the show with the same songs in the same order and doing the same "big finish" you did last however many times.

So, once the soundcheck was over, and the set list was either done or decided not to even be worth the trouble, we would have the black hole in the day.

If we had money to go get a hotel room, we would go get one. If, in an altogether more common occurrence, we had no money, and no friends in this town, then we were pretty much stuck at the club.

One can walk around a rock club only so many times in the early evening. One can look at the posters on the walls and check out the bathroom graffiti for only so long. We might play some pool. We might play darts or pinball. But all that got old.

Eventually, we'd wind up at the bar, opening up the tab for the night. We would put it off as long as we could, because it was a long night ahead of us and nobody was paying to see us on a stage plastered, but eventually our whistles would cry to be wet. There was no place else to go in the kind of neighborhoods we often played. There was nothing to see, nothing else to do. It was a bar. You drink in bars. And we usually wound up doing just that, watching a television we couldn't hear because music was blasting from a jukebox or a tape deck. And we drank plastic cups of keg beer, which was sometimes free to the band, and when such was the case, was usually some swill that ought to be free anyway. What the hell. A beer that's free and cold is a damn fine beer. And the evening would drag on. One hour. Two hours. Walk around again. Look at the posters. Three hours. Poke your head outside. Four hours.

Eventually it would be time to play. Maybe there would be people there already. Maybe not. Maybe we were in the mood to play. Maybe not. You might have woke up in a foul mood two hundred miles away, and maybe it had been a while since the Tomato Florentine soup and the free coffee refills, and maybe the cheap band beer was already making your head ache. Maybe the stage lights were on the same circuit as the PA, and everybody's amp was humming, and every time you touched your guitar and the microphone at the same time you got four million volts through you. Maybe you're just not real famous yet. This was the hard part, and it's a good thing it was hard then, and still is today. Were such a life any easier than it is, there would doubtless be even more people walking around with long hair and guitars than there already are.

\* \* \* \*

# 17

# come hell or hoboken

## (ten days in july, '88)

Every summer, there was this thing in New York City called the New Music Seminar. What happened at this event was that all the record companies, booking agents, managers, club owners, media people, performers and everyone else with *the look and the attitude* gathered in one ritzy hotel for four days of symposiums like "The State of Independent Promotion in 1988" or "College Radio at the Cross-roads" or "So, There's a Junkie in the Band" or "Freeze Spray or Mousse: Choices in the Spandex Age". Everyone paid out their life savings for an I.D. card and walked around "schmoozing". (They used that word a lot that week.) Every struggling band in the nation, and some who weren't so struggling, wanted to play in NYC that week because every music business heavy was in town, all the clubs were participating in the event, and careers could be made and all that. Thus, the rules we bands did business by went out the window for the weeks immediately before and after the Seminar. Every club-owner in the northeast gleefully knew we'd play any possible gig on the way there, and on the way back, for any price. A garbage can with a light-bulb in it in Baltimore? Sure, we'll be there. A houseboat in Southhampton? What time do we set up? Etc. etc. . . .

*Wednesday, July 13th:* We drove straight through from Bowling Green to Clifton, New Jersey. We found a HoJo for a reasonable price and slept. Clifton was right next to Passaic, which was right next to this, which was right next to that. There wasn't a reasonable boundary stretch of countryside between cities up there, like a Southerner would expect. It all looked like one big city for my money, and you drove from one into the other with no discernible change in the concrete surroundings. Sometimes, the only way to know which city you'd driven into was to ask the gas station attendants. Clifton is about ten miles as the crow flies from New York City proper.

*Thursday, July 14th:* We drove into Passaic where our first gig was, and also our first disaster. The club owner, a dead-ringer for Captain Lou Albano, was not a happy man. It turned out that the club "Sneeker's" was a METAL club. Captain Lou advertised on a METAL station. The Cheese had no aspirations of being a METAL band and said radio station, aware of this, would not plug the gig. To make matters worse, this was also the first gig for a band all the way from San Francisco motoring to the Seminar. Captain Lou didn't want to even open his club that evening because no one would be there and, even if someone did show, they wouldn't dig either band since neither was very METAL, etc. etc. We offered to play our limited library of Priest and Ozzy riffs, to no avail.

Oh well, he seemed to be a nice enough guy and we couldn't see building a future in his club anyway; so we drank a free Coca Cola, shook his hand and headed for nearby Hoboken to put up posters for the next night's gig.

Hoboken is a square-mile stretch of property on the Jersey side of the Hudson across from Manhattan. An astounding 60-thousand people live on this one mile of four-story buildings. It is the hometown of Frank Sinatra, and indeed it was his music playing in the club "The Beat n' Path" as we entered it. We borrowed a magic marker from a Chinese grocer and started customizing our pre-printed posters, writing "Friday 7/15 The Beat n' Path" at the bottom. We were duct-taping them to lampposts up and down Washington Street when a very short and very muscular pair of fellows walked past and up the stoop to an apartment house. One of the guys sported a pair of distant glassy eyes and carried a sackful of bottled beer. At his doorstep, one of the bottles slipped from his grasp and shattered on the pavement. We turned around and there he was, turning his gaze from the puddled debris and fixing a look of total, albeit glassy, fury on us.

He shouted, in very broken English, "You talkin't'me!?!? Wotchoosayin?! Huh?" Our reply was "We didn't say anything to you. Honest! We want no trouble." Billy actually walked up to him with a poster and said, "Hi, we're a band from Kentucky and playing at the Beat n' Path tomorrow night." This was to no avail because this man was obviously not a fan. His friend said, "Muscles! Drop it! C'mon upstairs. Forget it." We all sort of nodded agreement with

Muscles' friend. He didn't immediately drop it, but followed us with his gradually intensifying gaze until we were on the next block with our posters, at which point he went inside and we all breathed a little deeper.

There were five of us on this trip, the band and Chris Becker, the Shockboy. We were still nearby putting up posters when Muscles decided to come back out and play some more. He began shouting at us from across the street and banging an entire disengaged car bumper repeatedly on the sidewalk. Yes, an entire car bumper. He crossed the street towards us, thankfully discarding the bumper somewhere along the way. He was *really mad* now and shouting in some garbled combination of English and a language none of us knew. "Y'wannafukwitme! C'mon! C'mon! YerinHoboken! C'monwannafukwitme!" He actually started punching himself in his tattooed and very muscular arms and legs.

"C'monyerinHobokenwannafukwitmeCMON!" Our gait got a bit brisker as we forsook poster-hanging for the more pragmatic ideal of simply getting off Muscles' territory. We were practically walking backwards with Muscles five feet or so behind as we implored to him that we never said anything to him and we wanted no trouble. Muscles' PCP-like symptoms amplified as a group of five local Gotti-in-training types began to walk behind him asking things like, "Yous guys givin' him trouble?!!? Ya talkin' about Hoboken!!??" *Christ almighty, they're on his side.*

Muscles, happily aware that he now had friends, went farther into a crouch stance and truly became the Tasmanian Devil. "Dese guys got my back! C'mon! C'mon maddafukkahs!" Things were not looking good for the health of Government Cheese at this point, but wait, it got better! They all pursued us to the corner where four black gentlemen appeared out of nowhere. The newcomers stepped off the street onto the sidewalk and began throwing punches as casually as one walks up to shake your hand. Joe took a very loud and painful thump to the head, Chris took one on the chin and it was time to run, which we all proceeded to do in every direction! One block! Two blocks! Three blocks!!

Billy made it first to the McDonald's three blocks away. He asked the counter boy if he could use the phone to call the cops. The answer was no. He then kindly asked the short little turd to please call them himself inasmuch as four of his companions were being assaulted down the street. Much to his relief, all but I were soon by his side under the Golden Arches. I was spotted a half-block down at a Domino's, telling my tale to a delivery boy who interrupted me repeatedly with gales of laughter. It occurred to us all that we might be the only ones on the streets of Hoboken in this early evening hour (and there were plenty out and about) who had never seen anyone die violently before. Honestly, we had just been through what we considered an horrendous episode and no one we spoke to gave a flat rat fuck. The pizza guy wagged his finger at me and said, "Ya gotta be TOUGH in HOBOKEN. Heh! Heh!" Then he sauntered back to his delivery vehicle, threw the pizza in, turned back to face me, and threw his head back laughing again. What the hell!

The van was parked back down the street in front of Muscles' place, so no one thought it unmanly to ask the attending constables for an escort back to it, after which we got the hell out of Hoboken. We felt like M*A*S*H patients do on their return to the front; for we knew the next night we would have to come back to Hoboken (or "Bokie" as I'd heard it called) and play the damned gig, twenty yards from Muscles' place on the same side of the street.

*Friday, July 15th:* We returned to Hoboken and, except for a blown amp fuse, there were no mishaps. Good crowd, good show. No Muscles.

*Saturday, July 16th:* We arrived in Manhattan to play McGovern's on Spring Street. It was poster time again, so we were settled on a street corner, magic-marking, when we noticed a derelict lying on the steps of a building across the intersection. For minutes on end he was completely motionless, then he would suddenly spring to his feet, flailing his arms upward and shouting "GOGO-GOGOGOGOGO!!!" as fast as his glottis could crank it out. Then, just as suddenly, he would stop this strange behavior and become docile again. He repeated all this several times before we realized that his fits of "GOGOGOGOGO!!!" were related to the traffic lights. He was active during "WALK", dormant during "DON'T WALK". It rained that night, as it would do every gig until Lancaster, PA.

The whole Reptile bunch was at McGovern's, a little pub stuck in the warehouse district with barely a stage in it. Any music biz folks gonna find this place? Forget it. Susan played for nobody. The Dusters played for a few, and it looked like there would be a few more by the time we went on. It was raining. I was outside sitting in the driver's seat of the van resting my ears. Willis was rolling around in the back putting his stage clothes on. Tutt was out there with us. A knock

came on the window, which I rolled down a little way. It was the club
owner, who hadn't been too friendly all day but now was red-eyed
and smiling, the spitty rain splashing off his face. "Ay, any o' you
guys in there potheads?" He extended a pungent joint rolled with the
extra-large yellow rolling papers that no one ever knows where to
buy. What the hell, I thought. Won't be the first time I've smoked
dope before a show. I took a hit and was fine for about forty seconds,
and then it was like a lead cloak landing on my skull. Ka-thwunk!
Whoah. "That's not pot," I thought. "I'm from Kentucky. I know
pot. This is some sort of CIA Chokehold Brazilian Death Weed."
"You like it?" the club owner asked. "It's Hawaiian." Well, no
wonder they're so happy in all those commercials. I could listen to
Don Ho all day were I smoking this shit! I looked at him blankly,
giggled, said something along the lines of "What the fuhh . . . " and
dropped the whole joint into the puddle outside the van. "No problem," he shouted, happy as Bob Marley, "I'll be right back." He
came back with something from Thailand and stood there smoking on
the street in front of his club, being drenched in rain and not giving
even a sliver of a damn. At last we played the gig, my brain addled
and me feeling a bit guilty for choosing a New York gig to commence
my career as a Polynesian hemp connoisseur. I could barely spell my
name for the first half of the set. I remember trying to introduce a
song, "Hello New Yeerk and uhhh I'd like tuh drabnish flledle har-
redn, which uhhh . . . TAKE IT SKOT!" Oh shit. *I* start this song.
It's amazing that in the end, the few people there loved us, but they
were all friends of the clubowner and all smoking the same stuff, I'll
wager. *"Ay, these guys are great. (Cough, sputter.)"*

   *Sunday, July 17th:* We arrived at the Marriott Marquis on Times
Square for the beginning of Seminar schmoozing. Madonna's play
*Speed the Plow* was running across the street and we saw Ms. Penn
(at the time) herself bolt the stage door and hop into her limo amidst a
throng of admirers. Bigger thrills awaited as we saw Carmine Appice
and Michael "I'll be famous someday" Bolton drinking in the hotel
bar, which, like any convention, was where most of the action was.
The Dusters ran into Rob Halford of Judas Priest while setting up at
the Cat Club. We ate at Exterminator Chili on Church Street which
was run by a very nice fellow named Jack who booked our
McGovern's gig and sat us down for chow in the world-famous Elvis
booth. While there, we saw the Del Rubio triplets in the flesh, three
60-year-old identical triplet women decked-out in snow-white bouf-

fants, hot pants and go-go boots. They played three (likewise identical) acoustic guitars. Their latest album included versions of "El Condor Pasa", "Light My Fire" and "Neutron Dance". They played the Pyramid that night, and I will regret the rest of my life having missed it. They really existed. We attended the Nashville showcase at the Cat Club that evening. New Grass Revival, Foster and Lloyd (whose band included Byron and Marc as the rhythm section), Webb Wilder and the Dusters all played. All had a good time, no one more so than the person who made off with $200 worth of Big Dave Barnett's wardrobe from the Dusters' van while they played inside. In another piece of Seminar madness, Susan Marshall followed a Canadian hardcore band onstage at a country bar uptown. Chris had more bad luck. With the day off, he'd decided to visit his grandfather in Brooklyn. It was his mistake to take the Uptown subway instead of the Downtown. The street numbers got higher until he found himself in Harlem, then across the river and deep into the south Bronx, where he made a mad daylight dash across the street to the Downtown terminal and got back to Manhattan alive on the Downtown train.

*Monday, July 18th:* Joe met Paul McGuinness, manager of U2. I saw John Lithgow on the street and, seconds later, Lemmy of Motorhead. We talked and walked together a bit, and Lemmy proved himself to be an amiable fellow, if not slightly shorter than his pictures suggest. His comment on the New Music Seminar: "Buncha shit, man! Bu' at least I get to see the States." Billy got terribly worried about the van and took to considering its welfare his personal trust. So, in a novel way to pass time and guard the van simultaneously, he parked it in the limo driveway of the Marriott and dressed like a chauffeur as best as his wardrobe could be altered. For that entire afternoon and evening he stood by the van and told people he's Government Cheese's chauffeur waiting to take them to the airport. Yes, Government Cheese. *Perhaps you saw them on MTV six months ago. Damn straight, you did!* He made friends with other chauffeurs, and he and Chris saw Tommy Lee of Motley Crue walk by. They were amazed at the skinnyness of his legs.

I remember digging the afternoon view from Tutt's room. New York City from ten floors up in Times Square is an unbelievable view, giant stone and glass cubes and canisters of smoke, cabs below and buildings far and near. And then I turned to face Tutt sprawled on his bed, like he'd been the previous afternoon as well. He'd been up here for hours, as I had. The difference was he had a pass to get into the convention and I didn't. Joe had the Cheese one. Tutt didn't seem to go anywhere except the gigs. I remember thinking "shouldn't you be *doing something?* Calling somebody? *Anything?*" It's not comforting to see the guy who's signed you up for five years come all the way to New York to sit in a hotel room and not move. He said he didn't feel well, and I was thinking "Joe threw up before a frat gig last week and had some Delta Chi pouring Pepto-Bismol down his throat in mid-song. I've puked before a set and then again right after. So, in that spirit, maybe you could pop an Alka-Seltzer and *get the fuck downstairs!*" But I didn't say anything. By now I was afraid of him, afraid of his temper. Most everybody else was, too.

By this point, I think Tutt and I had both made up our minds about one another. I thought he was a well-meaning prick with a short fuse, and he thought I was insane. My all-time favorite Tutt quote is how he used to describe the band. "You see," he'd tell people, "in Government Cheese, you got this one guy. He's on Mars. He's from there and he's still there. He came to Earth, got three other reasonably normal guys, and persuaded them to *come back to Mars with him!*" I was the Mars guy in that story. After Tutt got in the habit of telling that one, I'd occasionally see the Marshall logo on my amp speakers half-covered with duct tape, so it read "Mars". Everybody had nicknames, and so for a while, mine became "Mars".

*Tuesday, July 19th:* We played at Kenny's Castaways in Greenwich Village. NMS madness was peaking as we, the Dusters, Susan and *four other bands* played that night on a stage slightly larger than a throw rug. (The Smithereens started at this club, incidentally.)

The vibe had turned dark around Tutt. He was throwing tantrums, and Susan's steel guitarist had had enough. While most folks gave Tutt room to rave, this picker, an older guy, wouldn't and didn't. He quit that night.

It was a gig that started terribly, got worse, and eventually became good only because we ceased to care at all and went ballistic. Joe broke a snare head on the first note of the first tune. I found myself, because of bad planning, stuck without my contact lenses on one of the more important nights of my career. Hence, an anarchic, fuck-everything rock and roll show. Government Cheese on a small stage in don't-care phase was insurance that there would be a large amount of bumping into one another, guitars getting knocked way out of tune, tables being fallen on and bottles and glasses flying. If that is one's idea of entertainment, then this show was no disappointment. Without my contacts, I was having to wear my glasses, and I saw them fly off my face and be crushed underneath someone's feet. It was the last thing I would see clearly that evening. Such chaos gave an edge to the final portion of the show, as four pissed-off gentlemen bashed through "B.G.", "Fish Sticks", "Skinny and Small" (with strip-tease) and a good old "Those are people who *DIED, DIED!*"

The vibe got more furious as we negotiated 2 AM Manhattan traffic downtown for a drink at McGovern's. Chris was driving. We told him to get in the left lane. He did. Unfortunately, a 1988 Saab was using it at the moment. WHAM!!! OK, Chris was now really mad. This had not been his week at all. He had been lost in the Bronx, punched out in Hoboken, and now this. The bumper was torn half off the van, and we could now credit about one-thousand dollars worth of damage to the Saab. We exchanged insurance numbers in the pouring rain and were glad our victim was a nice businessman instead of five friends of Muscles in a Nash Rambler or something. We decided not to tempt our fate further, abandoned the McGovern's idea, and returned to various hotel floors inasmuch as our own hotel room monies were long gone. We lashed the bumper back to the van frame with a bad microphone cable. It was bad from then on, anyway.

*Wednesday, July 20th:* Back in Jersey, Susan's steel guitarist left his hotel room as Billy and I watched. The phone rang. Susan's other guitarist, Mike, picked it up. "It's Tutt," he said. "Wanna say somethin'?" "Yeah," shouted the steel guitarist into the receiver from ten feet away, "Tell him to suck my Yankee dick!" And with that, Susan's steel picker was gone out the door.

The seminar was over, and we left the Marriott's revolving doors for the final time, behind Dave Stewart (Eurythmics) and his wife (one of the Bananarama girls). We journeyed to Paterson, New Jersey, home of the bat-wielding high-school prinicipal. Our next gig was at Realmonte's, which we discovered had a neon sign that said "LIVE GIRLS DANCING DAY AND NIGHT!" Oh boy, another one. The gig turned out to be quite nice, actually. The monitors worked, so the vocals did as well. I had a microphone on my amp, which, strangely enough, was something New York City clubs had not caught on to yet, and we got a sound check, another thing that was rarer than most in New York. However, only seven people saw this good-sounding gig, thus the novelty songs got a hefty workout and everyone loosened up. No live girls danced, though, not even voluntarily. Before the gig we listened to Iggy live from the Ritz on the radio. It was agonizing because our seminar passes would have gotten us into that $20 gig for free. Soul Asylum opened. And there we were with "LIVE GIRLS DANCING!!!!"

*Thursday, July 21st:* We played J.C. Dobbs in Philadelphia. It was our second time there and the audience was great. They asked for an encore. We gave them one. Things were turning around. A fellow raving it up in the front row was named Aldo. He played bass for the Ben Vaughn Combo and had a side band called Powderhorn and the Hellions. He was Powderhorn. They did a cover of "C'mon Back to Bowling Green", which we got a kick out of upon hearing about it. We had gin and tonics with some Lexington friends transplanted from there to Philly, and life was the best it had been since before we'd so lovingly welcomed Muscles into our lives.

*Friday, July 22nd:* We played the Chameleon in Lancaster, Pennsylvania. It didn't rain and the facilities were good. The people were nice, and we sold out of cassettes.

*Saturday, July 23rd:* No gig. No day, really, inasmuch as we slept through it. We all went to the movies except Billy, who did his laundry in the hotel bathtub. We saw *Coming To America,* as I recall, and knew Eddie Murphy's career was in trouble. Then we went back to the Chameleon to hear a Dead band. They were awful. I remember just walking around and around the club for three hours with all these preppy Deadheads, not speaking to anyone, not getting spoken to, not wanting to try any hippie girl's patience with my theory of the lead guitarist representing *Jerry-ness* instead of Jerry himself, although in that crowd I might have found a receptive, lysergic brain for my musings. I just wasn't into it. I was tired of bars. I wanted to be home.

*Sunday, July 24th:* We arrived at the Cedar Lounge in Youngstown, Ohio, and were perplexed by the notion that we were all thirty years younger than everyone else in the bar. Much to our relief, the entire staff and patronage changed over to our demographic within 90 minutes. The gig went well. We loaded the van and drove eight hours straight through to Bowling Green. We happily set our watches back to Central time. It was over. Five days later, we started a weekend stand in Lexington. Nine days later, the Library in Knoxville. Ten days later, the Mainstreet in Murfreesboro. Then back home. Then to Nashville. Eighteen days after Youngstown, we played Hot Shotz in Cincinnati, the very next night we were at Sloss Furnace in Birmingham, Alabama, then Picasso's, then Huntsville. Thirty-two days after Youngstown, we started a weekend stand at the Red Barn in

Louisville. And on the fortieth day, Picasso's, the forty-fourth St. Louis, the forty-fifth Nashville, and three nights after that we started two nights in Carbondale, Illinois, and *"I AM! I AM SUPERMAN! AND I . . . UHH . . . I . . . UHH . . . Uhhh. . . .*

*"ZZZZZZZZZZZZZzzzzzzz. . . . "*

\* \* \* \*

# 18

# this is my brain on drugs

*Another great night in Lexington. Play, get paid, load out. Go to a party soon. I'm standing at the back of our little yellow van, my little world tingling and weaving from a little bitta this and a little bitta that. Talk talk talk. Happy happy happy. Those damned white crosses, named so because of the plus sign stamped into their chalky-hard pellet faces. Ephedrine chlorhydrate. Get 'em over the counter, pal. Two of 'em and you're percolating the rest of the day. They make you talk 'til your throat feels like hand-rubbed tuna flank-steak, 'til your penis draws up like a raisin. Little collections of foam rise on the corner of your mouth. Talk talk talk. Happy happy happy.*

*That pre-show fatty is still in my head, yanking me out of concentration spans like that Vonnegut story where the alarm bell goes off every thirty seconds inside peoples' heads to keep the populace placid and unable to think of anything. I'm sorry, what were we talking about?*

*Boy, have I come a long way in a few short years. Straight whiskey used to make me throw up, and now look at me. I must say, I've become quite the agile matador in the bullring of the cheap buzz.*

*Oh, lighten up. Look at my arms, up my nose. We're not that scene, Mom. It's just a little innocent fun, is all. We're talkin' fungi here, whackus weedus, the dreaded Lysergic Acid Diaspora whatever. It's a* phase, *ferchrissakes! Don't shit yerself! I'm twenty-five, taking drugs for the first time really, and acting like an idiot on them for the first time as well, like any rookie, watching all the revelry and occassionally feeling like I'm a bit too silly too late in the game.*

I never did drugs as a teenager, and I never did nearly the amount our audience suspected. When you sport a slight Tourette twitch, an irrepressible streak at times, jump around playing guitar and sing a song called "Camping on Acid," people tend to conclude (reasonably) that you go through the line for seconds on the chemicals. Not really, though. That was just me.

I was raised in an exemplary clean-living home. To my knowledge, my parents never drank a drop in their lives. In general, it isn't good for the preacher and his wife to be seen boozing it up. Hellfire figured heavily regarding indulgence or vice. Eternal punishment for drinking a beer and similar moral algebra. This was a bit too cut-and-dried for me in later life, but it did ensure a reasonably safe and clean upbringing, for which I'm grateful. I drank a little bit back then, tried to hit off a joint exactly once, but that was the extent of it. I took notes of ways and rituals, but I wasn't in the same league with the varsity.

From the Cheese experience, I drew the opportunity to catch way the hell up, and if I discovered anything redeeming whatsoever that I might be able to pass on to posterity, it is this. God makes a couple of recreational drugs that, in my opinion, cannot be condemned wholesale. Man can't boast of matching this godly feat. Man screws it up every time, usually by upping the ampage dangerously and boiling something down to its purest evil, because the purest evil is what feels best and kills you quickest, and people who aren't in touch with themselves seem to want that. God's drugs are never something anyone necessarily should do either, because they can be abused and much harm done as everyone knows; but should the choice be made to do a drug of any type, time and experience have taught me that, the closer to the soil we stay, the safer and more rewarding the whole experience is likely to be.

I had never cared much for potheads until one day, I had to face the fact that I had become one. To his day, I'm not comfortable with the weed stigma, the glassy eyed, useless, couch-potato ambience. But hey, when I was in a van for seven hours at a stretch and there was not much to do except think about all the money that wasn't coming in and wonder what Tutt was or wasn't doing with the life of mine he completely owned, I often figured I might as well roll one up and get *real stupid* for a while. It never impaired my ability to watch cows one bit. I think it rather sharpened it. I've bovine mind-melded once or twice here and there, and it also improved the hell out of our one-speaker radio. I remember sitting red-eyed as we whizzed down I-24, completely *digging* "Everybody Wants To Rule The World" by Tears for Fears. Tears for Fears sounded *great* to me! That's the power of wacky tobacky for you.

Among the circles we travelled in on the road, pot was always only slightly less prevalent than a really good cup of coffee. I've seen it used as money, as the sacrament in social bonding rituals and as a dirty little secret that separated *those who did* from *those who didn't.* The primary problem with marijuana was that it made the people smoking it dumb as wood for the length of the buzz. Some people could use this stupidity for a fresh perspective, pulling interesting insights from the backs of their psyches. Others were just dumb.

I used to think it helped me write songs, and it might really have for a brief while, but mainly it helped me *think* I was writing songs when I was really just stoned and playing the same chord over and over. Some drugs have this first period when they *really can* affect your creativity and personality in a positive way. The minute you realize that it's affecting you that way is the very minute to put it away, though, because the honeymoon never lasts very long.

Before the nightmare rhetoric gets too thick for its subject, however, let's remember that this is marijuana we're talking about here, a plant state troopers look for walking back and forth through national parks, finding what looks like a lot on the six o'clock news and being very proud of themselves, thinking they've actually achieved something. It makes people happy, paranoid, stupid, friendly and lazy, and makes them think Jim Morrison was a hell of a lot more intelligent than he really was. Social mores tend to lump weed in with the big bad drugs and find it guilty of ills not its doing, but potheads do not sit in fetid hovels writhing in agony and sucking strangers off for money to get the next joint. Potheads drive too slowly. That is their main threat to society. There is no such thing as the punctual pothead. They are real "stop and smell the roses *all the time*" type people.

It will someday be legal, as all drugs will be, because prohibition doesn't work. Do we need another Volstead Act to prove that? People cannot be enforceably protected from themselves. If you want to hurt yourself in any way, or just want to relax in your chosen manner on your own time, go do it, just don't *shoot me* on the way to doing it.

As it stands in this country, the accepted rules of order are amazingly topsy-turvy. I can't walk out of a Mapco Express with a quarter bag, but I *can* buy a .44 Magnum, come over to your house and *blow your ass away with it.* I can buy any number of two-inch long exploding bullets for my small-arms collection, while the government swims in urine making sure that Nick the Postman isn't rolling a pin joint on the weekend. That makes no sense. The guy who drives the train, I can understand testing. The guy proofreading the phone book I *definitely* want tested; but perhaps, if Nick were allowed to catch a buzz, he might not show up with a Glock and *waste his co-workers* as often as he seems to feel the need to. It's worth thinking about.

It had never occurred to me, until it started happening, that people *gave* drugs to rock and roll musicians. Otherwise, of course, the musician won't have any since, as a general rule, said rocker hasn't the funds to get his own. People give you the same drug that they are taking so you will do a show in keeping with their own synaptic ohmage. This gave me the spontaneous opportunity on several occasions to swim out into further, deeper waters for the first time.

We were tuning up onstage at the Bottom Line in Lexington. I was facing away from the audience towards my amp. Someone tapped my shoulder and I turned around. A fellow was on the stage with me, with something cupped in his hand. "Here, Tommy," he said, "eat this right now."

He took my hand and emptied his own in my upturned palm. It looked like spongy flesh-colored dirt. I ate it. What the hell. I knew from visual appraisal on a dark stage that it was either mushrooms or bits of a ground-up tire, and since I'd never heard of any type of tire-munching fad going around, I figured it was that magic cowshit fungi I'd been hearing about half my life, that stuff that got the Native Americans going on a Saturday night, that Tom Robbins writes all his books on. I got the gnarly mulch past my throat and washed it all down with half a beer. I have a very nervous stomach, and I was just hoping the spongy brown pulp didn't come back up on me during the first song.

I gave a great show. Midway through, I was roaring. All the lights had pretty star filters on them. Colors were all rich and warm. I can't recall ever being so cheerful, loquacious and about to vomit all at once. I loved them. I wouldn't recommend doing them very often, or operating any kind of machinery while in the grip of what they do, but I think those little buttons do prove that the foulest-smelling manure is the most sacred in some way. God is saying something through those little ground-buttons, and its not for the squeamish. Three or four more times during the whole career of the band, I ate some of those. I was on them when they led Jim Bakker out of court crying. I sat on a motel bed in Carbondale, Illinois, laughing uncontrollably at the television.

Swim a little further out, and the waves get choppy from man's industrial-strength take on the magic mushroom. Better living through chemistry? The jury's still out on that one, way out.

One day in '87, I was listening to a fellow describe his misadventures camping on acid. "Camping on Acid". Now *that's* a song title.

I went home and wrote the lyrics immediately. The band learned the chords as soon as I thought some up, and it became a huge "hit" for us. Some people heard it for the satire it was (trying) to be, others were seeing it as some sort of affirmative acid anthem and that bothered me a lot, because I'd been responsible for the whole song, just like "Fish Stick Day", creating another monster that was funny a few times and then became the thing that wouldn't die, because by then everybody was irreparably bonkers for the song.

I fooled some people. I got compliments from hippies and acid-heads every show. They would come up to me reverently and laud my keen observance of what it was like to be having a bad trip in the woods at night with the crickets getting louder and the Coleman lantern captivating you for ninety minutes at a time. I had never done acid in my life. I'd just written a song, and appeared to have summed up the experience reasonably well for a lysergic virgin. But hey, *thanks!*

Eventually, it had to happen. My psychedelic deflowering came to be in Charleston, West Virginia, a town to make me forget Madisonville. Drugs, satanists, nitroglycerin ground-water. Always raining. Charming place. A fellow gave me a couple of little squares of red paper with a star printed on each of them. Put them in your mouth and let them dissolve, the guy said, and, for God's sake, don't look in the mirror.

We got in the van for the trip home, and by the Kentucky border the blue and green shades used in the highway signage were brilliant, deep colors. How had I missed that before? And wow, those leaves! Every one different as snowflakes, as individual as the fingerprint. We passed over the bridge at Ashland and its attendant industrial hellscape. *Gaaahhhhhh!* Blindingly lit and endlessly fascinating.

Seven hours later, I was still in the grip of it, feeling hyper with a wangy metallic taste in the back of my throat, seeing lights as intense streaks of lightning, and of course, the first thing I did when I got home was *look in the mirror.*

I immediately realized my mistake. My face. My God. My face! I never realized it . . . *looked* like that. Good God, what's that on my nose? How long has that been there? Look at those pores. Those huge pores! They look like apple-jacks. I stuck my finger in my eye and retrieved a little mucusish eye-gunk. Olive drab with a little off-white. Thicker in the middle, color-wise. Snot. Wow. The gear-greaser in the human thang. I stared at it while a record played in the other room. Side two, cut three or something like that. By cut five I was still looking at that snot on the end of my finger.

I did all the tourist things. I played my guitar. I even put *Sgt. Pepper's* on the stereo. I tried to get the whole experience down, regrettably missing out on any human companionship, which I'm sure is an integral part of the whole thing, and my only chance ever yet to happily put up with another acidhead. People on acid are obnoxious, not dangerous like drunks, just a little tiring to be around after five minutes. It's hard to be straight and deal with someone who is laughing at the wall, and occasionally making garbled pronouncements on life that surely sound like Shakespeare times ten to that person at the moment, but don't translate at all to anyone with his or her wits about them who might happen to be there having to listen to it.

An hour spent in the bathroom looking at muck on my finger was, on one hand, invaluable so far as gaining an insight into cosmic minutiae. On the other hand, it was an hour looking at muck on the end of my finger. It was thirty-six hours before I could think properly again, an incredible budget of time for what had been an interesting but hardly transcendent experience.

I go back and forth about man-made psychedelics. I don't think it is a good idea to take too much of a drug used by the seamier parts of our government for schizophrenia-inducement experiments. And, like all other "illegal" drugs made in basements, the lack of quality control is horrifying. As anal as my boss at Lee's Famous Recipe was with the flour in the extra-crispy batter recipe, I can only shiver to think how exacting the formula must be for a drug designed to make fucking buildings melt before your very eyes!

Once again, outlawing it does nothing. There's a guy in a basement right now making acid because somebody else wants it. His neighbor is cleaning out his basement to do abortions in the minute prohibitionist fools have their way about *that* issue.

I have to eventually say that it's simply big-league stuff. If you think you can handle it, good luck. You have to be *this tall* to ride. It's your ass. The original Swiss stuff, I've never had and neither have you most very likely, and when one is dealing with something God Knows Who made, it's best to just say it's *not good, and not good for you,* and dispense with the matter.

Eventually, you swim out into serious undertow territory.

Cocaine is a truly nasty substance, born of the coca plant, an innocuous bit of flora, Aztec speed in the chewed leaf form, I am told. This is one fully figured-out flower. It is pulverized, soaked, chopped, dried, and the purest wicked pleasure extracted from it. I like it. You like it. Monkeys in labs like it. It makes you feel like you are king of the whole wide world. It hoses every trouble you may have right off the front grille of your brain. Then it wears off and you feel extremely, extremely bad, and how extremely bad you feel is in inverse proportion to how incredibly good you'd felt only twenty minutes before.

January of 1988. The Empty Glass Pub in Charleston, West Virginia. Now, there's a formative town.

Raoul. He had a very, very nice suit, a silk tie, a beautiful girl-friend who hadn't eaten in years, and a little something in his pocket. After the show, he invited me into the restroom for a bump. My experience with cocaine had been minimal. I had smelled stepped-on Kentucky half-crank stuff once or twice. That was it. I never had the money, and I talked too much as it was.

Apparently, Raoul dealt directly with cartel representatives overseas. His stuff was flaky. Shiny. I've not seen its equal since. I snorted some off his car key, thinking I already knew what was what. I knew dick.

God, I loved that man. Within seconds, I wanted to know *all about him!* I watched him run a little tap water onto his fingers and snort it all up to get every last bit. God, he was beautiful. I loved him so. Right away! How's the family? Who's the family? Describe them. Really, that's wonderful! I ran a little tap water up my nose too, as if I already knew that was what you were supposed to do. While my hand was at my face I noticed I started drumming my fingers across the top of my mouth the way you do when you suddenly find yourself *SPEEDING LIKE A GODDAMN TASMANIAN DEVIL!* I was in Heaven. Heaven was a john in West Virginia. We left the bathroom and I didn't want to go. I wanted to stay there forever, just . . . *talking to Raoul.*

Load gear, talk, pack up guitar, talk, bound across the room, talk, not a soul in the place was unhip to the fact I had just been way nose-candied. Skot whispered to chill out. Sure man, no problem.

Joe man, you played great tonight. Hi, my name's Tommy, nice to meet you! We went back to the hotel. I gave everyone at the club our room numbers. About fifty percent of everyone invited came over, and I was the most outgoing, life-loving, histrionic, play-every-scene-for-all-it's-worth-asshole you would never want to meet. I interrupted conversations, roused hostile glares and could completely comprehend the fact I was making an unspeakable fool out of myself, and it affected my behavior not one whit. We had two hotel rooms, and I found that whatever room I was in, the people began to filter out into the other one. I loved myself way too much to care.

Raoul showed up with a supremely creepy, big silent fellow everyone was sure was a cop. The paranoia, which encroaches the minute the ecstasy begins to recede, the way endorphins feel when they just can't get hard any more—a *very very bad feeling*—hit me, and I was convinced he was a cop too. He was a big burly guy with a moustache and a windbreaker that should have said "DEA" on the back of it. Of course, he wasn't a cop, and if he was—hanging out with Raoul—he was the cop taking the payoff. But he freaked us all out, and *I had invited them both.*

Then Raoul and his "friend" upped the ante. They pulled out a glass pipe and various tools and began freebasing cocaine right there in the room. Well, well. *This* was a first. Their only concession to social nicety was to move into the corner next to the bathroom. Everyone panicked. Somebody threw Raoul and his gumbah out in the street, and Raoul was pissed at *me* because I'd invited him over and "told him it was cool", as if I had any idea he was going to pull out a freebase pipe.

Comedown was pure hell. Around four AM I crashed hard. I realized how I'd been acting, and now that the guests were gone, there was no one to make amends to. I had scattered my karma to the wind and there was no sweeping it up. Out in the world were new people who would run like hell when they saw me next.

It wasn't all nightmare. There was that happy chap in Houston, who kept dishing out lines to everybody while we passed around the guitar. He was a really nice guy. True, he had that cokehead spookiness, that slightly paranoid yet effusively courteous thing, but he was still a nice guy, and I had a hell of a good time. And the next morning

I was licking my fingers and wiping on every flat surface in the house, picking up residue and rubbing it on my teeth. I licked the entire living room. Every piece of furniture, every table top, every flat surface. I licked everything. I licked the dog as it went by. If there had been a turd with coke residue on it, I would have licked it off. That shit's dangerous when you've got a recent taste of it. You just want more and more right away. I had to sit and think about that one later. *I just licked an entire room.*

It's been years since I've seen that stuff now. I know people who spent a few party evenings in bathrooms snorting it, talking a lot for a while, and then they walked away from it without much thought. I know some people who lost their homes, cars and jobs because they couldn't put the stuff down. Len Bias had a great basketball future, did one line and fell over dead.

We were never a very druggy band. Some smoked. Some didn't. Nobody had a problem with any hard drugs. The main two Government Cheese staples were beer and white crosses. The beer intake was a steadily increasing factor in our lives. We didn't notice it to be excessive until it was several steps beyond that, at which time all of us had our moments of clarity, when we realized most people didn't live like this. Not that it stopped us.

Brief notes. Stops along the way.

Ecstasy is bullshit. I would probably do it again if it was free, which it never is, but I otherwise see no need to ever again be in a room with thirty screaming college kids all so incredibly *glad to see each other* that you just want to cut all their fucking heads off. I will only concede its use as a short-sighted social tool, a drug that completely eliminates the need to know whether or not you're truly enjoying the company of the people you're with, since you're too busy being insanely happy about something and you're not sure what it is.

Whippets and sundry rush-oriented things? For the life of me, I don't understand. Okay, just deplete oxygen flow long enough to get the head rush and maybe just kill your ass then and there. What the hell? No consciousness-raising. Nothing. Just some inhaling, then passing out and maybe gashing your temple on the table corner like William Holden so the neighbors can find you by smell in two weeks. Where do I sign?

I could boringly moralize about drug-taking and its preposterous illegality for pages, but there are much better texts out there, written by smarter people than me, for such reading as that. It's always been a choice, a glimpse of other views of ourselves and the world around us, and it's always been there for us to make rational decisions about. Nobody plays with their own brain too long and gets away with it; then again, vices are vices 'cause they're fun and bad for you, and we'll always have them, too. I don't think a viceless society's really possible or, for that matter, desirable. All I know is what I said at the top of the chapter, God seems to know what She's doing and Man has only the vaguest clue. And one more thing. Not once did I ever do a drug that made me any smarter.

*   *   *   *

# 19

# is this wednesday or texas?

The MTV exposure came and went. The record went up the college charts and then came back down, then it was history. Who knew when we'd record again? There didn't seem to be any immediate plans.

Tutt sat in his house off Nolensville Road, owning us lock, stock and barrel. Muscles stayed around as a crouching, shouting presence in our minds, to remind us of the impermanence of life.

So we'd done a bit now. The dream had partly come true.

It had been a long while since the innocent Pub days, when every day had been new, marked by some massive improvement in the band, either in our sound or our state of affairs. Now we went out, sounded pretty good, delivered a product and took the money. There wasn't as much suspense to it. We didn't sit at home and write songs so much any more, because we were too busy out playing the ones we already knew. The show, and our sound, were beginning to calcify.

Beth and I had improved our relationship, but I was still away from home too often to either make something solid of it or completely screw it up beyond repair once and for all.

Jason and the Scorchers kept making records and touring. We'd see their videos and see magazine articles on them.

Otherwise, it was the end of the world as we knew it (and we felt fine.)

So now I had a band—for two years already—what I'd wanted all those years and never really believed I would get. A band. MY BAND. I'd always thought that being in a rock and roll band would surely dissolve all my problems and hang-ups. I used to think that if I was in a band someday, then I would be suddenly taller and more attractive, and that birds were going to light on my shoulder. Things were going to be so much better someday, when I was in a band.

It hadn't turned out that way. I didn't feel a damn bit better, or cooler, now that I was in a band. I was having fun, to be sure, but I wasn't feeling improved or edified by the experience in any way. I was learning—very slowly—that low-budget hedonism was an empty-calories philosophy, and that a long string of anecdotal events was not the same thing as a life.

We were playing in Juanita's at Little Rock with Glass Eye, the group with the sickly pale, emaciated short-haired girl. I remember being very concerned about her, she looked so unhealthy. She looked like she could die any second, so I watched their set just in case she did so I could say I saw it. Even though they were obviously intent on coming off pretty arty, they closed their set with some AC/DC tune from *Back in Black*. I think it was "Rock and Roll Ain't Noise Pollution". You see, folks, we're really just *rockers at heart*. Nice people. The bass player was terrific, the Dead Milkmen's producer, I was told. I'm pretty sure they hated us.

Another house, and another nice guy with three cats and no litter box. Imagine the smell, then double it. We'd driven all the way through from Bowling Green and we were all dog-tired except for Billy, who was "dilating". That's what we called overdoing the white crosses.

It was four in the morning and *Thick As a Brick* was in the CD player. There's something grotesque about a record that's just two long songs. It just seems that much longer to have to lay through the whole thing. Our gracious host was showing Billy all his stereo equipment, and he had a mountain of it. It was all very cool, antiquated stuff from two or three eras before. When you crash with people on the road, it's a deal for them, and they're upbeat and hospitable and hey, God bless 'em. But every night is just like this one. And right now it's four in the morning and I want to sleep and, to tell the truth, I pretty much fucking despise Jethro Tull when I'm wide awake and in a *good* mood.

At last, it had been a good five or ten minute stretch of pure silence. Tull was still going, but that's different from conversation, which your brain feels it has to follow whether it wants to or not, like trying to sleep to the News All Night Channel or something. The guy was honking on his bong. I heard the bubbles. Go to sleep, Billy. This is Tommy's brain calling Billy's. Lie down, Billy. . . . Gooooo toooooo sleeeeeeeep Billleeeee. . . .

"What does this button do?" Billy asked. And off they went again.

Later, lying down, Billy sighed and said "I feel like an occupant in a space capsule," and then he laughed.

I rolled over on a couch and mumbled "Dollar."

It was code, Government Cheese code. Billy took his line from *The Right Stuff*, about those cool astronauts, confident, envied, and — unknown to the masses — tethered shamefully to smaller bodies on the ground, unable to make any autonomous decisions larger than when and how long they could piss in their own pants. Billy said "I feel like an occupant in a space capsule" because that was our situation too. We followed a plan. The Reptile Plan. The Scott Tutt Plan. We did what we're told. Don't think, Hill! Do it LIKE THIS.

I said "Dollar" because anybody got fined a dollar for saying the same damn thing they've said a million times already. The same joke. The same complaint. The same catchphrase. The same laugh. The same songs, in the same order, at the same clubs, night after night after night after fucking night.

The next morning, Joe took a shower and towelled off with what was apparently the only towel our host owned. That wet dog smell, like when dreadlocks get wet. One minute you're fresh and clean, the next minute unspeakably tainted. That one towel had served God knows who and what for God knows how long. Joe smelled like an old woman's hairbrush all the way to Texas. Nobody else showered.

And this is the road life. Binge on the moneymaking gigs, head out 'till you can't pay your way, then limp home. We'd just done Lexington, Louisville, Picasso's, Picasso's and Picasso's. Now it was off to Texas, by way of everything between there and home.

Down into Louisiana. Was it Monroe? Ruston? Was it Enoch's or the Trenton Street Cafe? Was it this third place I can see in my head but can't call the name of now? I know we were there, wherever the hell we were. Burgers in Louisiana came drowned in the indigenous Cajun sauce whether you asked for it that way or not, the same way you got salsa on everything in Texas. Hot sauce was on every table in Louisiana, because these people would catch whatever mud-dwelling crustaceans were running around behind the house and eat them, following a sound drowning in liquid dynamite.

We stayed in a mobile home with a cool couple, a guy and his girl. We got real soft Louisiana ground-water showers there. I blamed the soap at first. I just figured the woman of the house had bought whatever bar of stuff I was getting all over me and couldn't get off. Lotion soap kills me. It's a contradiction. Not that I'm into pioneer lye, but I'm also not into standing underneath a shower jet for ten minutes trying to rub soap off my face while it just clings ever more stubbornly. Then I realized that the water was ten percent crude oil, or something with a comparable slime factor. You've heard of soft water. This was goose down water. I was practically shiny once I'd towelled off. I dressed and popped the 4:30 PM start-your-engines beer, feeling soft and supple, trailing a playful hint of Eau de Bayou.

When you got sick on the road, you stayed sick on the road. You didn't get well 'til you got home. I'd gotten sick enough to snare a legit codeine prescription. One teaspoon every four hours, or maybe every two hours, or maybe every fifteen minutes or just maybe when I fucking feel like it, okay? In Ruston, I'd been a shambling idiot. Numbness in the extremities, momentary blindness, etc. I'd been telling all the funky local Cajuns these hilarious stories, and none of them were laughing. We'd play another song and I'd tell another story. A song. A story. It went that way all night. And nobody was laughing. Perhaps they were all morons. Perhaps I was drooling on myself. Thank you and here's another tune! Look! A silverfish running up the pipe! Get the Red Hot!

There was a frat fill-in date the next night and it was a thoroughly loathsome experience. We were doing horrible things to fill time, playing "Gloria" twenty minutes and suchlike. By this point, I was thinking there should be a reality-based television show where sorority girls were fed to Komodo dragons in a pit, legs first, so I could watch their last terrified, bug-eyed expressions and hear their last screams of *Like, this, like, lizard is like, tearing me apart! Like, eaumuhgawd!* Viewers could send in home videos, that sort of thing. I would set time aside every week to watch such a show. To be fair, I'd have to remember, not all sorority girls were useless tripe, not all of them serve no other purpose on this earth except to stand in circles and sing songs. Some were cool. And then some stormed up to us with all their five-foot-nothing bowhead dander up, hands on hips, wanting to know why it's *eight-o-clock* and we're, *like, not playing yet.* We were never musicians at these affairs, we were like the kitchen help or the landscaper, and we got used to it because frat-pay kicked club-pay's ass to the moon and back. It was worth it. You just smiled blankly while you tuned up, took their shit, and were glad for their sakes that you didn't believe in guns and didn't carry one. God, I used to be one of these people. Did we act this way?

Beaumont was cool. Good crowd, good show. Pizzas backstage, hotel rooms care of the school. Texas is a tonic. I've not had a bad time there. Everything's just a little over scale—a little more space between houses, a little more yard. You could see for miles all the time. It always seemed like you were on a hilltop in Texas. And it was hotter than frijoles already when it was still miserable, drizzly and cold in Kentucky. I actually started to get slightly well. My sniffle abated. I didn't exactly feel *good*, but that might have been too much to ask, given the recreational spice-rack I was sampling daily.

Houston was terrific. We played and stayed at Fitzgerald's. They had a band house and we used to just retreat from the world for three days at a time in there. A fortyish guy named Jim with a salt-and-pepper beard and a Mohawk used to roller skate all over the place, up and down stairs, carrying cases of beer. It turned out he used to manage the Jerry's Restaurant in Madisonville, back when I was a kid. He'd probably served me a hot fudge cake in his other life.

Cool things would happen in Houston that wouldn't even begin to elsewhere. We never really felt like stars anywhere we ever went, but in Houston we'd feel as if maybe we were being groomed to be. We felt appreciated.

We were guest-listed at a Ramones gig there when the Neighborhoods opened. *Come On Back to Bowling Green* had gotten a great review in a local rag. Things were firing on all cylinders. We got backstage, Skot walked up to Dee Dee and said "You don't know me, but I think you're a beautiful human being." Dee Dee, sunglasses on, smiled and showed his ghetto of teeth in a punk icon mouth. We'd heard he was on some sort of medication that made him throw up if he drank any alcohol, and that this left him angry all the time. Johnny signed a paper plate for Skot, telling him to only eat pizza on it. A fellow asked Johnny to sign his bass, and he said, "Sure, got a pencil?" I shook Joey's hand as he walked by. A wonderfully ugly guy. Put a wig and little red granny glasses on Dennis the Menace's father, kick the front teeth in and you have Joey Ramone.

The 500 Cafe in Dallas. Houston is day-glo. Dallas is khaki. Houston is danger. Dallas is bran. Houston has more music than it knows what to do with. Dallas doesn't know what to do with the music it's got. Might have been at least a decent gig if it weren't for some local hot-shots across town having their record-release party that night. Some Ecstasy-scene, hippie band having the big night of their lives. Our club needn't have opened. I couldn't remember their name. New Bohemians or something? Edie what?

Austin. This is *the* town for music in Texas. It never really was for us, frankly, and the minute I dis the place I'll sound like some loser running down a scene he didn't cut the mustard in, so let's just say we kept playing and waiting for the night when Government Cheese and Austin would click like a clock. It never happened.

We pulled into the motel lot and, down the line of rooms at the end, was a middle-aged lady loading guns out of her car and into her room. Big guns. Little guns. Automatics. Rifles. Pistols. One after a damn nother. A polyester, past-her-prime, varicose, stretch-knit bint, not the type of person you'd expect to be hoarding small arms for a coup. And there she was, going from her car to the room and back, a gun in each hand, trip after trip.

The desk clerk was a four-hundred-pound, black as Jamaica beans, flip-flop-wearing flaming star. He called me "honey". Billy wanted some sugar for his lobby coffee, and the guy said Billy looked plenty sweet enough already. We told him Edith Bunker was down the way hoarding enough firepower to make Ollie North spurt. "Oh, *her!*", he Bette Davised with a wave of his hand. "She's a strange one." And that was that. Another day at the office for Rasta Jollyfats Peter Allen here.

That place must have been in the Mobil Travel Guide for Hardened Criminals. The two guys next door eyed us gravely. They looked like they'd been living there a while, both of them well over three hundred pounds, hybrid steel-brawn and keg-belly. Their door was open, and we would soon notice that it stayed open. They were always scowling out. We tried saying "Hi" a couple of times, and got the picture soon enough that pleasantries weren't their bag. Bikers on Harleys paid them visits at all hours of the day and night.

Hello, Austin. Two gigs in four days. We were loading our luggage out of the back of the van, slinging duffel bags to the ground. One guy started slapping the back of his leg. Then another guy. Then another guy had to slap higher up on his leg. Slap! Another guy reached frantically in his underwear, chasing something around. Five crazy guys were preplexing the resident felons as we frantically all slapped away . . . something! We'd parked directly over Fire Ant Woodstock and sat down our duffel bags in the whole mess of them.

They came with us into the room, and for four days in Austin, we dueled them down to the last miserable one. Somebody was always slapping their leg in Austin. Jumping, yelping. Eventually, you started talking to them. Come on out you bastards! I feel you there, crawling up my ass. Come on out and fight like a . . . big ant!

At no extra charge, we had the American Triple XXXstacy channel. Dirty talk. Lesbian wrestling and patented gross-out, first-take's-a-keeper sex. More chips! More beer! Nothing cuts to the chase like a porno movie. One girl walks into the shot—let's say we're in a nice, suburban California home—and then a second girl walks in. "Hi, Connie." "Oh . . . HI, Cheryl!" says the sexy human quaalude. "Gee, Connie, I've been feeling SO horny lately." Cheryl whips off her shirt. Connie doesn't have to, because she's been naked the whole time. They french-kiss with their tongues three inches out of their mouths, as if anyone really does that. They stand with both torsos facing the camera, so you at home can see. They don't face each other dead-on, when it might be more exciting if they did. Then Bjorn the handyman comes in. He has a toolbox in his hand with one wrench in it and he announces to the two oblivious lesbians, "I hear you have a leaky faucet." IMMEDIATELY we cut to the three of them completely naked and going at it in various gymnastic combos. No lead-up. No motivation. Just cut to screwing. And then, here it comes, the dreaded *commingling genitalia from below and behind close-up!*

Why porno directors use this shot so much is beyond me. Women don't enjoy it, and the last thing I ever want to see is a guy's bare rump stuck up in the camera, plunging his ugly gray essence in and out of some woman's clinically exposed privates. It's not a pretty sight. And in the four days we were in Austin, we saw about five hundred of this same shot. I wonder if there's a class where somebody instructs on the nuances of it. Porno directors use that shot like Keith Richards uses open G. "Ewwwwwhh!" somebody would scream and throw a beer can at the screen. "Stop that! Why do they keep coming back to that?"

After an hour, you didn't want to see any more, Oh boy, more boobies. More piston-penis shots. Been there. Done that. What's on the news? Look at the *USA Today* for the eighth time. More beer.

A great show at the Big Mamou with the Fab Motion, a tremendous guitar band usually, who on this night just pulled out a bunch of brass instruments and did a Beefheart thing, improvisational blocks of noise on tubas and whatever was around. Absolutely incredible.

Trouble was, no one saw it. It had come a legendary rain storm, all the water bearing down sideways with horrific winds bending trees and carrying anything loose down the street. No one could get there. No one inside could leave. We split the door evenly. Eight bucks per band.

Went down to Sixth Street the next night. Austin was alive, but I didn't care. I didn't want to walk up and down the street seeing people going here and there, listening to bands outside the club because I couldn't pay cover, deciding to kick my last buck in for a death dog with everything. I saw White Zombie at the Ritz for a while. They did a Kiss cover. I don't remember what it was. I think "Calling Dr. Love", maybe. Everybody's just a rocker at heart, folks! Especially the rockers.

We played the Ritz the next night, on the small stage in what used to be the lobby. The PA was dogshit. The club owner actually took a vocal monitor off the stage and stuck it out the front door to attract patrons, as if the sound of Skot's lone vocal distorting a cheap, blown-out monitor was going to attract anything but industrial fans and pain freaks. It didn't stop us, though. We rocked that night.

It was just one of those nights when everybody felt evangelistic. Skot was bananas, Billy and Joe were tight, I was louder than God, playing good and greasy. Not many people were there, but the ones who came in stayed. Fifteen people became twenty people. Twenty-five. Hey, these guys are pretty good. Energy! That Picasso's kind of energy. Sweat, broken strings and song after song after song with no bullshit. A great show. We played an hour and a half straight before we took our first break. The jaded waitress, with a ring in her nostril connected to her right lobe by a gold chain swinging above her smirk, just scowled at us and told us to get back onstage for another hour if we cared about getting paid. No "great first set, guys!" or "what're ya drinking?" Just "get back up there, lackeys!" Baby, I'm gonna, make you a star! I got this TV show idea, you and a Komodo dragon. You'll love it. *Of course* your name is above the title! What am I, cruel?

Four in the morning. We'd sent one guy out for supplies and reconnaissance; he'd come back safely. We'd heard the burly neighbors earlier. Some yelling. A door slamming. Slap a fire ant. Huge Harleys roaring off to do no good somewhere. Small Arms 'R' Us down in Room 37. The lights were out, the television still glowing with the sound down. It had never been turned off. Five guys in a motel room

don't turn off titties. They'll all get in bed and tell the last guy awake
to turn them off. And then you can't tell who's asleep and who's not.
You try to go to sleep but the fake sex on the screen keeps pulling you
back to the surface of consciousness. You slip into a little nod, and
then you open one eye and you slap a fire ant under the covers. Gee,
it's been two minutes since I've seen a nipple. I simply must see another. I looked around the room and counted three guys with their
heads on their pillows and their glasses tilted funny on their faces.
The heads faced up but the specs went forward towards the television,
as if the lenses could record it and play it back to the brain later.

Oh heck, I'm up for a while. I'll get another beer. That means
slipping out of bed and crawling over whoever's down there on the
floor. Oh man, sorry down there. Grab a longneck out of the cooler.
Twist that cap. Hsssst! Step carefully back to bed. Slap a goddamn
fire ant. I tumble right over Chris. Sorry, man. I was walking backward so as not to miss any of the Texas Tit Parade.

I'm back in bed. Tomorrow night I may have the floor, but tonight I'm a BED GUY, sitting UP with my glasses ON. I swigged my
Bud and watched some Roman centurion get it on with two hand-
maidens. I found myself liking the big-budget porno movies better
than the cheapies. Period costumes and good lighting helped remove
a couple of layers of empathy for these people in the flicks. Cheap
ones, with the mic dropping into the shot all the time, made you look
at these people and know that some were junkies, some were runa-
ways. Some of them really, really didn't want to be doing this.

Who knew? You hitchhike to Hollywood with good teeth, round
shoulders and a dream. Wrap the straps around your wrists and yee
hah! You're going to be a star, and a few hard knocks and bad habits
later, you're in front of a bloomed-out klieg light, spilling seed with
another fallen flower from the heartland. Life's a bitch, then you fix
the lights and switch partners. Tough gig.

The rods and cones on the retina make up the movie screen of the
eyeball. They vibrate back and forth in millisecond swishes and
swings. They do this because the optic nerve at the back center of the
retina is the one place where there are no rods or cones. The surrounding ones twitch and swing in and out of that space, so you don't
go through life with a dark spot on the middle of your screen. When
you get drunk, the rods and cones get drunk too, and no longer twitch
and swing with their usual synchronicity. They basically act like any
big group of drunk people. They stumble and fall down with their

arms around one another. They swing in opposite directions across long tables like Germans in a beer tent.

The way the brain interprets this is that nothing looks stable any more. Things look like you're on a ship constantly, constantly, constantly rising up on a wave crest. Things swing ever upward until you feel like you're going to be sick, and that's exactly what Mr. Brain wants to happen. The alcohol needs to come out. You need to throw up, and the room's going to act silly until you do just that.

The titties were spinning. I hate this part of the night. I'm tired. I want to sleep now and I can't, because the goddamn room-spinning business has started. I can't lie down now. That was just asking for it. I'm up for a while. The eyelids droop. The head sags. Spin! No! The eyes come wide open! I'm awake again. Please be gentle with me, room. Please stop. Fire ant. SLAP! Miss. I lost the grip on my bottle. God! Why am I *still holding* a bottle? Five AM. I *GOTTA* sleep. This is ridiculous. Damn the rod/cone mod/rocker riots. I have to lie down now. I stretch out and lay down, heaving great draughts of air like you do to settle your own stomach. I put my hand against the wall like everyone says to do. So much for that theory. I put one foot on the floor. Strike two. Maybe if I put BOTH feet on the floor. Well, shit, maybe I'm just sitting back up again. One eye comes open. I give the carnal shenanigans another peek. It's a cheapie ugly porn movie now. Well, they're all ugly now, aren't they? It was three sub-basements below mere sex at this point. It wasn't exciting at all. It was like watching an undressed G.I. Joe ramming Barbie. All the humanity'd been stripped away. I'd gotten too high, and I couldn't feel it any more.

I rose unsteadily, staggered to the television, reached one skinny, searching hand out, and pushed in on the on-off knob. Wrong one. Push this one. Nope. There! That's the one. I declared my independence. I sealed off the spigot. The sun was peeking through the windowshades. In the distance I thought I heard Harleys, maybe some gunfire. Maybe I was already dreaming. The room settled down. The sun bit through the shades in spots. Slap, scratch.

Wake up, slap it, scratch it. Pack up and head out. Gotta go home. Back to the same old same old. Gotta go back to Kentucky, make some money. Louisville, Lexington. Picasso's Picasso's Picasso's.

New Orleans. No gig there, we just stopped in on the way back. It wasn't exactly on the way, but hey. Bourbon Street was cold, and we admired the French Quarter at a stiff pace, with our heads low, our hands rammed down in our pockets. The voodoo paraphernalia was interesting. Gator heads for sale. Different prices for different sizes. Beautiful homes with all the wrought-iron railings. A small black child was running through the crowded street, diving and spinning around people. He charged right up and stopped under Chris's nose. He froze, looked up at Chris, and shrieked *"DAMN! You ugly!"* And he was gone.

*    *    *    *

# while you were out

> *"If you were the salad*
> *And I were the dressing*
> *I'd give you an oily vinegar blessing.*
> *I'd take your croutons in my hands*
> *And give them sweet, soft tickles.*
> *I'd run my fingers up and down*
> *Your long and luscious pickles.*
> *Your peppers are so cool.*
> *Your onions are so boss.*
> *Wanna get in a bowl with you*
> *And just toss . . . toss . . . toss . . . "*

*A smattering of applause. Seventeen people spread over the whole place. What's the definition of an anticlimax? The third set at the Hangar. The first two sets, we rocked. It was good. Now it's 1:30 AM on a school night. Everybody's gone. Our contract says three sets, so here we are. We're playing things we haven't played in a while, like the "Love Boat" theme. That's right, the "Love Boat" theme. Gavin McLeod, Gopher the congressman & Isaac, the bartender who never slept. You got it. And we have the chords right, down to the last major 7th. Go figure. We get the chords to "South Central Rain" wrong, but "Love Boat" we kick ass on. The show is stopped while Skot's trying to tune his guitar, and I'm doing poetry at the mike, smoking a cigarette, killing time. Billy, would you like to say something to our distinguished audience?*

*He leans into his mike, clears his throat, thinks a moment. "No."*
*he says. "Why don't you do another poem, Tommy?"*

*Very well.*

> *"I know a girl. She's four feet tall.*
> *Sexually experienced and talks about it all.*

*You think your woman's mean?*
*My woman is the meanest.*
*She doesn't say weiner.*
*She says penis.*
*Penis! Penis!*
*It's not so uncouth.*
*You could say it too,*
*If you were Dr. Ruth."*

*And on and on. Three verses of that bit. Another smattering of applause. Thank you very much. Somebody yells for "Fish Stick Day". We haven't played it yet, and we're not going to, 'cause I'm tired of it. It's not funny any more. Hey, buddy! I got yer fish sticks right here! Fuck you! This is art! We're ROCK STARS. Perhaps you saw us on MTV eleven months ago. Damn straight you did.*

*At last, Skot is in tune. We're ready to play something, except Billy's suddenly not here. There he is, coming back onstage wearing the case to his bass rig. It's a homemade cardboard & duct tape contraption designed to fit around one of his massive speaker cabinets. It has holes in the sides for the handles. Billy is wearing it, with his arms sticking out of the holes. It's all we can see of him except for his legs. He can't see where he's going. He looks like one of those dancing cigarette packs from the golden age of television. Joe leaps up and guides him to his mike, where Billy begins singing. I can't tell what tune it is, because there is a layer of cardboard and duct tape between Billy's voice and the microphone. It appears to be a garbled filigree medley of the "Flintstones" theme, Bobby Goldsboro's "Honey" and "Bess, You Is My Woman Now."*

Carbondale, Illinois. Carbon-Hell, we tagged it. The worst motel we ever stayed at. It was so miserable we had to keep going back. Very Charles Bukowski. I don't recall the name, and it honestly might not have had one. It was a courtyard-type arrangement where you pulled in and there was one level of rooms on three sides of you. You knocked on the locked door of the office, and you knocked again, and just when you were almost about to leave, a guy in his shorts and undershirt would come out from the back with a frozen dinner tray and a fork in it.

Carbondale out-nastied the competition. Folks threw their wadded bills at the convenience store guy. He threw the potato chips in a bag upside-down, crushing them, and shoved the bag nastily back.

Many of the students were brat-farting Chicago bottom-feeders. Loud, rude, very genuine people.

The Hangar 9 had a stage four feet in the air and, as often as not, the steps would have been taken away by someone for some other purpose, meaning you had to haul yourself aloft. A dollar cover in Carbondale was pulling teeth. A big night at the Hangar was when the local home for the disabled brought all the paraplegics in. There would be a dozen people in wheelchairs (and, once or twice, beds) lined up haphazardly on the dance floor below us. They were adults, and by God they could drink if they wanted to. People would be crashing their wheelchairs into one another on the dance floor. It was dangerous for any normally ambulatory healthy folks to get in their way. Payback time for the discriminating able-bodied. A don't-give-a-shit orderly would lounge in the corner, in case one of them turned over and couldn't get back up.

I got into a conversation one night with a guy who had two little bowed legs at the end of his hips, each about ten inches long. No arms. Not even knobs. Nothing attached to his shoulders but empty short sleeves. His feet were like apes', curled around inwardly and amazingly adept at grasping. His dwarfed midsection was bent from a lifetime of curling concave to bring knives, forks and, in this case, beer glasses to his lips. The only thing full-size about him was his head, and it therefore looked huge. His name was Artie.

We talked music. He knew hardcore bands through and through. I listened to Artie dissert on SST and Alternative Tentacles and 'zines and other hardcore things. Before Carbondale, I'd have thought anyone confined to a wheelchair would know nothing about slam-dancing except, of course, second-hand insights. Seeing them in action on that floor proved me mistaken.

Artie finished a beer, I got us fresh ones and he downed his before I had time to look at my own. That little fucker could put it away. After twenty minutes, he asked "Can ya help me take a piss, man? It's no big deal."

"Sure!" I said, while in my brain I was screaming "*No way in hell am I helping you piss, man!*" So we went off to the Hangar's men's room, which is about as repulsive as any other rock club dumper. There was usually one stall with a full toilet and a long porcelain or aluminum trough, with one of those pink things in there as an enduring testament to the futility of man. One little pink disc is a spit in the ocean for two to three hundred heathens consuming and releasing liquids in unventilated velocity. And there was usually only one toilet for a reason, the lack of any kind of privacy. (It was common practice to have to leave the club and walk half a block or more to find a suitable place to do any more than whip it out and have target practice on cig butts.)

So we got Artie's wheelchair in the almost too narrow door, made a difficult hairpin turn and got inside a stall. Here's where it hit me. I was going to have to do *everything* for the guy. I grasped him across his chest, pulled him up and clutched his back against *my* chest, then kicked around the wheel chair to put him in firing range. I briefly had to set Artie's nimble but none too strong feet down gingerly on the toilet seat, keeping him leaned backwards against me. If I let him lean forward, he was going to pitch forward into the bare chrome plumbing pipes and crack a tooth at least, maybe put an eye out or worse. And so he did his thing. We returned to the side of the stage, where he continued to match me beer for beer.

All the gear was loaded up and Joe was heading out of the back parking lot with Dianna, his girlfriend at the time. He was going off with her in her car and told us he would see us at the next stop. He whipped around the gravel lot into the street and stood up on the brakes. There was Artie, lying like an overturned bug in the street, unable to do anything but squirm. His upset wheelchair was behind him, still on the sidewalk, where he'd struck a bump at what for wheelchairs is drunken warp speed. The craft had pitched forward on its face and thrown Artie a full three feet into the street. Joe had spun around into the road and screeched to a stop right before he squashed Artie's outsize head like a ripe melon. He got out, set Artie back upright in his craft, and left him to his own drunken, paraplegic devices.

The rest of us went to a Hangar 9 employee party, where we saw a girl stop a ceiling fan with her tongue. The blades hadn't been swept of dust bunnies in years. She stood on a table underneath the spinning blades, angled her head flat back, protruded her taster as far as it went, and, the minute she made contact, the dust started flying. The blades made a static visual impression for just a second, and then kept spinning. She stabbed with her tongue again, and the blades went static once more, and more dust flew, and the blades began to slow, the tongue began to win, and, as the whole packed house went crazy, she completely stopped a spinning fan with her newly gray and lint-ridden licker.

Cicero's in St. Louis. A basement club under an Italian restaurant. We'd had some nice gigs there and some hell nights. We knew from experience that the girl who booked the place was nice but bubbleheaded. This would be different from all the times before, though. This time, we'd sent her posters two weeks ahead of the gig, and even sent her notes about where to put them up *in her own town,* though she should already have known. We got to the club and loaded all our stuff down the fire escape in the garbage-strewn alley pit behind the club. Cicero's was a bitch load-in. And as soon as we had the stuff inside, here she came up with the stack of posters and big smile. "Hey guys! I've got the posters here! Want to go help me put them up?" The gig was in five hours. Sometimes you just sit down and bury your head in your hands. What else can you do?

Down into Kentucky and Tennessee for the usuals, Tewligan's, Wrocklage, Big Apple, Picasso's, Picasso's, Picasso's, Exit/In, Library, Quarterback's, Tuscaloosa and the greatest motel in rock and roll, the Dill Motor Lodge, every room a fridge and a couch and two full beds.

In Lexington, I'd been detained on the street by several policemen because I exactly matched the description of a local feeler-upper. My road schedule provided an alibi for all this guy's past offenses. One cop asked me what band I played in. I said "Government Cheese" and the youngest cop said "Oh, cool!" The older cops scowled at him and he got mean-looking again.

In Murfreesboro, I became the only member of the band to ever throw up onstage under the lights in mid-song and keep playing. I claim that for myself. Other members threw up offstage before a show, or left the stage in mid-show and vomited, but mine was under the lights and I played the lead break on "Inside of You" during it. Milk and fish don't mix. Milk, fish, Rumpelmintz and white-crosses especially don't mix.

Birmingham, Alabama. Saturday, September 24th, 1988 was the all-time worst Government Cheese show ever. Shooter's was the club. There was no publicity and barely a PA. No lights. The stage was completely dark. Why we didn't refuse to play I can't tell you. The beer flowed hard. We did one set and I wound up stripped to my underwear and wondering why I was that way. Billy's sister had come in from Huntsville, which intensified the embarrassment through and through, because the next day I had to remember that I'd been cavorting onstage in front of Beth Allen Hill in my skivvies, and it wasn't funny or meaningful, it was just a pissed-off guy in his underwear at a joke of a gig that came too recently after the last joke of a gig, in what was slowly but surely becoming a joke of a career. It was one of those first real good hints. If you looked directly at our career, it still looked hopeful, but out of the corner of the eye, entropy was marshalling, surging and thickening.

Oh, by the way, where the hell is our new record?

We'd recorded a night of live stuff for possible insertion into our much ballyhooed, long-promised debut Reptile long-player. It wasn't live in a club. We'd brought an "audience" into the studio and recorded a live set there at Chelsea Studios. The "audience" had to stand carefully around in the big room and be gingerly about not stepping on wires and standing too close to microphones, while Joe was in his windowed broom-closet behind his drums, Billy could only hear his bass through the headphones, mine and Skot's headphones kept falling off, and that damned acoustically correct carpeted room still had no live ambience at all. So we were all a bit surprised when we'd heard the entire playback and it was for some strange reason *already better* than what we'd been laboring over in maddening stop/ starts for more than eighteen months now.

It was suggested we release the whole thing as a precursor to the studio album, which we'd been assured would be done and ready for release in fall '88, a year after the four-song *Bowling Green* EP. We hadn't heard any of the tracks from that record in months now, and since we hadn't been allowed to bring cassettes home with us, we couldn't even remember exactly what songs we'd recorded any more, much less how the hell the tapes sounded.

Only Skot was vocally against going through with the live record. "Let's just finish what we started," he felt. He didn't believe for a minute that Tutt could release this live record as a mini-album, then turn around two months later and put out the finished studio record. That was the line Tutt was feeding us, though, and Skot didn't buy it for a second. I bought it.

The way things were planned, we'd put out the live record and call it *Three Chords, No Waiting,* then the regular studio album would follow it by a couple of months. That was the plan.

We went back into Chelsea one more time after that live session. We fixed a few things, such as when headphones fell off and we couldn't sing, or when somebody yanked his cord loose, and for the two and a half remaining years we sat under contract, this was the last time we ever entered a studio with Scott Tutt.

We weren't there for the mixing. We were on the road too much. There had actually been arguments about whether we'd be allowed to attend the mixing *at all*. Tutt didn't think our presence there was necessary or constructive.

We heard the whole record a few weeks later at Tutt's house. We approved it, as if Tutt needed us to. He didn't, but it made us feel better to act like we had a hand in it.

And that was months ago. Any moron knew that the studio album wasn't just around the corner any more. And every time we asked about the status of the live record, we heard that it was going to be mastered next week, or that we're waiting for cover art, or this or that. Every week, it was *next week*. We lived through one next week after another, as if next week was this figment to aspire to more than something real on the calendar. It seemed to me a complete mystery. You go to Masterfonics, you master the damn thing and write a check! What's so hard? Could it be that *check* part of the equation? Is that what's holding everything up? We couldn't get a straight answer.

A word of advice for any young musician out there who someday may be waiting for a record to come out day after day: don't do what I did. I just sat on my couch night after night getting angrier and angrier. Not good. There are too many books to read and too many movies to see to ever spend a second of your life wondering where your record is. Besides, whose shoulder are you going to cry on? There won't exactly be a line around the block outside your door waiting to give you sympathy. In a world of strife, mass famines, ethnic cleansings and other assorted miseries, nobody gives a greasy rat's ass if your record comes out. But I was obsessed with it, thinking about it day in and day out. Where's my record? Smoking cigarettes on the couch at four in the morning, fuming, ranting "Goddam sonofabitch Tutt!" That is no way to live.

Centre College. Another wonderful frat gig. Freedom of Expression next door was much more fun. Better bass speakers. Better quality everything! Jah, mon.

Sal's in Nashville two nights later. A brand new club, and all the waitresses had on skimpy mini-dresses that hardly had enough fabric to be called dresses at all. They made Hooter's girls look dowdy. In their honor, I took a moral stance from the stage, shedding my pants and playing the gig that way. If they were mired in sartorial sexism, I'd join their ranks. The waitresses completely didn't get it. They thought I was making fun of them. One of the girls had to be called off from attacking me.

The gig was a bomb anyway, nobody there, and by this point we had a nice following in Nashville too, so there were questions to ask. Skot tore off the stage and lit right into Tutt with all kinds of "what is this bullshit?" and "what are we doing here?" sort of questions. Tutt said we were trying to break a new club and Willis exploded. *"Fuck breaking a new club, especially in Nashville! Break us!"* I didn't know about the altercation until later, because I was too busy slamming blue ocean waves and dodging pissed-off waitresses. I just remember wondering why Tutt and Susan left without saying goodbye.

Tewligan's again in Louisville. We were winding up the show with our usual jumping-around crazy behavior, and Skot was spinning the microphone in five foot arcs like Roger Daltrey, as he'd recently taken a liking to doing. There is a good reason why Daltrey always wrapped tape up the mike and down the cable length, which we discovered in classic learn-by-doing fashion when Skot's mike took off from the cord at high speed and brained Lisa Dunaway on the top of her skull. She went down like a tree. The show stopped and we all went to the emergency room. She turned out okay after a few stitches, and didn't sue.

On up to the Canal Street Tavern in Dayton, for the bi-yearly attempt to stir up any interest there. Our picture was in the paper, that horrible old dorky shot where we all looked preppy and young. We'd been furious about that picture from day one. It was the first thing Tutt ever did for us, and his first major boner too. We called it the Menudo shot, and it followed us around everywhere.

We went to a student party somewhere in the stony wilds of Dayton. A damnably tough nut to figure, Dayton. I never saw people on the streets downtown. It always looked like that Arby's commercial where the guy's looking for people in an abandoned city and they're all at the Arby's Roast Beef Sale. Modern buildings are everywhere, the traffic lights are working, but where is everybody?

We found the party in a driving rainstorm, popped the beers and proceeded with the good times. Two very cool art student types lived there, kind of like Skot and Ken's old place. Things hanging from the ceiling, incense going, Escher prints on the walls and a genuine human skeleton in the corner with Christmas tree lights in the eyes. I was enjoying drinking beer and sitting cross-legged on the floor talking to them, but where was that infernal clanging coming from? And then it sounded like a ratchet hammer at the end of a hallway. And then AAGHHHH! Eight guys banging on sheet metal! JEEEsus! What in the hell *is* that? I asked. Oh, you like it? They responded, passing a joint on. It's this new band from Germany named . . . *You mean this is a band? This is on the stereo?*

Yes, sometime while we'd been out doing the Kerouac thing all over Dixie, industrial music had come to be. Somebody had mixed and mastered *this!* After an hour of hammers banging on I-beams and engines coughing and metal saws screaming as they bit into scrap iron, and then, of course, the sheet-metal chorus, I had to excuse myself. That night in Dayton, way past the age of 25 — and sometimes lately *I* couldn't keep track of how old I really was — I knew that the world was moving on . . . while I was out.

The Wrocklage in Lexington. We'd developed the habit of missing the opening bands, not out of disinterest, but because after soundcheck a guy's gotta eat and, if lucky, shower. This time, we caught the opener, and felt lucky about it. A three-piece with the bass player from hell. Freakout, over the top, mayhem funk with Monty Python lyrics. Frisco guys on their way to New York City to snare a record deal. Primus? What the hell is a Primus? Isn't that what they called a camp stove in *Kon-Tiki?* We looked at them and thought hmmm, give them a year and they'll be somewhere, and for once in our stinkin' little lives, we were right. We got the unenviable job of following these mutants. Joe counted us off and immediately plunged a stick through a snare head. "Pose!" he yelled, "find me another snare drum!" "What?" Chris yelled (Pose was Chris' latest nickname, and nicknames came and went so fast *I* sometimes forgot who was who). "Find me a snare!" Joe screamed, as if there would just happen to be twenty snares lying around in storage nearby. "Go find those Primus dudes! Go! Go! Go!"

So off went Chris, and we played a couple of numbers with Joe banging on his toms and sounding like shit, and here came Chris, ramrodding his way through the slamdancers with various pieces of spare drum equipment, looking for some reason like he was one heave away from spewing puke in every direction. "Don't make me go see those guys again!" He screamed. "Wha's yer problem?!" we screamed back, still playing. "Aren't they nice?" "Yeah, sure!

They're nice . . . but the *SMELL*!", he screamed back, slapping a head onto Joe's abused snare. "Oh God! They haven't done laundry since California, and they're cookin' godawful couscous Moroccan vegetarian shit inside the trailer! Agghhhh!"

Down to the Tip Top in Huntsville, when we were rocking out with a good crowd and suddenly everyone dove to the ground. With the lights in our eyes, we didn't see the guy waving the gun around. Other people pushed him out the front door and slammed it on his arm, so that the arm (in serious, limb-severance-type pain) still waved the gun around the club, while the whole club was lying on the floor except for the four of us onstage. We thought everybody was doing the gator; that's how bright we were.

Atlanta. The White Dot on Ponce De Leon Road. We were lucky enough to catch the opener again here, since we were broke and had nowhere to go anyway. Three black guys and a white guy they'd later get rid of. Probably the most incredible band I ever had the pleasure to see in all our travels. Their soundcheck ran the gamut from hard-core funk and balls-out metal, to a country weeper with a dead-on nasal twang seriously caucasian type vocal. It was the second gig they'd ever played. Their name was Follow For Now. We came back to Atlanta in five weeks and open for *them,* and the place was packed. They got big quick.

Down through Johnson City for a stop at the Pub Out Back, with the Iraqi manager who made lousy pizza, at least he was Iraqi until the Persian Gulf war when he became, I swear, an Iranian overnight. He should have just thought ahead enough to call himself a Jordanian and been done with it. The opening band featured a very very cute fifteen-year-old preppy girl singing a song called "You're My Anus!" The song was all about her alimentary canal, with the title aperture being both the chorus and big finish, literally and figuratively. The only line I can remember is "When I eat food, I think of you."

From Studio B in Greenville, South Carolina, where we did a great show and went down a storm for all five people, to Rockafella's in Columbia, South Carolina, where we did so well covering for no-show House of Freaks the first night that the club asked us to stick around. The next night we opened the triple-bill of the Connells and Dash Rip Rock. What great guys! Dash Rip Rock's sound check and half their *show* was Spinal Tap covers. I don't remember much about the Connells, except that they were nice guys and they covered some Fleetwood Mac song off *Rumours.* I don't remember any more than I do because I made the silly mistake of trying to drink with Dash Rip Rock, a bad move back then. By the time the Connells went on, I was a slobbering fool. I remember shaking hands with the lead singer, walking about five paces behind the club and vomiting violently.

Speaking of puke, let's go straight to Charleston for two nights and watch Joe throw up in a seated reclining position uphill behind the hotel, aiming it all between his spread legs. At least the drive through Virginia was beautiful, but you had to think that maybe this imbibing-'til-your-stomach-inverts thing is getting more than a little out of hand. The next night, Joe and I swam fifty yards out in a lake to a stationary pontoon, where we held on for dear life, totally spent from the short paddle. We looked at each other, both about to die. Hey, this was supposed to be a fun little swim, and we'd barely made it.

Coming up to the stairway outside the hotel, we passed a fellow about our own age sitting in the driver's seat of his car, masturbating unabashedly. Later, I was cross-legged on the bed talking to a girl who'd just returned from Russia on a school trip. She showed me her ruble. The phone rang and it was the parking lot jacker. He invited me down for a bit of backseat buggery. I took a rain check.

Back up to New York City. CBGB again. For some reason, this trip to New York seemed like just another milk run. There was no elation this time, no touristy yearnings or need to explore. It was a dirty city that we got in and out of as quickly as we could. It's sometimes not the fact that romance dies that strikes me, but that it dies as quickly as it sometimes can. This was the New York I worshipped from afar as a New Wave sophomore, and now what do I feel for this big ugly place? Billy and I were drinking beer, looking outside at Manhattan, talking about the state of the band, and he was sounding pretty down. Man, I'm tired of being broke. I'm tired of broken promises. I'm tired of a pipe-dream future. I'm just tired, man. I know, man. I know.

Newark. Rutgers University. We played in the student lounge with a speedmetal band called Insaniac, who screamed "Alright Rutgers!" between every song in speedmetal speak. *"Owwwriiiight! Rrrrrrrrruttgahzzz!"* Really nice guys, though. They're the only speedmetal band who ever sent us Christmas cards.

Eight jillion straight miles and four days later, the Nick in Birmingham, where a guy used to bootleg us onto videotape with a microphone plugged into a VCR. On up to the Don't Care, in Huntsville. The club was named after a White Animals tune. The soundman at the Don't Care was an original. He had a canned audience applause cassette. At the end of a song, this wild crowd from some *Price is Right* taping faded up into the PA speakers; and if he personally liked our song a *lot*, he'd leave the applause on a while and even turn it up louder. "No! Please! You're too kind! No! Really!"

How's the record going? Oh, we'll know something *next week!*

Athens, Georgia. R.E.M.'s home. Ort's home. I'd waited a long time to finally play this town. This was like going to Lourdes.

We opened for the Flaming Lips. All they did for soundcheck was test the smoke and bubble machines. Cool.

Ort had plastered the town with posters, utilizing our logo and WLBJ's old broadcast pattern map. He took us all over town. We met up with several folks we'd known in other towns. Athens was a magnet. People came there and didn't leave. Ort took us to the 40-Watt. The Montanas were playing, and as I turned around at the bar, I saw Peter Buck right behind me, talking to Barrie the bartendress, whom he'd later marry. I considered for a minute saying something. But it had been such a long time since the Opry House, and if I had to keep a list of all the stars I'd made a fool of myself over, or felt like I had, Peter's name would be right up there. Anyway. Who is he but a guy with three BMWs who smells worse right now than I do? And that's saying something. I can smell him right now turned fully way from him. No, wait, that must be this guy here. Hey, maybe it's me. So I stood there at the bar stupidly refusing to turn around and say anything to him because I figured I'd said enough stupid shit to him the first time. A uniquely American disease, this star-lionization thing, especially when applied to guys whose main accomplishments are mastering three chords and keeping their hair.

The Ross Theater in Evansville, Indiana. Now *that* was surreal. I saw *Million Dollar Duck* here when I was seven, and now I was on the stage in front of the movie screen for Saturday midnight punkfest. It was a massive, Depression-era movie house, and the sound system we had would have been barely adequate for the back of a car. But it was a lot of fun bopping around on a huge stage, with honest-to-God kids in the front row instead of burnt-out drinking age types like we'd had to get used to.

On to Hot Shotz in Cincinnati, where Skot was a mad whirling dervish all over the stage, and all over the front tables, and then in the middle of "This Life's For Me", he leapt off a banister and cracked his skull on the bottom of the overhead video projector. Down he went, fifteen feet to the dance floor, where he lay cold for thirty seconds while we played the turnaround over and over. Then he hopped to his feet and picked right up where he'd left off. He never knew he'd been out. For him there was no blank space, whereas for us there had been thirty awful seconds where we thought he was done and brain-dead. No worries, as he bounded up and finished the show with no more than a goose-egg on the top of his skull and no more brain death in him than we were already used to.

Down to Memphis and the Antenna Club to open for Love Tractor. Back to Nashville to play at Tommy Smith's new club on Printer's Alley, the T.S. Emporium. All the time asking, "where's the record?" All the time hearing "*next week*, we'll know something! *Next week!*"

Back to Cincinnati and Bogart's, to open for They Might Be Giants. Funny guys. Liked 'em. Had my last bowl of Cincinnati chili and swore off it for life. I'm sorry. I like Little Kings, I like the Reds and the Bengals, but the chili? Never has a town been so proud of something so bad as that town is of its chili. You want instant Cincinnati chili? Drive through Wendy's, get a bowl of their chili, eat it, wait four hours, shit in the same bowl, stir in some boiling water and let it stand for five minutes. That's Cincinnati chili.

I celebrated my birthday onstage in Louisville at the Red Barn by getting booed by a bunch of frat guys after I made some vitriolic leftist political statements. Given how small a band we were and how little anyone gave a shit, there really wasn't a place for it; but Bush had just won and I was angry. But hey, I couldn't stop there. I had to open my mouth a little wider and announce that I was quitting smoking for my birthday. I threw half a perfectly good pack of Marlboros out into the crowd. They spent the rest of the night throwing cigarettes back at me. Backstage, people who ran from me when I was in a cigarette-bumming mood came looking for me, to dangle a juicy Marl Red in front of me. But I held my ground for three solid weeks. And then I took up cigars, which is a move that mystifies me to this day. I was grossing my own self out with them, but I wouldn't go back to cigs. I'd just smoke those horrible big old Swisher Sweets. God, if it's not puking by the roadside, it's cigars. What the hell is going on here?

The first year or so, it didn't seem like that much changed. We came home, we went on the road. We came home again. We saw folks while we were in and every so often somebody moved away; but it took a while before we first came home and sort of asked . . . where *is* everybody?

Skip had moved to California with Cathy. Ort wasn't around much any more. Half the people at Record Bar were new. And who were all these little people? All these freshmen and sophomores I'd never seen before, and they'd never seen me, and Government Cheese was either a godlike band to them or they hated our guts.

We'd used to play at clubs under Bowling Green's old statutes, where 19-year-olds could get in to dance but not to drink. Ken Smith was convinced he was getting his balls way busted for having minors in Picasso's. He checked IDs diligently, but they could be faked, and all it took was one apple-cheeked wag to glom his way in, have a drink at Ken's bar, and then go out and wreck Daddy's Mazda, and all Ken had worked for would be down the dumper. He came to believe that either *he himself* would sponsor a measure to restrict nightclub ages to 21 across the board, or he'd watch his own club be taken down by the boys in blue. So he sponsored such a motion, and the city commission passed it, and the music scene in Bowling Green essentially died.

Government Cheese was the only band to make it out onto the alternative chitlin' circuit in time. All the other Bowling Green bands who hadn't made an out-of-town name for themselves yet got sunk.

In this new and tougher tundra, the next crowd had been fostered. Clubs were no longer the scene, except on the all-too-rare all-ages nights. The new bands came to be in backyard parties, and apartment jam-sessions, if and when they ever came to be at all. We saw it all from the windows of the van, Jane Pearl's curtains sagging inward, now long faded to almost nothing on the outside, from miles and miles of sunshine, all ripped and spotted from flying flecks of life itself.

The first local band in our wake, James Jauplyn and the Park Avenue Dregs, had lost their leader when James Hall cut loose and headed for Atlanta, where he formed Mary My Hope and got a deal with RCA. The band whittled down to Johnny and Pete, who in turn pared the name down to the Park Avenue Dregs.

Johnny Thompson. He came from a good family in Nashville who'd maybe had more stockbroker-ish designs for his future. That was a lost cause now. He'd dropped out of school and holed up in an apartment, speaking softly, growing his hair short on the sides and down far in front of his face and finding his own muse. Rumors began sifting around that he had indeed found *something*. It may have been way too far out in left field to call it *muse* technically, but it was definitely *something*.

The first shows were bombs. When a local fanzine pans you, you've either pissed somebody off or you're really dreadful. But they got it together. Keith Heric picked up a bass for the first time. Johnny sang. There are singers who learn by the rules and those who throw the rulebook out the window. Johnny burned the rulebook, jumped up and down on it, threw it out the window and then spat after it. The closest one can come to describing his voice is that it as closely approximates a baby's cry as can be done while still sounding completely manly in a fey, sensual way. Confused enough?

The harmonies were dark, their music a walk through some gothic whore's forest. Smoke and mirrors everywhere and trippy shifts of rhythm and tone. They sounded the way Black Sabbath's first album cover *looked*, with the lady and the stone house and the dark woods and the film on the lens. Johnny had retreated into his apartment and not come out until he'd spun an amazing web full of dramatic shifts in time-signature, lurches from fast to slow, light to dark, heavy to light. They hated comparisons, especially the dreary, easy ones like "oh they're like early Floyd, man." The only way to *get* the Park Avenue Dregs was to hear them, and the only way to hear them was to come to Bowling Green and wait around for it to happen. Maybe they'd play at Picasso's or Mr. C's, maybe they'd play in someone's backyard, or at the annual and soon-to-be notorious Halloween party. You just had to be there when it went down.

The Dregs used to drape the stage in ivy garlands. They used strobe lights. It was the Electric Kool-Aid Acid Test by way of Nosferatu. They promoted shows with strange, cryptic-lettered posters on campus-neighborhood phone poles. A few old ladies complained to the police about the satanist propaganda. It took Beth, as a newswoman, to set them straight downtown about who was making these posters and that no one was drinking goat's blood that we knew of. Chill out, grandma.

I was now the generic holdover from a blander, safer time, the old guard. Last year's thing. I'd go to Dregs gigs on Tuesday nights and there'd always be someone behind me in the crowd, expecting me to be jealous. I was, but not of the adulation.

They could do anything they wanted to. I'd made it out of town. I had a "manager" in Nashville, and I could see how they sort of envied that. But they had no concept of how all my options in life were closed off now. I could "tour." They couldn't. I could sell records and see my name in the college charts. They couldn't. But they could do the shitty cool cheap record I longed to do, and do it over and over 'til they got it right. I couldn't. Not with Scott Tutt around to "produce" it. I couldn't just hang around at home and get to know people, feel a sense of community. They could, and were. And I wondered where we were playing next week. Carbondale again? Oh boy! Maybe if we play there fifteen more times we'll make it big? Is that how it goes? And I wondered if the record was going to be mastered *next week*. And, strange as it may have seemed, I was envying the guys who didn't have the blessings I had, the ones who couldn't leave town. Maybe they were better off where they were, and maybe I would have been too.

\* \* \* \*

# 21

# the crash

*"He not busy being born is busy dying."*
—Bob Dylan

I can almost pin it down to the day, this smacking headlong into a cinderblock wall of reality. It was November of 1988, and basically I woke up one day and knew the band was over. One day I believed. The next day I didn't. That was about it.

What was there left to say? We had stuck it out and made records and toured. That alone was enough to leave plenty of people with egg on their faces. We had achieved a certain decent enough musical cohesion. We had even gotten on MTV. We had done it! We'd proved we were German shepherds in a dog-eat-dog world. Past this point we'd have to piss in the tall weeds all the time. It was going to take things like "vision" and "talent."

With the focus and clarity of any crazed zealot, I had always believed we would eventually be a great band. There is no point in *not* believing it. You've got to picture it before you can make it happen. You had better be obsessed and go after it with all your heart, because the odds are actually with you for a while in a strange way.

Everybody is awful when they start out, not just at music but at whatever they go for in life. No matter what it is you want to do: painters, archers, mafiosi, they all start at the bottom with all the other schmucks. Even savant prodigies have that first day when they don't know their asses from holes in the ground. Practice makes perfect, discipline makes your character and anything, *anything,* is possible for a young soul who believes in what they are doing.

Those first practices and wretched early gigs? Put them out of your mind the minute they go by. You don't just live in the now, you live in the three years from now! You don't hear how out-of-tune the guitar is *today,* because you can hear what's *gonna be.* Let the small-

minded around you deal with what *is*. That is how I lived every day of
my life, right up to November 1988, and that was when I guess
dreams just weren't good enough any more.

Four years had gone down since it was Toby and Skot and me in
my apartment on 12th and Park, bashing out R.E.M. covers and getting complaints from the theater majors downstairs. Four years.

Had it been fun? You bet your ass it had been fun! Grueling, to be
certain, but unbelievable fun. As a matter of fact, touring the country
had turned out to be so much fun that we had failed to progress one
whit as musicians, as writers, or as people since the whole rolling
cavalcade had begun. It was still fun, but just dry-kibble fun, bloodless, unfilling, momentary pleasures and nerve-center strokings. No
growth.

I know what tipped me off.

I was sitting in Tutt's living room one day hearing *Three Chords,
No Waiting*  on his cassette player, since dropping by his house was
the only way I could hear my own record. For the first time, a nag-
ging feeling enveloped me.

This record kinda . . . sucks.

I could blame Tutt for the production and Big for the mix, but
that was *my own* mediocre guitar playing: strings buzzing, in and out
of tune, bad beer-commercial distortion tone, clichéd licks. I had a
long way to go, a lot to learn, and I wasn't alone. Three years ago,
I'd have only heard what was gonna-be. Well, *gonna-be shoulda-
been* by now.

We all had different directions. Tutt understood us as a comic twist
on basic blue-collar arena rock, which was level-headed but dry. Joe
wanted to be Aerosmith, which bored me. Skot wanted to be Iggy Pop,
which at least meant he could be the mobile frontman and we wouldn't
have to teach him guitar parts any more. I wanted to be XTC, which
was completely out of touch with reality. Chris, when he was with us,
just wanted us all to be one big happy Soul Asylum and stop bitching.
And Billy, as far as anyone could tell, just wanted to go home.

And then I thought of other insurmountables, for what seemed the
first time ever.

There was the name. Government Cheese. A poverty metaphor
slapped on a bunch of suburban white guys. Gee, that was less than
brilliant! As a matter of fact, now that I thought of it, "unseemly"
wasn't a big enough word for that image. The more I thought about it,
the more it appalled me. Government Cheese! Why hadn't I ever con-

sidered all its ramifications before? How could I go three years and it never occur to me? What kind of sick bastard am I? Who thought that name up, anyway? Oh yeah, me.

And then, of course, there was Tutt. By this point there was no use even pretending about him any more. With him at the helm, we were untouchable. A sad consolation was that the only thing rescuing Tutt from complete music-industry pariah status was his own relative obscurity. He was working his way through the list, though. He'd meet somebody, insult them, throw a fit and we could cross another name off. I saw it over and over again.

And then there was my own unfortunate tendency to write songs about fish sticks, and comedy songs about drug use fifteen years after they were last *au courant.* You see, in rock and roll, you're either funny or you're not, and the minute you're funny, you're not rock and roll. Immediately, stamp 'em clowns and write 'em off.

It seemed that once I'd had my moment of epiphany on Tutt's couch with the cassette, all the other curtains rang down. Everywhere I turned, a new red flag was popping up with "It's over!" stamped on it. I chose at first to ignore it, and it wasn't long before ignoring the truth took so many mental calories out of every day there was precious little energy left to do anything else.

A real man would get up and leave, right? Not me. I was afraid I might be wrong. Maybe things were fine and I was just tired and suffering from a prolonged conscience attack brought on by inebriate, libidinous road behavior. Maybe that was what was going on here. But then I would think of how the next record sounded, and I would know the truth in my heart again.

And then I thought about how lucky we were. No one just forms a band and hits the road. The road has to *come get you.* It was a very lucky thing to be able to make a living this way; and only the vilest lackey would pick up his rucksack and bug out when the going got rough, right? So I stayed, or at least my body stayed. My mind went off looking for any sort of destructive distraction it could root out. I became a truffle-pig of bad habits.

So here I was, with the band I had dreamed of falling apart on me, my relationship with Beth and other various dalliances—romantic or not—in entropy. And I did exactly what I did when I played alone as a tot: classic passive, depressive behavior. I folded my arms and watched the whole thing go on like it was a movie, like I wasn't even part of it.

I smoked too much and drank way too much coffee and beer not to be full of shit in conversation, and I spent most of my evenings in smoky bars when I should have been home reading a book. I like bars. I liked them then, and I like them now. But you can't practice your guitar in one.

Beth and I had split up, sort of. I had my own half of a dump duplex off Kentucky Street. I cut up newspapers for curtains. One night, while I was out of town, I had a burglary. They pried open the back door, went through the house and didn't take a damn thing. I was now an object of pity for small-time criminals. That is where I was in life.

All the good times I had not had in high school? Well, I had pretty much passed everybody up, hadn't I? All those supercool, peer-group dudes in high school were eating my dust now. I played on the road and had a *good* time! I was a rotten husband and I hadn't even been married yet. I spent my money on cigarettes, staggering through back-porch keg sessions, engaged in some pseudo-intellectual conversation I wouldn't remember in the morning; I was pretty much an asshole. And then *this* had to happen. This . . . *realization.* We weren't going to be brilliant! We weren't the New Beatles. We would just be this little local band that came and went.

But people can't know that. The public must be deceived and pleased. Hi folks, everything's great. The record? Oh, we should know something next week. Thanks for asking, and have a lovely day.

Living a lie makes you crazy. Living in direct contradiction to all the morals you knew as a child makes you crazy. Being regularly disgusted with yourself makes you crazy. Doing them all at once makes you crazy, flustered and pretty busy. As I finally began to go honestly 'round the bend for the first time in my short life, I learned all these things. I thought I knew what crazy felt like already. I knew nothing. Low-grade depression is one thing. Crazy is a whole other deal altogether.

I stopped going out. Given that I was smoking cigars, few people missed me. I cut all my hair off and looked, as a friend noted, like some preacher's son in a Flannery O'Connor short story. That's good, I thought, since essentially I *am* one. Maybe I should blind myself and round out the whole mad, Southern picture.

I grew paranoid. I stopped seeing people, except during gigs. I sat in the living room with my guitar, writing confessional sop with embarrassing chord changes. The other guys stepped back and waited for me to work it out. Months started going by, and I wasn't working it out.

One day I had long hair, Peter Buck black vests and a belief. The next day I was a rock and roll atheist with short, greased-back hair, an overcoat and a cigar. I looked like a fey Polish mobster. Young folks don't like other young folks who smoke cigars. People tapped me on the shoulder and I jumped a foot in the air. I was nuts. I felt tremendous guilt. In 1988, I planted not one single tree. In 1987, I had helped not one lady across the street. In 1986, I had done nothing to help the homeless, or Big Brothers, or AIDS research, or voter registration. All I had done was fall in and out of a van, toe the company line, entertain folks when I petulantly consented to, follow my id and, in late 1988, collapse into a year of hermitage, an incubation of shame.

Peter Gabriel once shaved his head as a sort-of sackcloth-and-ashes thing, his open confession of marital infidelity. Then again, Peter Gabriel used to dress up as a sunflower onstage, with giant petals spreading out from his face. Cute.

The bald idea did strike me when I read about it, though. There was the purgative aspect of it, and I'd always been mildly curious as to what the top of my skull looked like anyway. But I still wasn't going to actually do it without making at least twenty bucks on a bet, I figured.

We were playing in Atlanta, at the White Dot. It was March of 1989. The record was still always coming out *next week,* six months of next weeks and counting. Ever since I'd crashed into my moment of realization, the gigs had sucked royally, one after another. I hadn't meant to sabotage anything, I just had a lot of trouble faking the orgasm. And Mr. Crowe's Garden was hanging around our gig tonight, Steve Gorman's bunch, only they were the Black Crowes by this point, signed to Def American and bound to be huge, at least for a few weeks, we figured. At the time, they were just the most recent smart-asses on the scene to score a deal.

I like the Black Crowes. They've got soul, and the two brothers seem to be as talented as they are ostentatiously dickheaded, thus justifying their art if not their lives, which, not knowing them, I can't comment on. The only one I ever knew was Steve. I don't remember talking to any of them that night. By this point, I knew just to avoid other bands and bandmembers out on the road. There are rules of cool you wouldn't even dream of among musicians on the road, and not a cool bone in my body. I learned just enough over time to keep from getting my ass kicked and I backed off from then on. Somebody pointed them out and I said "oh, that's nice"; besides, I had a half-pint of Wild Turkey in my back pocket and was well on the way to getting very negative for the rest of the evening.

We were last on a three-band bill and the middle band were flaming assholes. I can't remember their name now. I wish I could. We had worked with them before and wanted to kill them with pain before, as well. They were a five-piece, and their lead singer loved himself with tragic passion. Their stock-in-trade was to grab the middle slot and take eight days to set up their equipment, thus being the star attraction on Saturday night. The greedy bastards had done it before. It was dirty pool, but it worked like a charm. They started playing at midnight when they should have been on by 11:15.

So, we got onstage at 1:30. Half the crowd was gone, and we were angry and too beer-soaked to be worth much. Adding to that equation, we knew exactly what the Black Crowes were going to do. They had taken a front table—and there were a few to choose from. They were going to listen to our first thirty seconds, and, given the lateness of the hour, unless we immediately chain-sawed a live pig or something, they were going to get up and leave. Ahh, they suck. Let's go. We chainsawed no pork, and they gathered no moss.

So now my camel's back had been out-strawed. We'd been played for chumps and fingered as losers both in the same evening. This called for some completely unreasonable gesture on somebody's part, and I was the guy.

Act one. I figured I would try to smash a guitar to end the night. I had never done it before. I discovered why Pete Townshend started with fragile Rickenbackers and worked his way up to solid-bodies; it gave me a whole new perspective and respect for the solid, durable workmanship of the Gibson Les Paul Junior, and it tore the absolute shit out of my lower back. The pain was intense and immediate.

Pain or no, I got three or four good swings in before Skot intercepted. A great stage move it may have been, but we hadn't the money to replace a Junior with P-90 pickups, so he caught the guitar by the neck on the final downswing and nipped the whole idea in the bud. My back was howling in pain and my arms were trembling in post-trauma, like a guy in a cartoon shaking back and forth from striking a gong. I was in pieces and the guitar was fine. Rarely have I felt like less of a man. All of the knobs worked, and the capper was to plug it back in and discover that it was still reasonably in tune.

We couldn't find a hotel room until Marietta. It was ridiculously late, around four-thirtyish. The other guys settled in front of a television set—*Shane* was on—and got ready for bed. They didn't notice what I was doing until it was too late to turn back. I'd gotten out all my blue Gillette disposable razors. I rooted around in my bag and found my Edge for Sensitive Skin. I regarded my head of hair, somewhat grown out from last fall's Pentecostal 'do, and sprayed a great glop of Edge all over my Nixon peak. I took the first blue razor and went to work.

Act two.

Chris was slumped in front of the television, perfecting his imitation of the little kid in *Shane* along with Skot. It was a contest to see who could do it more high-pitched. Then he looked around and caught my reflection in the bathroom mirror. I looked like Dr. Frank N. Furter from *Rocky Horror Picture Show*. Lots of hair on the sides, bald as a damn cue ball all the way back to the crown of my skull.

Chris's scream tipped off the others. Billy hopped up on top of bed and started jumping and screaming "He's doin' it! He's doin' it!"

I had threatened to before, and now I was making good. I was shaving my gol-danged head! Good eggs that they were, everybody took up a position on the various sides I couldn't see. What a bunch of guys I had around me! They wanted to make sure I was shaved *real good!* And I was, by golly. We crashed just as the sun was dawning, with everybody laughed sore and tired and me very bald.

Aw shit. Beth was going to slaughter me. This was definitely going to turn our on-again, off-again deal way the hell off. That's me in the mirror, isn't it? I had to put on my glasses and look for sure. The earpieces stuck in no hair as I slid them across my smooth head. I looked back in the mirror. Good God, I'm Gandhi.

I discovered in the spring of '89 that hair just beginning to grow back tends to stick in the pillowcase, and drag it around as you toss and turn in bed. Your head and the pillowcase become like Velcro. Also, I noticed that I got cold quickly without hair, and always had to keep a thick cap with me.

*Three Chords, No Waiting* did at last make its debut to the world. It was rather off-beat: a studio effort, recorded in forty-five minutes live with an audience that was exceedingly well-miked. The back cover was nothing but a strange and ridiculous stream of verbiage, courtesy of me. I wrote and wrote and wrote. One perusal gives away my state of mind, trying to make excuses for the band, the record, me—everything. At the time, I really felt that if there were detailed liner notes telling what kind of record this was and that it wasn't really the debut album but in a default way, it is and I kinda wish it was this but instead it is *this* and yadda yadda yadda . . . and I was hoping in some demented way that people would read this crap and say "Oh! *That's* how I should listen to this record!" A week before it was printed, I was still revising it. This was not rational behavior.

I imagine there are former college radio staffers out there, and plenty of other media folks, who to this day shudder with fear at the mention of the Reptile name. They were murderous, bloodthirsty bastards, and that is a compliment. Tutt would do anything to get a record played. He threatened a picket-line around D-98 in Bowling Green if they didn't play the record. They didn't, and one of the station's employees took three of their five *Three Chords* promo copies and sold them at Pac-Rat's, pocketing the money for himself. On a national level, things were, thankfully, more hopeful.

"Camping on Acid" made the college singles top-forty chart although it was never actually available in that form. The album itself made the thirties, started back down, and then did an almost unheard-of resurgence, starting back up the charts. It gave the band a whole new lease on life, and I must admit that my hardened opinion of Tutt softened ever so slightly when I could look at the CMJ chart and see Government Cheese, right there between Pussy Galore and Vomit Launch.

This boost of morale was not yet in evidence the day we released the record, however. We had another party at Picasso's, and again there was press and television, even a letter of congratulations from the Governor, Wallace Wilkinson. I remember Bowling Green mayor Patsy Sloan asking me, somewhat nervously, "You guys aren't any real *druggy band,* are you?" "No, no! Not at all." I laughed as I took a Sharpie marker and signed a record for her, right next to where it said "Camping On Acid."

Compared to the *Bowling Green* party almost two years before, however, the mood was sullen. We did one of those shows that were increasingly common, where we didn't look at each other, like four guys playing instruments in an elevator, looking up at the floor numbers ticking by.

I had my own most shameful moment a few weeks later at the Birmingham Botanical Gardens. We had somehow been booked to play the graduation party for a medical school. This was our Spinal Tap at the Air Force base scene.

Any other time before, when things had gotten this bad I'd always done something that was at least destructive in a semi-interesting, life-as-art kind of way. I would stand at my mike and talk unceasingly 'til people threw things at me. I would disrobe. Whatever. Not tonight. This night in Birmingham I simply did . . . nothing.

Nothing.

I stood there and played my instrument and didn't look up except to sing. I was the marital partner withholding conjugal rights to the bed. I simply offered nothing at all that would qualify as a performance. I did some lowlife things in my time on the road with Government Cheese. I kissed our manager's ass and hated him behind his back, I did drugs, I drove drunk, I cheated on my wife, I took pot buds out of people's bags when they weren't looking, but this was the lowest of the low for me. That night in Alabama, I became . . . dull.

Flat, deadly dull.

Joe quit the band that night. He had a speech all rehearsed to lay on me, about how he'd really thought I'd had what it took and he was sorry he was wrong. But he couldn't find me after the show to deliver it. I'd just taken off, wandering around the gardens, smoking, cursing and kicking things. The next day, we just continued, with no mention of anything. Just a little more scum at the rim top of everybody's pot where it had boiled up to the top and then cooled back down again. Everybody'd had it, not just me.

We shot a video for "Mammaw Drives the Bus". This time there were no big crews and tons of extras, just Billy's little super-8 camera and a 16-mm that Santos Lopez operated. It was a charming, almost homely response to the the sleek, big-time "Face to Face". Most of it was done in Billy's parents' front yard in Horse Cave, since it was much more doable to come to Mammaw than have her come to us. We got close-ups of her behind the wheel acting like she was driving, then far away shots of Joe doing real driving in a white Mammaw wig.

Billy and Santos did the editing and it was sent off to MTV in New York. A few weeks later, Tutt said we had been given the thumbs-up.

I have heard of people claiming they saw it, people from far-off places who have described scenes in the video accurately, but I have never actually spoken to one of them. I heard MTV used the music as background in an Earth Day special. Again, there has never been rock-hard proof of that furnished to me. As a matter of fact, to be honest, I've never seen irrefutable evidence that ''Mammaw Drives the Bus'' ever made it up there in the mail.

* * * *

# part three

## the road home

# 22

# the final descent

*A year goes by. Nothing changes at all. The gigs come and go. The contracts drag on. The sun rises and sets. I'm walking down the street in Bowling Green, stalking the wild antidepressant, with my long stringy hair blowing in my face, wearing my ratty old jeans and the green army jacket Skip gave me. I cross at a light where a Lexus is stopped. A mom with two kids is in it. As I walk in front, I hear the "kattala-dunk!" of four doors locking simultaneously. I stop for a moment in the middle of the intersection and smile. This is quite an achievement for the preppy, myopic dweeb. For the first time in my life, my physical presence scares the crap out of another human being. It's the coolest thing that happens all year.*

In the summer of '90, everything came home. Our troubadour cesspool lifestyle jetted and spattered like frothy shit-mousse on the sides of the tank. The summer of 1990 was the tour from hell. The Nightmare of the Reptile. Hot months of asphalt mirages, warm beers, broken bones, smashed vehicles, hangovers, delirium, great gigs, awful gigs, vomit, confusion, moral and physical poverty, tantrums and sad resignations. We were the command module re-entering Earth's atmosphere, a shield on our ass blazing up sparks past our ears, and all around us the feeling we had to only tilt slightly the wrong way and all would fry.

The eighties were over. The gig circuit was really starting to suck. Money was drying up. Our price was going down. It was partly the recession, and partly what was obvious for anyone looking at us. We were fried like won tons.

There had been literally hundreds of one-nighters, arguments on and off-stage, kamikaze shooters and mornings waking up wondering where the hell we were. We played all the time. We had for years.

That was what we did. There was no sense in talking strategy, how it was useless to play Birmingham on Tuesday for six people. It was *what we did!* Get in the van and go play. For years now, every weekend. Get in the van and go play. The same places, in the same two-mule towns, for less and less money. We didn't work part-time jobs. We played for a *living!* To back up now and get jobs would be admitting a crushing defeat.

Eviction notices, however, will beat out being crushed any day of the week so far as motivation goes. The hierarchy of needs and all that.

Skot was first to capitulate. He went to Nat's and got his old job back. Chris went out to Tender Touch Auto Wash and got a job with Pat, and to their incredulity, Billy and I weren't far behind them. And there I was, wiping down car bumpers on Scottsville Road.

I preferred vacuuming to wiping, which was sun-burning, shin-splinting shit work by comparison. Vacuuming meant bending over a lot, but you were at least in the shade, under the vacuum bay overhang, and there were slack times not enjoyed by the wipers. So I schemed my way into the vacuuming clique. Billy was already there. Chris stayed up front. He actually preferred wiping.

If anyone had told me when I started that I would still have that vacuuming gig in two years, I might have just jammed a shotgun under my chin and blasted away right then and there.

We always thought our big break was two months around the corner, or that we would make some sort of sensible decision in a short period of time. No decisions came. We washed cars and sometimes the van picked us up on the way to a gig. And we came back and we washed cars some more. We would leave on the road for several days and come back and wash some more cars. When it rained, we got to sit at home and be glad we weren't washing cars. And we never thought we would still be doing it at the end of that summer.

The car wash people were generally full of far more interesting stories than you could ever hear in any office job. You'd be wiping down a bumper next to a guy with half a short story bic-pen tattooed all over him. You would get acquainted. "So, where ya from?" "Jail, man. Just got out! Man, you play guitar in the Cheese, doncha? *Whutter yew dewin HERE? Yew motherfuckers JAM!*" Well, thanks. High five.

One guy was the Valium king of the Mid-south. He sucked on them like Life Savers. Another lived with his mom in a motel room and used to get greedy with anticipation an hour before closing, because Mom would have a *cold fifth* waiting for him back in the room. He'd show up on acid in the breakroom at seven in the morning hollering "The world OWES me, gott-dammit!" There was Howard, who ran cars through the back entrance and operated the high-pressure hose—a skilled job, because you didn't want anybody with that weapon peeling off paint like I had a tendency to. Howard had a beard and never took his cap off. Then there was Roy, who took everybody's abuse. You'd feel bad for him, but he'd keep walking into it. Then there was Wormy, who was fifteen and essentially supporting himself. There was Billy Fritz, who had a dance named after him. You sang the "Twist" tune: *"C'mon baby, let's do the Fritz! C'mon baby, let's do the Fritz! Just hunch on over . . . and walk like this!"*

There was Billy Basham, who owned every Metallica T-shirt ever printed and drove a car with TRIPPEN spelled across the windshield. Ricardo, who was nicknamed Julio, I think, just because a guy had to have a nickname, even if it was no more or less exotic than his real one. There was Robbie, who fed his dog gunpowder "cause it makes 'em crazy, you didn't know that?" There were Lisa, Gail and Karen staying in the back, trying to keep order, and Darrell and Russell up front.

It was a musician-friendly job. We washed cars when we we could and, if we weren't there, then the managers all figured we must be playing someplace, and most of them dug that we were the Cheese, as far as I could ever tell.

Over the years an acceptance of us had pervaded the real town of Bowling Green, the off-campus people who would just as soon forget there was a college anywhere around. The art scene on campus may have burnt out on us, but the real citizens of town were proud of us now. We'd met them halfway, learned to get in tune, hold a steady beat and rock like men without any bullshit, and because of that we had become something to them.

The Chamber of Commerce had done an article on us when "Camping on Acid" went college top-thirty nationwide. We were in the brochure they sent out. A half-page article and our publicity picture. This, after "Camping On Acid". Go figure.

Some mornings, I just didn't have it in me to go out there to the wash. It wasn't the work. It was the look you got when you opened the door for an old friend from school, some girl you hadn't seen in five or ten years, and you had to ask her if she needed full service.

Inside and out? And she would ask how the band was doing, and I would say "Great! The band's doing just great! Would you like an air freshener today? *I'll have to charge you extra for the mud!*"

Whacking a car seat with a big orange vacuum wand left a guy with plenty of time for reflection. I'd just get in the car, suck up Froot Loops out of the upholstery (you could always tell the cars with young kids in them), and just take a lotta stock in myself and everybody else.

Ort was staying back around Georgia nowadays, looking after his mom. Skip was somewhere in the United States or Canada, selling comic books with his girlfriend Cathy. Sweeney listened to records and watched basketball and swore one of these days he was going to have had enough of this pissant town. Gorman was off getting famous. Beth was on at 6 & 10 weeknights. I was working at a fucking car wash. Mom and Dad were getting grandkids by all the kids but me. The Berlin Wall came down. We fought a war that was timed to start with the evening news. Gene Simmons was breathing fire and getting a gut.

Whack the seat covers once for the Georgia boys. R.E.M. How did those bastards get so lucky? I swear, they had to be the four luckiest sonsabitches that ever found each other. Every record they made did better than the one before it. They never compromised jack shit. They tried and tried to make records that would stymie their career, and every time out they sold more and got bigger. I still liked them alright, but they weren't any religion any more. Their ascent was so perfect and the music so consistently good that it got boring after a while. Michael Stipe started enunciating his lyrics and they turned out to be (can you guess?) *great*, and Peter Buck kept learning how to play guitar and it turned out he had it in him to be *(SuuurrrPRISE!)* great, and Stipe became the Great God of all things politically correct, and this happened after we'd spent all these years watching them, thinking "Yeah, I can do that. Yeah, they're just those guys from Georgia. We can be that good, that smart, that cool." Fuck 'em! Just fuck 'em! What could they brag of that we couldn't, I'd wonder, whacking with my vacuum wand. What in the world made them so special, aside from having a great manager and being, oh, about eighty-seven thousand times better than we were?

Whack at the floor mat for the local inspirations. Jason and the Scorchers had stumbled under the weight of all the usual rock and roll maladies: indifferent record companies, bickering, playing two hundred gigs a year just to come home and say "Broke! Whaddya mean we're broke?!" Nobody gave harder or longer than they did. I saw them every tour, and over time even Jason, clean-living Jason, started looking a little crispy around the edges, and by that point the other three looked like they'd been hung up in a smokehouse. I saw some tired shows and was sad about it, even though a worn-out Jason and the Scorchers still mopped the floor with most everything else out there. Warner was a guitar hero now, with longer hair, a big stack of amps and all that goes with being a guitar hero. One day Jeff the bass player went out for coffee and didn't come back. He quit? He got asked to leave? Who knew, and what difference did it make?

They made another record as a five-piece for another label. It was alright. They went to Europe and—from what I'd heard—just came back on separate planes and didn't talk any more. There was no press release, no final gig, no ceremonial pyre. They were just . . . *gone,* just like the other ninety-nine point seven percent of the bands who don't achieve R.E.M.ness. They just got shot out of the sky, and you could send the purple hearts to any relatives you could find. Jason and the Scorchers were gone. You want justice? Fuck you. There is no justice.

Whack the wand on the arm-rest for myself. By then people were writing our epitaph, too. Oh yeah, the Cheese, those guys, the fish-stick guys, what kinda deal did they sign, anyway? *"They were! They were Supermen. . . ."*

It had been a year since *Three Chords* had come out, and we hadn't recorded a thing with Tutt since. We'd done a bunch of our own demos and paid for them ourselves, and Tutt didn't even want to know about them because they didn't involve him. He seemed to think we were just going to wait around like placid little mice until he figured we should record again. As far as we could tell, he was still thinking the sessions from two years ago were our next album. I hadn't even *heard* that stuff in two years. God help us.

I could kill eight hours whacking seat covers and rationalizing about having signed with Scott Tutt. What possessed us to sign five years of our lives away to this guy? What in the hell were we *thinking?*

Well, I'd remember, we'd needed hope, and Scott Tutt was never—and I mean never—at a loss for a motivational seminar off the top of his head, even if it was peppered with bullshit speculation and/or flat-out lies. But who was I kidding? We'd known who he was when we'd signed that deal, and we'd known *what* he was, if we'd ever wanted to think hard about it. I knew it the first day in his office. All it took was a good look at Scott Tutt to tell the difference between his promises and how much he could have really delivered. He had the publishing rights on four Alabama tunes and some jerkwater minor hit Roy Clark and Anne Murray had done. That was it. That was his working capital. Had it ever been enough to finance *an album a year for five years*? For us, Jerry Dale McFadden, Susan Marshall and the Dusters? And manage us all? And do everything in-house? Sure. It was possible. It was technically possible for a cow to jump over the moon if the cow's back legs were strong enough to muster the thrust to push it out of the earth's atmosphere. I wouldn't bet on it, though.

We had signed away the farm and left it up to Tutt to shop deals for us, for big booking agents and a bigger label and T-shirts, etc., and we always wondered whether or not he was actually doing it. He would say, "Be patient, guys. Remember, you're always fresh, new and untested so long as a major label's not dropped you yet."

Piss on that. By now, we just wanted a chance, even if it was a guaranteed failure, where a label signed us for a tax loss and we got a two-week tour of the West Coast on a bus and then it was all over. Slamming the coffin lid in such a way was better than the holding pattern life had become. The pressure would be off; we would have failed, and could get on with our lives.

It had sunk in fully how we were being used to advance Tutt's interests rather than the other way around. The Dusters and The Cheese were Tutt's two main playing cards for his entire grand "Dist. by" vision: to manage a major band *and* get Reptile a big distribution deal, *and* make Tutt's mark as a record producer, *and* to do this and to do that as all part of *one big deal.* That was his dream, for the sleeve credits to read *Produced by Scott Tutt for Reptile Records, dist. by Somebody Huge, All Songs Scott Tutt Music BMI, A Scott Tutt Production in cooperation with Scott Tutt Enterprises,* and until he was convinced that no major label was going to give him all that to get either the Dusters or us, he would not let either of us go to anyone.

He was never going to get that dream deal in a million years, either. No sane major label executive in the United States was ever going to let Scott Tutt produce a record. But until one did, neither

Government Cheese nor the Dusters were going *anywhere*. And there wasn't a damn thing in the world we could do about it. Fuck it. You want justice? Watch *Matlock*.

I'd whack at the steel floors of the pickup trucks and think about Susan Marshall. She was still a sweet person, five feet tall with a round top of curly blonde hair, but she never ever ate, and that Barbara Mandrell face had stress lines way beyond her years. Susan had eight different jobs at Reptile and no life. She was a country recording artist, Tutt's secretary, Tutt's girlfriend, a record promotions agent and a booking agent for the bands, Tutt's cook, Tutt's housekeeper, and on and on. The running gag was that she worked only half a day on Sundays, twelve hours.

She'd get up in the morning and go to work downstairs, and not be done until sometimes one or two the next morning. She had no world outside Reptile, no pals at a bar, no girlfriends to have lunch with, nothing but Reptile and Tutt.

Tutt used to order Reptile's greeting cards in black and white, and when they came in, Susan would sit up until the wee hours with a green Sharpie marker, inking in the green parts of the lizard on the front of each one. It would be two-thirty in the morning, and she'd still be coloring between the lines for her man. All she wanted to be was a country singer.

I could whack the seats and think about the other guys. By this point, we were all pretty darn tired of each other. Everybody knew each other's little innocuous habits that you don't think about until one day you realize you're going to kill the miserable bastard if he ever does it again, and we all had one big thing that drove the others crazy. I was a first-class moper, always looking miserable and bringing everybody down. Billy had gotten to where he considered a shower and ten beers a full day. Joe was chewing everybody out like a football coach, and Skot had grown incapable of uttering a complete sentence without some withering barb of sarcasm swinging from the end of it like a cudgel on a chain. Whack the seat covers and catalog the years of slights, gibes and other meaningless shit that takes on meaning when over-examined.

Someone gets at you, yells at you, whatever, and you mark down a little notch in their column. You owe them one snide remark. And if you don't aim and fire right away, the moment gets lost and you wind up with a debt burden. After a day or so the anger at the person dissipates, but there's a little film around the top of your pot that wasn't there before. Then somebody aims and fires at you again, and damned if you don't get a return shot off in time again! The coals in your oven flame on some residue there that ignites well, like desert camel dung.

And then it passes again, but there's more film at the top of your pot, and a little bit of lingering smolder, and it happens again and again. And you vow on your mother's grave that you will not be snapped at, gotten at, embarrassed by, told what to do, sneered at, irritated by or whatever by this lowdown sonofabitch, or any of the other lowdown sonsabitches, one single more time without retaliation.

You rehearse retorts in your head, applicable to different situations. You practice with flashcards in your brain. You spend your whole day in a mental three-point stance. You're ready to pounce. You won't be gotten at again. Then one day somebody says something like . . . "Hello" and you say "Yeah? *Fuck you!*" Add beer. Shake well. Take the act on the road.

Now it would stand to reason that, considering Tutt hadn't recorded us for an elephant's gestation period, the contracts were good for little more than wiping on said pachyderm's butt. After all, Tutt *did* have to record us once a year. The contracts said so. True enough, but mitigating circumstances mitigated the hell out of those circumstances.

Nothing was so simple as going down to the courthouse and suing someone. There was no agreement among the band as to how to sue, what for, who was going to pay for it, or what we'd expect to gain.

To complicate matters further, for the past two years, Joe had been working at Reptile.

It was his job—a place to go in the morning. It kept the parents off his back and let him know he was working for a living. Joe was a firm team player. The Cheese was a company, and Tutt was the boss, and that was that. Yeah, Tutt's behavior bothered him too, but by this point, Reptile's work (strictly on behalf of Government Cheese) was partly his work too. Hence, a screw-you to Reptile partially stuck to him when flung that way. Nobody liked it that way—not him, not me—but a kind of line did get drawn in the sand eventually. He was getting a first-mate role thrust on his shoulders as the rest of us toothless swabbies were plotting mutiny.

The fans knew what time it was, though, and eschewed diplomacy. Somebody in Murray, Kentucky, was printing and giving out

*Piss On Scott Tutt* buttons. I still have one somewhere. Mr. Big knew what time it was. Suddenly, one day we all found out that he and Tutt weren't speaking any more. He didn't run sound at Reptile gigs any more, he didn't engineer Tutt's sessions. He was just gone.

But if we had to deal with Tutt, he had to deal in turn with the aluminum and brown glass recycling program Government Cheese was running. It was a common sight-gag occurrence to open the sliding door on the van and have several malt pop vessels fall out onto the asphalt. Beer wasn't an indulgence any more. It had become a way of life. We didn't hit the stage bombed every night, but we always hit the pillows that way, in motel rooms done in early longneck, with empty six-pack cartons everywhere and the remnants of ice melting in the sink.

And what was I still doing here? Didn't I have a moment of clarity about eighteen goddamn months ago? Didn't I realize that I could blame Tutt all day long and it wouldn't change the fact that we weren't exactly the *new Zeppelin* or anything?! What was I still doing here? It was the dream. That sled was way gone, and I was just running to keep up. I couldn't undo my wrists from the straps now. They'd bitten through to the bone. There was still, I found, some crazy faith in me that this would all work out someway, somehow. There was no letting go of the dream now. No way in hell do you let go of the dream. You just hope someday it lets go of you.

The Night of the Reptile tour was conceived as a throwback to the days of Dick Clark package tours, or the Stiff Records tours in the late Seventies. A rolling cavalcade for the whole summer: Government Cheese, the Dusters, Susan Marshall. The whole label. T-Shirts, records and stickers available at the door. Come one, come all.

As noble an undertaking as it was in intent, its execution made the summer of 1990 a savage, drunken sleighride to hell. I will never forget a bit of what little I can remember of it.

It was flawed from the outset. A summer tour of Southern college towns was a terrible idea. The audience was at the beach, and the only question was whether the tour would lose a little money or hemorrhage great gouts of it.

Business being down was the reason for the tour, as Tutt saw things, a real "in numbers there is strength" sort of operation. The Dusters and Government Cheese together could command a bigger price at the door than either could alone. However, the price would have to be double our regular fares to put us right back where we started, and this wasn't going to happen in the summer in Tuscaloosa.

And then there was Susan. Yes, the Susan Marshall Band would open every single date. Oh boy. So take our door price and spread it over the care and feeding of another four-piece band who would have to work their way up to drawing no one.

Six weeks. Good night or bad night, four hotel rooms, three vans, and whopping ten-dollar per-diems every day on the road for a grand total of sixteen people. Okay, make that fifteen.

One day, the Dusters' soundman, Todd, strolled into Tutt's office and made a supremely ridiculous weekly salary demand for doing the tour, four hundred a week or something like that. Tutt turned several shades of purple, called Todd a number of choice names and threw him out. It had been calculated. Todd saw it all coming, and there was no way he was going on that tour.

On paper, by some magic, it all balanced out. Tutt could sit at his computer and calculate the guaranteed wage from the club versus the expenses. And it all looked like it would just barely work.

But one blown tire could upset the cart. One blown gig could turn it over. All it was going to take was one thing: one stiffed guarantee, one medical emergency, one wrecked van, one unanticipated day off. Just one little thing. And every one of them was going to wind up happening, too.

The tour started at Picasso's and wound up in Nashville six weeks later, so at least the first and last gigs would probably be pretty good. T-shirts were printed. White ink on black pre-shrunk cotton, naming all the acts, with the big Reptile dwarfing all the acts' names. On the back were all the dates.

A big booth with banners was set up at every gig. It would amuse us how this booth, with a big green Reptile Records banner and sectioned, varnished-wood, quick-assemble pieces, seemed to take priority over the band equipment. Brian Rohrer ran the booth. He lasted four dates, after which he tore off running across a hillside without looking behind him. Once he was gone, unfortunately, the responsibility of running the booth fell to various band members. There would be intense jockeying and illness-feigning so as not to be fingered as the sap who got to be the cool musician onstage one minute and the nurtz behind the counter the next.

There were two guys on the crew, Chris and Chief. Chief had

roadied for the Dusters since he was about fifteen, which is right around when he started being able to raise a beard in half a day and get into bars without being carded. Chief had a smile for everybody and a reputation just behind Bishop Sheen on the nice-guy scale. I don't think he was quite 21 on this tour. He might have been, but just barely, if he was.

Chris Sherlock was the Dusters' drummer then, and a great guy, a genuine human being. A real rocker, with long black hair, real skinny with a lot of energy and a great smile. Sherlock loathed Tutt. It drove him crazy to breathe the same air as the guy. Hiding it took all his mental energy and he didn't hide it very well. It wasn't long into the tour that recruitment started for the various camps.

There were the Reptile folks, the middle-of-the-roaders and the Tutt-haters, for whom Sherlock was a titular point. The Tutt-haters had secret meetings where they drank away their frustrations and wondered why the others couldn't see this man was leading us all to hell. The Reptile people seemed to be genuinely unaware of any problems. The middle-of-the-roaders ate nervous meals and wondered who was who.

One thing made an awesome difference those first dates of the tour. The Cheese van stereo lived again. Creedence be damned!

For years everyone had been bitching, and no one would pay to get it fixed, so one day I did. It's probably the only thing I paid outright for in the history of the band. I took that damn van down to some stereo place and got the cassette player fixed, the left speaker re-connected, the whole works. Charged it. The whole atmosphere in the van brightened up. We all brought tapes. Being lifted out of one-speaker, classic-hits radio did as much to keep that tour going as anything. *Physical Graffiti* from Zeppelin, *Black & Blue* from the Stones, *Tim* from the Replacements, Big Star's *Sister Lovers* and Ice-T's "The Girl Tried To Kill Me" will be forever linked in my memory with that van and that tour.

The New Daisy Theater in Memphis—a huge place, approximately nine hundred and fifty times the size needed to accommodate the people who showed up. A fourth act on the bottom of the bill, the Rock Roaches, were a curious quartet. Two Latin-looking types and two Germanics, all wearing Beatles-type matching suits they had apparently owned for years. The bass player was either not the original guy or had gained a lot of weight, because the buttons were bursting on his skin-tight suit. Billy kept calling them the Roach Rockers onstage, which made me feel bad for them until I came offstage to find they had drunk all of our beer.

Forrester's in Oxford. Packed. Some wag cranked on the heat, and people were being carried out and dumped on the sidewalk in limp, wet heaps.

Kat Man Doo in Puryear, Tennessee, just south of Murray, Kentucky, on the wet side of the border. We didn't want to be playing there. Home was the Big Apple up the road, but Reptile had gotten into some argument with the owner there, so here we were in this redesigned aerodrome quonset hut with its mix of collegiates, Bubbas, and dangerous people.

Billy and Sherlock were becoming quite close, with a lot of commonly held opinions. Skot was increasingly furious. He had definite ideas how a tour should be run, and this was not the way. He knew how a manager did business by now. He was no babe in the woods any more. He wasn't seeing things go down properly, and hadn't for a long while. There were already enough people out here on the road wondering where the pot of gold was at the end of this fucking rainbow. C'mon! Where is it? There had already been enough frustrations. Five more weeks of this tour? At ten dollars a day? No way! That night, getting dressed in the attic alcove of Kat Man Doo, Skot mentioned the notion of quitting to me for the first time.

As I remember, he asked that if he bailed out, perhaps by faking some mysterious tropical disease, would I hold his job open 'til the end of the tour? I asked him what made him think I was hanging around if he bugged out? Fuck you, pal! You go, I go. Thank you, he said. That's touching.

So we did a tense gig. Three songs in, Tutt walked onstage and completely stopped the show. He seized the moment to point out the booth with the Philly Eagles-colored Reptile banner and all the purchasable goods therein. He stopped the show cold for this. Skot was so pissed he heaved his mike stand at Tutt. It missed by inches, and Tutt gave no notice that he even saw it. It was the first open act of revolt. The atmosphere onstage was like a one-hundred-degree kitchen with the all the gas jets on the stove turned all the way up for ten days. No one had to light a match. Just *think* of one for a second.

We got to the end, hauled Chris onstage to play Skot's guitar, and swung into "Search and Destroy". Skot was a raging shaman loaded on white crosses and fury. He was all over the stage. He couldn't have been more mobile with a jet pack on his back. He was ready to kill, run his head into a wall, eat dirt and hurt somebody. He was alive!

The tempo raced. Faster and faster! I jumped back, hit a wild chord and ran my forearm across all the amp knob dials. Suddenly, every knob was 10, 10, 10, 10, 10, 10, 10. Chris was banging the shit out of Skot's guitar. Harder! Faster! Louder! Skot was rolling on the floor, diving into the audience, just going bats.

Those times when you got completely lost in the noise, the rhythm and clang would begin to spin the whole room. It made everything worthwhile. The Perfect Moment. When everybody was kicking ass and I was thinking inside "Oh, yes! Yes! *This* is the reason I do this! There IS still a reason." We had it. We'd needed it. And then, right at the end of the song, when everything was rocking so hard and beautiful—train wreck.

Billy lost the ending. He didn't know where he was. The song skittered to a stop like a runaway truck coming down Monteagle Mountain too fast, slamming into the sand, coming to an impotent end of the line.

I looked around. The music was over. The audience, which rarely knows a mistake at jet-airplane volume, was going bananas. Joe was up out of his drum chair, furiously hurling sticks at Billy's feet, and screaming curses I was too deaf from noise-aftershock to make out. The moment was *over!*

Aw Dammit! Okay, okay. Now I'm pissed. I was pissed at Billy for blowing the ending. I was pissed at Joe for reacting this way. I was pissed at Skot and if you give me a second I'll think of a damn good reason, and I never wanted to see any of them ever again. And the first person I never wanted to see again was Scott Tutt.

Option #1: Break up just to get out of the tour. Option #2: Sue to get out of our contracts as soon as the tour was over, if we made it that far. Option #3: Get four guns and three bullets, load all but one of them, pass them out and blow each others' pathetic brains out at point-blank range, with the cold blue metal barrels poking into blanched-out temple skin. Whoever got the empty gun could sell the van and make up a story for the police.

On to The Nick in Birmingham, Alabama. The Nick was a great club in some ways. The staff was superb, and anyone wanting a hint of danger could simply go out the front door. We pulled into the lot once just as a crack deal had gone bad and one guy's ear had gotten either cut or bitten off. The main problem with the Nick was that no one ever went there on the nights we played.

Solomon's in Tuscaloosa was part of a strip of clubs across the street from the University. The clubs do a bang-up business, and each one has a band. Often there will be a band inside and another out back on an outside stage. It was the University of Alabama, Roll Tide and all that. Fantastic-looking women, handsome, scrubbed young men. All of them had two beers and got paralytically stupid, but they looked great while getting that way.

It happened every time we played there. In Tuscaloosa, the students carefully examined which bands were where on the strip. Who is playing here or there? Who's at the Tusk? The Chukker? Where's the Dead band? The reggae? Where's the original rock band? They would judiciously survey the whole scene, make their decision, pay the cover (if there was one), and once inside, pay absolutely no attention to the band at all. It happened this night just like it always had. We did our show while the audience did their usual autistic wall-hugging beersuck routine. We finished up with "People Who Died." I swung my big Les Paul out of the way, grabbed my crotch and shook it so hard I racked myself. *"Fuck you, Tuscaloosa!"* I shouted, and the next thing I know, I was being restrained in the dressing room after having broken about fifteen beer bottles against the wall.

Bangtown in Chattanooga. Mainstreet in Murfreesboro. The Tip Top in Huntsville.

And the second week was over. Tempers were, if not cool, at least incubating in some docile manner. If things stayed this much in control, maybe we could cruise. Of course they wouldn't, though. Guys pulling down ten dollars a day make for a 39-gallon eight-ball side pocket of stress sooner or later.

We traveled in three vans and kept in touch via CB radio. Tutt's CB fed back like a bad Bach trumpet whenever the mike was keyed. Communicating with their van got to be so loathsome that we stopped doing it, and kept them from contacting *us* by having me give dramatic readings over the CB. Day after day, night after night, I keyed open the mic and read from whatever cheap paperback was around, totally monopolizing the frequency. One night I recited the first scenes of *The Godfather* from memory, Bonasera's intoductory bit followed by Brando's first lines. I stopped, and some far-off voice— not one of us—crackled over. "Keep goin'. Don't stop now."

Billy and Sherlock pooled per diems and came up with the Night of the Reptile Diet Plan: Coffee for breakfast, vodka for lunch and a sensible dinner.

Three days off. The car wash and the girlfriends. Three days of Billy and Skot avoiding the landlord. Billy was losing his mind with money worries, getting up early to go vacuum at Tender Touch on every day off, whacking seat covers and cursing nonstop. I kept getting stuck up front, wiping and getting a sunburn on the back of my legs.

Thursday, June 28th: Ella Guru's in Knoxville. A good gig. Joe's brother Toad put us all up at his massive hilltop apartment complex, where things got foggy. Toad lived in a huge house subdivided into many, many apartments. The building was in three wings that surrounded the pool in the back on three sides. Toad moved in halfway through college, and several years later he was still there. I couldn't blame him. Everyone in the building knew each other, and the collective fun was enough to knock the most driven pre-law student off course.

A jam session in one room went on until three or so. Then there were the eight people in a dark room with a bootleg of the Dead in Hamilton, Ontario. It was the second night, second set, and this obnoxious but very beautiful blonde girl in a mini skirt was getting everyone to dance to it, offering running commentary on the Dead genius. *"Oh! Listen to Garcia's lick coming up!"* Give her credit. She knew this tape, and there would be the lick. *"Oh! Listen to this drum fill!"* and there it would be. I would have enjoyed it a lot better had she shut the hell up, but she was tripping her pert little boobies loose and so I had to excuse her. All the lights were out and everyone was dancing. She insisted on it. The only way to get her off your back was to simply stand up and dance some goofy, loose-limbed shuffle.

I woke up on a couch at eight-ish with this same obnoxious girl standing over my head, screaming that she'd lost her car keys. I take it she found them, because when I woke up again she was gone and everyone else was in the pool. I wound up playing guitar on Dylan tunes with Mike, who'd wind up the lead singer of the Screamin' Cheetah Wheelies in a few years. A day off in a life that wasn't really going anywhere, but seemed to have stopped in a very pleasant place for the moment.

Louisville, Kentucky. Huntington, West Virignia.

Three weeks into it, three weeks left, and Skot Willis was one day away from his ticket home. He would have been glad to go, but he might have thought twice, given the way it would happen and the amount of solid food he would be passing up for a while.

Wednesday, July 4th. The birthday of our country, and every in-bred, alcohol-sodden West Virginian sonofabitch was down at the Charleston riverfront. That night in Charleston was the feeling you get watching *Gimme Shelter*. Astrologers had to be losing their lunch that day. Somebody was going to get their ass kicked.

The streets were crowded and the riverfront was packed. Families were everywhere and having seemingly good times. It was innocent revelry, but nothing in Charleston is ever so sweet-natured as that. Little bits of angst creep up under the sidewalks there. People in the bars who usually didn't go to bars were there that day as we set up our gear. Guys who smiled while their eyes stayed blank. Missing teeth. CAT caps. Guys who stared first and dared your ass to do any-thing. *Anything.* Guys who usually don't get out of the mountains were there, and what were *you* gonna do about it?

First of all, *Susan* nearly got in a fight. *Susan!* America's sweet-heart was pulled in off the sidewalk by Tutt as she threatened some local tough bitch with her silver-toed stage boots. Well, I thought, there's a first. Charleston's the town for firsts, alright.

Ken McMahan was on the whiskey. Bull plus china shop. I re-member sharing a Wild Turkey with him at the bar and us saying how much we liked each other's bands. His arm was tight around my neck. It was nicely comradely but made breathing a bit difficult. I felt a pinched nerve in my trapezoid every time he went for his drink with-out loosening his grip on me.

Ken could drink whiskey and play great. I couldn't. The Cheese pretty much sucked that night. Skot was shitfaced, but doing pretty well as a frontman when not falling over. A pretty girl was up front. This wasn't unusual or disturbing. What was a bit unnerving were the three guys watching her. I remember them. I couldn't pull them out of a lineup, but I do remember them, standing in the crowd off stage left. Watching Skot, watching the girl. Watching the girl watch Skot.

They were nursing the notion of knowing this uptown lass in the most fundamentalist, biblical sense, perhaps in a gang-biblical sense. Their brains could barely find words for their rage. SHE LIKES THAT FAGGOT THERE! That short little fucker on the stage! Ain't right.

Later on, the gig was done. All the stuff was packed up onstage and we were waiting for the vans. I was in the back alley, next to the door, playing horseshoes with an inverted cardboard box and Allen's head. Allen was Susan's guitarist, and he was slumped in the corner, dead drunk. I stood about ten feet away, tossing a cardboard box at his head. I can't remember who I was playing with, but I had a partner, and I was winning. A girl came running up our alley from the parking lot beyond. She was hysterical, screaming and crying. "Omigod! Omigod! They've almost killed Scott!"

I guess I'm stupid. I was used to lots of Scotts. Davis, Tutt, Willis, Fitzgerald, Turow. Scott Chandwater. (Sorry) So I made no immediate connection. She ran past me inside. I took a gander into the parking lot, saw no one, and went back towards the bar to see if the girl was getting assistance. Then it hit me. Skot had just left to get the van. She didn't mean "Scott", she meant *Skot!* I was just far enough inside the bar to turn around with everyone else who now realized something very bad had happened.

I made it back into the parking lot just in time to see Skot being helped in. He's looked better.

His jaw was obviously wrong, going in weird shapes like a jaw just doesn't do. His nose looked smashed. One eye drooped. Blood ran from his scalp, from his nose, out his mouth. One of the guys carrying him had blood all over his t-shirt. Skot's clothes were torn, caked in dirt and blood. He had a glazed expression like people have in old films of ghetto riots when they are covered in blood but can't scream and trivialize pain that's too intense to feel.

Then again, Skot couldn't feel *anything* yet. He had still been mercifully drunk when the three sons of their own sisters shoved him against a wall, pushed him one way and hopped on him the other. They got him to the ground and kicked him like a dog. They kicked him in the head. One heavy boot after another, straight into his face. They broke his jaw, made a bloody mess of his nose and generally ripped and scuffed the skin on his skull, ribs and legs.

One of the bartenders, Sam Spade, had torn out of the darkness to Skot's aid, taken a few blows and delivered a few. He handled an alternating two at once, and, in a tangle of fists, curses and flying flecks of blood, made the difference. Big Dave Barnette, the Dusters' bass-player, dove into the fray, tipping the odds to the home team. The white trash cut their losses and took off. Skot lay on the asphalt with blood everywhere, looking more dead than alive.

The bar exploded with activity. Skot was laid out on a table. We all hovered over him. Snapping our fingers, waving our hands in front of him. Skot! You there? With the number of Kamikazes down his throat, he wouldn't have been much there if he *hadn't* been kicked in the head God knows how many times.

A typically efficient and rude ambulance team showed up. One guy, and a girl who looked and acted like she could have kicked all three hillbilly asses herself. She cleared everyone away from the table and enforced a butch Hitlerian order around the scene. They took him to the emergency room.

Skot couldn't be drugged because he had drunk half the bar. His body had to detoxify first before they could wire his jaw. His nose, it turned out, wasn't broken; it just looked like eight kinds of hell. I told him everything that had happened to him five separate times. His short-term memory was down for servicing. By five AM or so, he'd developed a hell of a headache and kept forgetting how he'd gotten it. We all sat out in the lobby. The sky went dark blue, then it did like the dawn sky always does. One minute, it's dark, then you look away, look up again and it's light blue. ''Damn,'' you think. It always goes light in the split second when you're not looking.

Chalk up another one in Tutt's ''good'' column. The minute he heard what hapened, he grabbed a mike stand with a big metal bottom and charged out the front door ready to stomp ass. He may have been a prick, but he never ran from a fight. Then he came to the ER and stayed through the night. For a while, all the other hassles dissipated in the stark reality of what had happened.

Skot was sent home with a wired jaw and prescriptions to die for. Surely we weren't going to continue this tour. Surely we're going home. Somebody say something. Somebody say we're going home. This is a sign from God. Let us go home and get jobs, take stock, let go of this whole rotten, depressing situation. Certainly no one thinks anyone is still going to get rich or famous or anything but their butt kicked out of this whole venture. Somebody say something.

So far, the whole thing had gone about as badly as expected. Press attention was minimal. Radio play was slim to nil. Nobody was making any money whatsoever. Tutt was handing out the per diems from his pocket. The gas was going on his card. The hotel rooms were going on his card. He was losing his ass, and his first public tantrum of the tour came outside a Cracker Barrel two days later. It was a bizarre sight. A dozen hung-over, sunglassed rockers with cowboy hats and bandanas, rocking back and forth on the front porch in those charming rocking chairs they provide, and Tutt started screaming at Susan about how the radio station somewhere didn't have any of the records and it sure as hell wasn't *HIS FUKKIN' FAULT*, now, was it? Maybe *SOME STUPID FUKKIN'GODDAMN <u>WOMAN</u>* forgot to send them, but it sure wasn't *his* fault! Tutt was screaming full-out. Old retired couples were making wide arcs around him as he raved right in front of the door. Susan just took it, like she always did, and the rest of us rocked back and forth like hell's grandpas, pretending that there was nothing in the world wrong with this picture.

Johnson City. Somehow, with no one actually deciding anything, it was resolved that we would continue. We played the songs Billy sang, and the songs I sang. When we got it polished up in a couple of weeks, it was fun, in a way, but it wasn't Government Cheese. Skot and I certainly hadn't gotten along very well the last few years, except for those magic moments when we were both in a good mood at the same time. He was a bastard, but I liked the guy, and I missed him. I didn't want to play.

Friday, July 6th. The Wrocklage in Lexington. Chris picked up Skot's guitar and gamely plucked through songs he wasn't sure whether he knew or not. The gig was a triumph out of despair. "A Little Bit of Sex" should have been recorded on that night. We all had a nice time at the Congress Inn that night. The Shockboys were among us with their wit, Black Sabbath tapes and amusing demonstrations of Lance machine gang-rape.

Next we went to Asheville, North Carolina. That gig stunk. The room sounded terrible, and we didn't even know what we were supposed to sound like any more, considering our lead singer was at home with a wired jaw. Why hadn't somebody questioned the wisdom of continuing? Why didn't somebody speak up? Tutt was already losing money hand over fist. Government Cheese pulling out of this tour was the best thing anybody could do for him. But we didn't. We played that lame-ass show in that awful little closet of a room, and then I sat down with my book and a beer at a corner table.

I read all of *Moby Dick* on that tour. I think that safely demonstrates my desperation. I would rather have been on a ship with a pegleg loony captain and a pissed-off whale than on that tour. Read, read, read. All the time. Even with the Dusters blasting forty feet away and the promotional Miller Beer girls walking around in hotpants shooting everyone wih fire extinguishers. Ken was tearing off blistering leads at megadecibels and pretty girls were all around and I was in a booth on page two hundred with Ishmael and Queequeg and that big, egocentric blowhard of a fish giving everybody a hard time and determined to take the whole ship down with him.

Wednesday, July 11th. The Cotton Club, Atlanta. Dan Nolan owned this place. He also owned the Nick, which is why everybody played the Nick, because everybody wanted to play here. We'd done plenty of Nicks and no Cotton Club, and I was learning to hate Dan Nolan more than anyone else I'd never met before. We did an okay show, still trying to figure out what the hell to do as a band. We told Tutt we were staying in a hotel uptown with some friends and he could cancel our room wherever they were staying. Were we glad we did that! There was a major lecture from Tutt in one of the hotel rooms the next afternoon, on conduct, speed of transition between acts, alcohol abuse and other matters. It had quickly turned into a heated argument, with Chris Sherlock finally losing all grip on his tongue and outing himself as a Tutt-hater.

The stars were in some weird wishbone formation again. We did the show at Shannon's in Rome and went down like a storm. We were getting better at this new act. We did "Like a Rolling Stone" and every single thing Billy sang that we knew. He started singing "Mammaw Drives the Bus" like he'd used to before Skot took it over. Everybody had a good time. Only two things went wrong.

First, there was Benny, who ran the club. A great guy, maybe not the most attentive businessman, but a great fellow just to hang around with. He taught me you could sing "Green Acres" lyrics to the tune of "A Day in the Life". Tall, lanky, and balding before his time, Benny liked the Cheese and was always glad when we played. He'd dropped acid in honor of our coming, not knowing he would have to deal with Tutt. It came time to settle up at the end of the night. It had been a good night. If there ever was a night when we beat the guarantee at the door, it was this night. It should have been easy. But Benny was tripping, and Tutt was Tutt.

Benny had neglected to provide the food platter at the load-in in the afternoon, as the contract rider required. It wasn't much, just some sandwich meats, some bread, condiments, sodas. But Benny had forgotten.

Tutt raised hell. I remember his giving Benny all sorts of terrifying Tuttness at close quarters as I steered around them, taking guitars and amps outside. Even though the damage was done and this was hardly an issue to burn a bridge over, Tutt was going to torch the whole vicinity.

I was heaving some luggage into the back of one of the vans when Benny came flying out of the club. He was walking backwards, flailing his arms and speaking in a high tremulous voice. "Guys," he screamed, "Y'all are all welcome to come back *enny tiiimme,* but you keep that asshole *at home!* And I'm not doin' any business with his ass *no more!*" He kept walking backward repeating variations of that to us. Down the street he went. We didn't know where he was going. He didn't, either.

It was the final straw for all the folks who had been in on that day's hotel room argument. There had been way too much stress for ten dollars a day. Migrant fruit-pickers made out better than this. Anyone sitting on a fence about Tutt now had to deal with how he had handled this situation. Club owners are not easy people to deal with in the best of conditions. Arguing with one on acid about a deli tray is just about the definition of useless.

Tutt finally managed to alienate Joe for good. It was the fatal sacrifice on his part.

Since we'd not seen fit to show up for that meeting/riot in Rome, Tutt had petulantly not booked Government Cheese motel rooms for that next night. We'd had to secure one for ourselves. I remember very distinctly sitting in the van after the Shannon's gig, watching the summer Georgia moon through the windshield, drinking a Miller Genuine Draft and smiling as Joe referred to Tutt as a stupid two-year old something or other. Ahh. Glug. Erp. He's one of us again. The belch of unity. The beer breath of a new tomorrow.

Athens, Georgia. Hi, Ort. Bye, Ort. I wanted to crash with Tim Vinson, but I was told it would upset Tutt if I left the herd. Tim's still waiting on a call from me. Tim, man, I hope you see this book someday. Call me.

Auburn, Alabama. I remember taking a swim at the Heart of Auburn Motel with Big Dave Barnett and Chief. There had always been this code between the Dusters and us. We didn't talk about bad things, just good things. No more of that now. "So what are *you* doing after the war?" Dave stretched out with the water lapping at his breastbone. He looked skyward and mused, "God. I always wanted to be in a band. But this isn't what I had in mind." Lying up against the poolside, lagoons in our pasty chests, we came to terms with rock and roll. We didn't need any of this. We could walk away. We had legs. They touched the ground. I could put one in front of the other. But we were like draftees now, at the front, and when this was over, when we had done that Exit/In gig on the 28th, we could walk away. All our lives we had wanted it. The rock and roll dream. OUR BANDS. We had had them, they had had us, and under no circumstances do you let go of the dream.

Driving back from Auburn, Billy swigged madly from a Colt 45 the size of a small oxygen tank, stammering with the rage of his own moment of clarity, of seeing the light truly, of saying "My God! We're lost. Will somebody please admit we're lost?"

Another week of the tour was over. It was afternoon. We had left Joe in Nashville and it was me, Chris, and Billy in Billy's monster car. I was driving, since the other two had been drinking since noon and I hadn't started 'til two or so.

"All these years of denial! 'Things'll work out! We're going places!' This is so lame! This is so fucking lame! God, those posters! *Can you believe those posters?!*"

Billy was referring to the black and white 11"x14" Reptile Records posters on sale at the booth every night. They were going for a dollar apiece and appeared for all intents and purposes to have been run off on a copier. "*Fuck* this!" Billy continued, "This is so lame. I'm not gonna lie and say I'm happy any more! I'm not gonna be associated with this any more. I . . . I . . . I . . .

*"Quit!"*

We drove on. The sky went to dusk. Mars winked on the other side of the sun. The sky went red and purple and summertime tapestry. Billy had quit the band in Tennessee. We crossed the border and he quit the band again in Kentucky, just to keep it official. The sky went a shade darker. He swigged the Colt and quit the band again. I turned on the headlights and Billy quit to us in the car louder, swigging the Colt and spitting the words out hard. All the way back he kept up the mantra. Swig and quit. Swig and quit! Like he was convincing himself he was really doing it. Like he was psyching himself up to tell the others. Like he was getting up the gumption to tell Joe he was not going to Texas. Nobody was going to get him out on the road any more. He was not going on the rest of this tour. Billy Mack Hill was Frederick Douglass, stealing his body back from his master, heading north into the hills if necessary.

For two days, no one spoke. No one did anything. We saw Skot, and laughed at the wired-shut, clenched-jaw laugh he now had. But I didn't see Billy, and he didn't see me.

The day before we were supposed to leave for Texas, I tracked him down drinking at the Shocks' house. I struck a deal, more like a promise I hoped I could keep. This was it. Get through the tour and then no more Reptile. No more Tutt. Somehow (and I had no idea how), we would get out of all the contracts. Just come on this last leg of the tour. At last, he agreed and went home to pack his bags.

I don't know why I did it. This was the out. Billy was willing to kill the beast and be the bad guy. I guess I just didn't want Scott Tutt to be the guy that made him do it. We had had a life before Tutt that was rich. Maybe we could have one after him.

Besides, believe it or not, all this still beat the hell out of working for a living. It was still a rock and roll band. Better than some. Worse than others. See us on a good night and we would rock your socks off. Even with all the squabbles, and all the bullshit, it was still a good show for your money.

And call me a pervert, but I wanted to see what was next. Who would go crazy? Maybe somebody would *die* before it was done. The craft re-enters amid flames galore, and maybe we needed to go through this last bit. To COMPLETE the severance. To . . . I don't know . . . fulfill prophecies or something like that. We needed to go do it and totally flame out. There was a certain exhilaration in all of this emotional chaos. After this, we all knew it was over.

Billy went home, packed, popped a beer and quit the band all over again. Ahhh! Billy, what're you trying to do to me? At last, I got him in the van. Off we were, once we found Chris; and even he took a bit of doing to unearth, as I recall.

The Texas leg, and what a scabbed-up, hairy old leg it was. The van would never see Bowling Green again. For 10 days we skittered in the command module just across the ozone. We glanced at each other with tentative wonder, mouthing silent prayers that the chutes would open in time.

\* \* \* \*

# 23

# re-entry

*Wednesday, July 18th. Little Rock again. I am watching Sherlock drum. He has this funny thing where he throws his long, lanky arms behind him, looks at Dave and Ken really quick—like a squirrel watching other squirrels play tennis—and then he hits the last thwack of the song. We've all seen each others' sets so many times we know everything backwards, so several of us, at various places in the bar, raise our arms all the way back and hit the downbeat along with him.*

*On that same note, during one of her songs, Susan sings a line that goes, "You gotta be rough, you gotta be tough, if you wanna fall in love these days." On "rough," she raises her right arm and flexes her little bicep. On "tough," she raises and bends the other sadly malnourished twig up to join it. Two weeks into the tour, we were all doing it with her, at discreet distances in dark corners, lest Tutt catch us and not think it so funny. Since then, someone's connected that a flashbulb goes off at this moment every night. It's Tutt, getting his documentation shot. We've loosened up about getting caught. We muscle-flex with her every night, five or six guys within eyesight of each other at various places around the club.*

*My cousins Tony and Steve are here tonight. They're the only relatives who have ever seen me play. The last time I saw them, they didn't shave yet. Now they have kids. Tony asks me how things are going. My eyes are red, my hair's greasy. I haven't changed clothes since Kentucky. "Great, man. Things are great. Let me have another cigarette."*

We were out chasing the dance macabre. Conjuring the grotesque. Nightmare Part Dos. The Texas Leg.

From Little Rock we went straight on to Houston, which is a haul, and a show that same night just rubbed it in. I barely remember Houston. I have a flash memory of being onstage dedicating a song to

Tom Wolfe for some reason I can't remember, and that's it. Then I got my sick wish for some more life-as-art, in the form of a ludicrous mission to Shreveport.

Shreveport was, at the time, an interesting civics lesson—and that was about it. None of us had ever been to this club we were booked at before. Humphree's? Where and what is a Humphree's? We'd heard about Shreveport. You didn't fuck around in Shreveport lately, roaming around looking for something on unfamiliar streets, as the town had been rife with drive-by shootings and other types of fun. Fortunes, careers and minds were going southwards, thanks to the belly-up oil industry. In the wake of Charleston, nobody was in the mood to court death any more than we really had to. All the way from Houston for this gig? That's a lot of map. And guess what. *There's no gig!*

Tutt asked Susan if we had a signed contract returned in the mail from the club owner with his signature visibly scrawled on it somewhere. She said yeah, she thought so. He asked her again. This time she said yeah, I'm pretty sure. Every time he asked her, the answer got strangely more positive when it should have gone in the other direction, and he never checked for himself.

And so we found Humphree's, a dump in shooting vicinity of Shreveport's worst area, the kind of intensely dark neighborhood social club where opening the door causes an insulting light-saber gash. There were sepia stools and pool tables, but no stage and no PA. There was a friendly little man behind the bar, and that was it. He didn't know where the owner was. He didn't care.

The first question to ask was who booked this turkey. There had never been a rock band of any import play this place in its history. We were certain of this because there was obviously nowhere inside for them to play. Tutt got livid. He tore around the gravel parking lot, where all the vans were rounded in the best conestoga circle three vans can manage.

"I'm sick and tired of being right all the time!" he thundered. "We should never have come!" We wondered what he was right about, exactly, since he was one of the very few people who should have made sure to lay his eyes personally on a signed contract before we drove two hundred and fifty godforsaken miles from Houston, where we could have all still been, happily farting, with six packs, on beds watching titties via satellite, this very second.

Tutt made us all stand outside. The nice bartender ordered us a bunch of Domino's Pizzas courtesy of the club. Tutt forbade us to enter the bar and eat them, because he didn't want us taking anything free from the club owner. One by one, we flaunted Tutt's ever-flagging authority, went inside and ate pizza. Paper beats rock, scissors beat dynamite and hunger beats Tutt hands down.

Sherlock and I split a pepperoni pie and, being a veggie, he took all the red pepperonis off his slices and gave them to me. They were little saucers of wretched testament, gastric zingers from a kitchen way below government specs. I wasn't eating them, I was only putting them into my body for a while, so they could sprout like gremlins and try to kill me later.

We waited in that parking lot an hour for the club owner to show, because Tutt wanted to kill him, I believe. One hour became two hours. No one was talking to Tutt, and various cliques were not talking to each other. This was beautiful. Here we were, all just hanging around behind our vans, hiding from the street, pathetically presuming the van chassis would stop any stray welcome-to-the-neighborhood bullets.

I remember we were listening to Muddy Waters' *Hard Again* out of the reconstituted Cheese stereo when the pizza began to hit me. My stomach muscles began to ripple, and I felt that tightness in my throat. My forehead started to go warm, then cold, then warm again. I started breathing deeply, trying to stabilize. Oh no. Oh please no. BLAWWWWWWAAAGGHHHH!

Nothing in this earthly realm sucks quite like food poisoning sucks. It's like a retail store's inventory strip-return for the body. The central warehouse wants everything back. Not most of it, all of it. You retch 'til you let it go. There are little guys with clipboards running all over your alimentary canal making sure it all goes. Your stomach starts taking back orders from the duodenum trying to get it all. It tastes awful, it feels worse, and it doesn't stop happening. It goes in phases. The hunched-over-retching phase, followed by the sea of tranquillity, followed by the choppy seas and deep swells again, then unholy upheaval, bargaining with God, and back to the beginning.

We waited in that parking lot for another hour. Now if you were a club owner, and three bands you probably never wanted anyway were in your parking lot waiting to play, or get paid without playing, or maybe just break your balls, period, and they were headed up by a crazy man stomping around screaming, would you for a minute consider going near the place? Of course not. The guy ain't comin' 'til the bartender calls him and says the gypsies from Tennessee have collapsed their tents and shuffled on down the trail. And yet, we waited. It started getting dark and I was throwing up vital organs, leaning against the front bumper tucking vomit-flecked hair behind my ears, and trying to keep my glasses from falling in the little puddles of puke I was leaving everywhere. Step lively with the gastric bombardier amidst.

Eventually, common sense did prevail and the mission was scratched. Eddie, Susan's bass player, made contact with his cousins near Monroe. We could go there, he said.

Just before we headed out, Joe and I were trying to have an argument about our future, and, amazingly, considering my pukefest, I was winning, or thought I was.

"Listen, Joe . . . " I panted, my pale head hanging out the open window, looking at the purple Louisiana sky, "We're gettin' outta here, outta the deal, outta all this. I don't care how. . . I don't . . . "

"Hey," Joe said, "I'm not suing Scott Tutt in court unless *you're paying for it.* Do you know how much it cost Jerry Dale to get out of his deal?" Joe then cited some exact exorbitant figure I can't remember, somewhere between two and ten thousand dollars.

"Joe," I said, catching my breath, my head out the window, looking up at the winking planets and stars, smacking the taste of watery stomach acid on my tongue, ready to just . . . retort! Really let him have it! Here it comes. "Joe, let me tell ya somethin' . . . " Here it comes! I opened my mouth . . . "Joe . . . BLAWWWAAR-RGGGGH!" And that was the end of that conversation, and the end of the paint job down the side of the van. Not that it would matter in a few days.

Eddie came from a nice Christian family and they had a beautiful spread, including an immense game room where our whole bunch of depraved road mongrels played like little kids: video games, ping pong, pogo sticks. I got to know one of the bathrooms very well from knee level, and that was the extent of my explorations. But I did get a bed in a room all to myself that night.

All the way back to Austin. I got my per diem at the club on Sixth Street, took it across the street and drank it down in ten minutes, a dollar a minute. I was joined by Big Dave and others. Gus Moore showed up that night, Skot's old roommate and cycling buddy, a sight for sore eyes. We talked about Tom Robbins novels and sundry hippified cordialities, about the way things used to be at home.

I remember before the Austin show that Chief was trying to figure out where to put the amps on the stage. He was pacing around on the stage and at one point he, under his breath, said "I think. . . ."

That's as far as he got. Tutt cut him off. "Don't think, Chief! Don't think! For every time you've thought, I've thought three times! That's why *I'm the boss!*"

Then there were two solid days off in Austin, which is not a bad place to kill time. I could hear the screams outside my hotel room door, though, the sound of Tutt's wallet, hemorrhaging and mortally wounded. The Shreveport debacle, coupled with a few hoary disappointments in gate receipts, tripled with two straight days off in Austin, quadrupled by knowing every single musician was going to be looking for the salary packet promised upon completion of the tour. It was a billfold retching its bowels in mortal agony.

There was a great jam at Keith Christopher's house. Keith had done stints playing bass with lots of folks, including the early Georgia Satellites. (At this writing, he's in Shaver.) He hunched over the bass with his hawk nose, a crooked grin and a big mane of brown hair that hung everywhere. A devil-may-care, *jene se quois*, and other four-syllable tags kind of guy.

Quick story. Keith is responsible for the lowest score ever on a *Star Search* episode, a Blutoesque zero point zero. He wasn't the featured contestant, he was just in the backup band. In the closing segment, when all the acts waved at the camera behind Ed McMahon, Keith had reached out and gestured behind Ed's ass, playfully cup-cupping with his hands. He and the act he was playing for got fired. An effeminate stagehand had later come running up to Keith screaming "Mr. McMahon has screened the roughs and he is *livid! Livid!*"

So anyway, in Austin that night, Keith was playing some great rhythm acoustic guitar. The bass drum was when he stroked it in the back, and then he would hit the snare drum farther up on the guitar. Sherlock had set up various coffee cans, beer cans, bottles, whatever, and was drumming on it all. We did a lot of Beatles. Everybody sang whatever they could think of. It was a good time.

The night grew deep and late. I bid my goodbyes and caught a ride back to the hotel room. Joe, Big Dave, Keith and Keith's girlfriend took off in the Cheese van for Sixth Street and more revelry.

Crossing a side street between Sixth and Seventh, another van leapt into the Cheesewagon's path. What followed was the usual awful standing up on brakes, the slow-motion crunch, the sound of glass flying, metal tearing and bending, steam suddenly escaping, the hopeless wish that you could turn back time just fifteen seconds.

The van was a gnarled, twisted front-end piece of worthless junk. The police came and never noticed a quart Jack bottle wedged between the back curtains and the window glass. Big Dave, who had smacked the windshield, was pronounced okay. And the mop-up operation began. I'd been back in the hotel room the whole time, asleep. The next day, several guys went to the wreckyard and stripped the van of everything we'd ever use again. I didn't go. I wanted to remember that smelly old heap as she was.

We rented a big Ryder truck. Tutt's wallet screamed some more. Two uncomfortable seats, a faulty air-conditioner and a shitty Philco radio. The good part was that all the gear could fit in it, and so from then on the Dusters' van became a rolling party shed. Susan's band, who had had to ride with Tutt and Susan in the green van up all the time to this point, bolted en masse. For hundreds of miles at a stretch, they'd had to sit and watch Tutt drive, see him every so often hold out his hand silently, Susan obediently placing a naked, unwrapped stick of gum in his hand; and then—occasionally, without warning—Tutt would scream his head off at her, and she would just take it. There are more pleasant ways to ride around the country. Slumping on the metal floor of a van using Ken McMahan's redolent dirty laundry for a pillow is just one of them. I rode in the Dusters' van some as well.

St. Mary's in San Antonio. Photos of the Alamo have to be very carefully cropped, so that it always looks like it's in the desert when it's actually recessed within two major metropolitan business buildings. We saw it, went back up the street, and played for nary a soul.

Dallas on Wednesday. Club Clearview had a moderate reputation, made on previous, different nights, I suppose. There had been no small amount of trouble even finding the place in downtown Dallas, because Tutt's van had to be doing the leading and they had no idea where they were going. We drove around in circles. Susan would key their whiny, feedback-blasting CB mic as we'd try to listen for commands through the static, screaming feedback and Tutt yelling his head off at her like he was always doing and she was always taking.

Drinking became a quest. There was the place across the street where I asked the waitress if she knew where I could find a hit-man. She said yes, too. This was exciting stuff. But I hadn't forty thousand dollars, much less enough for a third beer, so the contract never closed. Big Dave, bless him, whipped out his credit card with a damned audible swishing noise. I remember listening to a homeless man's poetry at a sidewalk cafe. Big Dave and Billy were sitting with me there, trying to rationalize the predicament we were in. I was sitting between them. Billy was in no mood for rationalizations. There were none. This was rock and roll Vietnam with no clear objective. Billy was right, but he was also crazy. Zoned. He'd been drunk so many days running now, he couldn't keep any emotions straight.

Then he stood up from the table and said "I've had it with this bullshit!" He gave me a hard look, like I was the enemy now, like I couldn't be trusted, like I hadn't proclaimed my allegiance to the underground subversive movement staunchly enough. I was carrying information back across the lines. Like, what are we gonna do, Billy? Blow up a goddamn bridge or something? Billy stormed off down the street like Benny had done in Rome, with no more idea where he was headed.

He walked off down the street in mid-town Dallas like he was going to walk all the way back to Bowling Green. I could picture him in three months with a scraggly beard, looking at the Pacific surf and thinking, "Hmm, maybe it was back the other way."

He came back, but I didn't find him until showtime. It wasn't hard. I started with his guitar cord. It snaked down from his amp in a straight diagonal line without touching the floor of the stage. The long, black cable wrapped around the back side of his amp and down a small flight of steps. Then it traveled about ten feet into the darkness, where it led to Billy's bass, slung along his back as he had all six feet six of himself bent double into a garbage can, heaving and retching violently. In a strange juxtaposition of decadence and professionalism, Billy was plugged in, tuned up and doing the pre-show vomit launch. I waited for a lull in the heaves, reached gingerly down inside the container, tapped Billy on the shoulder and said "Showtime!" into the bassy confines of the green, plastic dumper can.

Monroe, Louisiana. I almost got to see a fistfight that night, something about a thrown drumstick almost putting somebody's eye out. Eddie's relatives came back out. Hi, this is what I look like without vomit on my chin. Nice to see you again.

Shoney's. Three-day old Tomato Florentine soup with sad, soppy pasta shells. So there we were, across a great long table, all looking like different folks than the ones we were almost six weeks before. The dark circles under the eyes looked like badly applied stage makeup for a high school play, and they were real. All the greasy hair, and one cowlick per guy hanging down freely into his food. Chris with the sunglasses on. He always had his sunglasses on. All of us were nervous in a public place with Tutt any more. In some restaurant somewhere recently, his coffee hadn't come quick enough, so he'd just started screaming from his table *"COFFEE!!"* (For the rest of the tour, guys would pass each other and fake-scream under their breath *"Coffee!"*)

*USA Today* headlines on the table, the corner of the paper wet with spilt ketchup and vinaigrette dressing. Brent Mydland of the Grateful Dead had become the fourth Dead keyboardist (literally). Rosanne had mangled the National Anthem at a ball game, and the only two people who had thought it was funny were she and that loudmouth who had attached himself to her career and called it love.

Hal and Mal's. Jackson, Mississippi. The Cheese had played there once for about five people. Or was that Starkville? Regardless, this time was better. I believe the Dusters had a following here. This last gig of the New Cheese was the best one. "Like A Rolling Stone" sounded pretty nasty that night.

There was no backstage, just a tiny little alcove in which to sit and drink the case of Miller Genuine Draft that arrived for the Dusters every night. The Dusters were a "Miller Band." We had once been looked at by the company to possibly become one, but "Camping on Acid" had nipped that idea right in the bud real quick. Miller bands got support for touring from Miller Genuine Draft. They got free musical equipment, help getting gigs, a trip to Milwaukee to play at the convention every year. It was a sweet deal. The catches were the usual capitalistic routine, posing for brochure photographs that folded out into big posters with the Miller logo almost as big as the band's name. The band posed with one of the members holding a Miller Genuine Draft bottle. The top could be off but no beer drunk out of the bottle, and you held it with your fingertips raised away from the label. Then you got a case of Miller Genuine Draft backstage at every gig, and it was in the best interests of your career to not have anything onstage but Miller bottles. We in the Cheese were part of trickle-down economics at this point. The Dusters had first crack at the case, and then we all dove in like pilot fish, taking the scraps.

We headed home to Nashville. That last gig was a smoker, the best show of the tour. We had our Skottie back, his mandible newly unwired and open for business. The whole Cheesehead battalion from three or four states seemed to be there. The Exit-In was jammed.

The Cheesehead rumor mill had been cruising at its usual blinding level of speed and wild inaccuracy. Skot was a paraplegic now, blind in one eye, stuff like that. Billy had been rushed to the hospital in Texas with an overdose, etc. etc. In light of that, when we strolled out for that last Nightmare of the Reptile gig in Nashville, I swear I saw palpable relief in that crowd, looking from face to face out there. The worst wasn't true. There we all were.

I didn't know everybody in the audience that packed Exit/In night—it was the Dusters' crowd and ours put together—but I knew enough of them. For five years I'd been having quick conversations in bars with all of them. For five years I'd been trading bits of philosophy with each of them as fast as I could, always trying to get conversations quickly rolling into deep water because *we're going on soon and there's not much time, man!* All those people I knew by face, and maybe a dozen names if I was lucky. All those people who'd given a fuck about me and my friends. For five years they'd come, show after show, and here they were relieved, honest to God relieved, that we were all up on stage here, all in good health. Government Cheese lived, man.

It was strange, I had to think. I'd spent the last eighteen months getting so used to my bittersweet perspective on things, how the whole picture looked from my angle, how I knew that, no matter what, we were going to pull up short, be the *guys who gave it a good try, gosh darn it didn't ya love 'em.* And I guess I could think that way, if I wanted, all day long.

But tonight? Tonight, there were a couple of hundred people out there in the Exit/In who didn't think that way at all about us. They thought Government Cheese was the coolest thing since pockets!

They didn't know anything I knew. They didn't care about Tutt and our contracts, and that everybody was tired, pissed-off and punch-drunk. They didn't care about any of that whiny-assed shit. They weren't burned out on the three chords and an attitude way of life, with all its empty calories and philosophical dead-ends. All they cared about was that they'd paid five dollars tonight to see if Willis was on his feet, and if we were all okay, and if we could all throw down in the four/four-time key of A for twenty minutes, and go "Those are People who *DIED! DIED!*" one more time.

They didn't get bummed over the impossible sociopolitical implications of the band's name, they didn't get bent out of shape over "Fish Stick Day". They didn't have guilt-trips about living an irresponsible, libidinous life. They just knew that Billy and Joe were a tight, tough rhythm section, that I knew well enough which end of a guitar to blow into, that Skot could mop the floor with any frontman out there, and that Chris, when he got up with us, was getting pretty damn good too. Some of them went back to the Pub days, some of them earlier than that. They loved us, and we'd earned it. We were a rock band, buddy. A real one. You don't get that every day.

"Search and Destroy" brought everything bashing to yet another red-faced, bone-jarring close. There is a day-after-show condition known to all headbangers as "Gig Neck", a cramped-up condition of the trapezoids and a feeling like nine vertebrae are crammed into the space of six. In extreme cases, you can't turn your head. Gig neck occurs the day after a serious, cranium-throwing rock and roll jihad. I knew, coming offstage, that I wouldn't be able to turn my head come the dawn, but it was okay. I had no plans to turn my head.

There is a speech Kevin Costner does near the end of *Bull Durham*. He knows he's washed up. He has just quit his baseball gig. He tells Susan Sarandon that he wants to take off for a couple of weeks. He wants to, he says, "just be". No thinking of what happened, no wondering what might happen in the future. "Just be."

I loaded Beth's car with all my gear. We couldn't see out the back window for all the guitars, amps and wadded-up raiment. All the goodbyes were said. People hugged and said nice to get to know ya, even like this. Yeah, you too. Take care, take it easy, take a bath.

I looked around for Tutt to say goodbye, and couldn't find him. He'd already split. Right after settling up, after six weeks of complete hell, he and Susan grabbed their stuff and left without a word. I wouldn't see them again for almost a year.

A day later, Beth and I took off with a tent and two sleeping bags, to just be.

\* \* \* \*

# 24

# splashdown

And that was pretty much the end of it. We stopped touring like we had done, and just played on the weekends. Joe kept going down to Reptile's offices and helping out, at least for a while. One day he just walked away from it.

Tutt didn't send a letter notifying renewal of his contract options for another year. Legally, he had to do that, otherwise the deal was immediately voided. He has since told people he intentionally didn't send the letter, which I doubt is true since he had also forgotten the letter the year before, and that was the only reason we suspected he might forget again. The minute the deadline went by, we had a lawyer waiting with a nice letter of our own, and it was all done very quickly. It was over. Tutt was out of our lives.

We worked on making another record by ourselves, going back to that old basement, Marc Owens' place, where we'd done that first E.P. a lifetime ago. No more 32-track digital and big expensive room. We went back to those eight analog tracks and the low basement ceiling, and we worked on it a little at a time, whenever we had the money or the enthusiasm, both becoming disdainfully rare commodities by then.

We saw the Dusters in Huntsville when we both played the state fair, the two bands in a big tent pitched on asphalt with about ten disinterested farmers staring at us. We talked about the old times like it had been ten years ago, instead of six weeks.

We saw Mr. Big occasionally and hired him for old times' sake to run sound a couple of times. We didn't see Tutt or Susan until a Metro awards show the next summer. Now that was a quick handshake for you. Then, the next month we played KDF's "One For the Sun" at Starwood Amphitheater. Cheap Trick and the Outlaws were way up on the bill, and we and the Dusters were way down. Everybody saw each other and talked. It was cool. Everybody'd moved on. The Dusters had a new record out. They and Susan had actually gone on tour in France, where they had record deals.

Chris became a full-time member of the band, and we noticed how he mainly got the looks from the girls now. I remember running my fingers across my head and knowing full well there used to be enough hair up there to tease and spray, and now it seemed a little thin to want to do anything. We used to never say no to an after-gig party, and now, more and more, we just went off to bed somewhere. Sometimes I found myself at a party just tired and disinterested, holding up the wall, but not wanting to leave and admit that I was old.

Winter came. Working at a car wash in wintertime means wet shoes that freeze, and slipping loose change down the inside of your glove with the other hand because you drop it if you try to fit a bulky gloved hand into your tight pocket. You just stick it down the glove. Later on, when you're alone, you empty the glove. I never took change unless it was under a floor mat or stuck so down in the seat the driver couldn't possibly know. Yeah, yeah. I know. Like that makes a difference.

The record turned out pretty well in spots. It's the only thing you can get on CD. It's self-titled, just *Government Cheese*, and Chris Heric helped us with some computer graphics on the cover. Some of our best songs are on it, "Sunday Driver", "For the Battered", "No Sleeping in Penn Station", our cover of "Search and Destroy". We spent most of 1991 working on it. Skot was mainly in charge. He mixed it with Marc. I couldn't be depended on to care any more. Parts of it turned out really good, though. Billy's voice sounds great, and I'm proud of "For the Battered". You want a copy? I have a full box somewhere. I haven't seen it recently but I know it's around. Call me.

I jogged a lot, wondering what I was going to do when it was finally over, wondering who was going to step forward and be the bad guy, slay the beast properly and say he quits, wondering where the hell my twenties went, wondering if there was time to start over anywhere. I had a path mapped out around campus and I jogged a rut into it, from winter with long underwear and sweats and a cap, through spring with just sweats, into summer with shorts on, back into fall and winter again. The buds turned into leaves, and the leaves bloomed and went all different colors and fell off the trees, and I was a year older. We were playing on weekends and working on this record here and there, and some days I went and washed cars, and some days I just didn't.

It was a couple of days after Christmas, '91. Joe stopped in Bowling Green in transit from one family Christmas to another. We went to Mariah's to have a drink or eight. He said maybe I ought to consider coming to Nashville and living with him. He had offered before. He said "Why don't you come down there and find some guys to play with, you know, like, some good players, real musicians you could get a clean start with, you know what I'm sayin'? Take a step up and try to knock one out of the park."

"Whut're you sayin', Joe?"

He said, "I'm goin' to Bolivar, Tennessee. I'm gonna learn how to fly planes. I've always liked planes. I wanna fly one myself. Yeah, yeah. That's it. I quit."

We agreed to stay together as a band as long as it took to put the record out in local stores as a souvenir. Staying together for the sake of the children, essentially. That turned out to be several more months.

In March of 1992, Beth heard about a job opening at Channel 5 in Nashville. The morning anchor. She applied, and got it. She had been the 6 and 10 anchor in Bowling Green for several years now, and it was nice having the two of us on the same side of the clock. No more of that now. We had two weeks to move.

I didn't know I liked Bowling Green until I knew I was leaving. It was a boring, beautiful, dreary and utterly idyllic place, in its own static way. I jogged around my path every day, looking at the new buildings coming up on campus, and knowing how next year's freshmen would never know how the yard outside Pearce-Ford Tower looked when I lived there, back when I listened to the Sex Pistols in Scott Troop's room, back when I looked out the windows and played my guitar through the Soundesign stereo speakers and there were Clash buttons and ultrathin lapels and anything was possible, nothing had been tried and I had no idea how the real thing could be.

Channel 5 paid for the movers. It was a class, big-budget show all the way. Three guys boxed up everything we owned. There were big boxes, little boxes, medium boxes. It was a cardboard art-piece exhibit in that apartment. They even boxed up a wastebasket with the garbage still in it.

One of the nimnul movers had stacked one massive and very heavy box directly on a floor-furnace grate. Not good. Beth discovered it, tried to move the box and there was no way. She did the only other thing she could. She turned the thermostat all the way down. It wouldn't turn off, just down.

Later that night, I came in from Karma Dogs rehearsal, completely unhip. (The Karma Dogs were a loose acoustic aggregation of me, Billy Mack, and others.) I bent down walking through the dining nook to scratch Chelsea's big furry belly. She was this fat fixed cat that had been de-clawed by previous owners. If Chelsea came in the room when you were there, that meant a lot, because she was unarmed and scared of her own shadow. I rubbed her stomach and went on to bed. That was the last we ever spoke.

Some people swear by coffee, until they try fire once. You'll be out of bed and moving like you never thought you could. I'm just glad I was wearing pajamas already. Neither of us had time to grab our glasses. With the kitchen already blazing, the fire spread like one will when the entire apartment is cardboard. Beth called 911, watching the curtains melt, while I madly dashed upstairs to rouse everyone in the building. The next thing we knew, we were sitting barefoot in the (quite cold) street watching an uncorrected and very myopic image of, basically, all our stuff burning up. We were shivering, holding each other and seeing great orange tongues eat through the front living room windows.

Chelsea was dead, her little mouth and eyes red and cold. My first pet ever. She hadn't burned, but the smoke had gotten her. The whole living room was gone, the kitchen wasn't there any more, the bathroom was all brown. Some of everything was gone. Friends helped us pick through it all, and amazingly we still moved to Nashville that day, but it didn't take a van. Two cars and a friend's pickup truck hauled it all easily.

Now everything would be different. My jogging route was gone. My band would soon be over. My car wash gig was done for. I couldn't even wear the same old clothes. They were either gone or smelled like smoke, indelibly. Talk about a fresh start.

Something curious happened in that last year of the band, after all that went down, after the young years and the slow ones, the good times and the band, the explosive shows and the catatonic ones. Right when you least expected anything to happen and we were just playing Picasso's for the rent, when we were old hat and nobody cared any more, we got a second wind, a new optimism.

It never lasted too long at a time, but in spurts we would feel young again. For a while after Tutt, it felt like we could go for the brass ring yet again. It all seemed possible again. We even talked to Tom Sturges on the phone once or twice.

But we had changed from the young, power-garage-pop band he'd once loved. We'd locked into a mature groove, become a genuine kind of grizzled, amiably thick-headed, Marshall-amp band with an obvious affinity for six or seven major punk albums, and we were starting to get the sound legitimately down too. We added nothing new to this well-tilled genre, but practicing it honorably earned us a dignified death, I think.

We even learned a Kiss cover. It started as a joke and we wound up meaning it. "Rock and Roll All Nite." I wished it had been a hipper choice. I was hot for "Shock Me," but we learned the former because nobody had to be taught it so much. We did it pretty well, and it felt pretty good. I felt connected to my ninth-grade self again.

So in the end, what can I tell you about this band you've read so much about and never heard a note of? Were we really worth a damn? Damn straight, we were.

We had heart. We were exciting, and on a good night, brutal. We made some people believe in us. We had a family come up around us, and they made us feel like we were coming in from the cold when they came to see us play. People sent us money. Not to buy anything, just money in the mail! In good faith. If I got started thanking everyone now, I'd leave someone crucial out, I know. But it was touching, and it kept us going as long as we did, knowing that, for a thousand-odd people in the southern United States, we had real value.

Skot Willis was a magnificent showman. He made a lot of highly-paid rock-star frontmen look like the cosseted, lily-livered pussies they are.

I once saw Skot leap off a stack of PA speakers so high that he sailed into a spinning ceiling fan and knocked a blade off with his head. He landed on the dance floor about a second before the blade did, and he never stopped singing. I saw him walk across bodies and swan dive into slam-dancers with no more fear that you'd have dropping into the deep end of a pool.

One night in Murfreesboro, Tennessee, a fight broke out down front and Skot took less than a second to hurl himself offstage, throwing his arms and legs wide like a flying chimp. He landed on one of the combatants' torsos as they duked it out, getting swung back and forth like a long-haired, sweaty back-pack, and he never stopped singing. It was a common occurrence for Skot to chip a tooth in the process of doing a regular gig. People don't know the agonies he went through: the back pain, the sprained this or that, the doctor visits. He gave all, refueled, and gave all again, time after time.

Billy and Joe locked together as a rhythm section. Billy used a lot of treble on the bass. It was half boom-boom and half nong-nong. Joe came down hard and solid, with the hi-hat cymbals open and nasty. When it got going, the sound was a locomotive that had gotten ideas of its own and was hurtling down the tracks at you. It was the sound of rock and roll AND the sound of things shaking off the shelves and hitting the floor. Billy was a marvelous songwriter and is more of one now than ever. Joe was the most solid of us all, a great Charlie Watts/ Mauro Magellan meat-and-potatoes drummer, who never asked more of others than he gave of himself.

Me? Well . . . it certainly wasn't my playing or singing, but I did bring something intangible and valuable to the table. Being our most extreme in demeanor, I was the band's spiritual master and emcee. Things were great when I was into it, and they sucked when I wasn't. Mainly, I wasn't afraid to act like a complete fool. I seemed to do it enough without meaning to, so I just turned on the juice wide-open during shows, and it sold tickets. I uncovered my crazy side and turned a nickel after all. Not much more than a nickel, usually, but I did do it. Together, the four of us—five when Chris was around— were a damn good show many nights.

Harmonies? Love songs? Fuhget about it. You didn't come to a Government Cheese show for supple fluffery. You came to get bludgeoned. Pummelled. Along the way, we delivered good bathroom-humor yuks. Skot would inflate a condom on his head with his nostrils. I did poetry. Maybe everybody would be jumping on tables by the end of "People Who Died". Maybe we would have a packed club of soaking wet people who had stopped dancing, and all they were doing was standing there twitching a little, completely worn out. Two hundred people with the shit beat out of them and liking it.

Jumping around on a stage with a guitar is a hell of a lot of fun. Few people get to do it. That last night at the Pub, with everybody jumping in unison. That last night of the Bottom Line, with us holding that last A-chord and jumping up and down while the bartenders sprayed everybody with the seltzer hoses. That night at CBGB, standing where Johnny Ramone used to stand, and about three or four hundred other instances I can call to mind if you give me a minute, all those times I never thought I would really get in my life, and I did.

Seven years. Seven-hundred-odd shows. God knows how many miles in three vans. God knows how many guitar strings, drumsticks, cases of beer. Why? Sometimes I wonder. It went on a few years too long. It all went to hell and I lost interest, or I lost interest and it all went to hell, or something like that. I'm just elated and appalled that it all happened. Everybody take a bow. And as long as there is somebody out there who remembers us, who we gave a good time to, somebody to put an arm around one of us years from now and say "Damn! You boys shoulda done as well as them boys, they *suck!*" — who am I to say they're wrong?

It has been almost ten years since I was in that basement working on that first record. Some kid who was conceived then is walking home from school right now. That bothers me. Some sperm and egg were saying how-do while I was tying that broken string back onto the bridge. Now that kid's talking and getting ideas. He might even be thinking of growing his hair already, as I'm keeping mine long while I still have it to grow at all. Before long, I have to think about having my own kids, and what I'll tell them. Not that it's such a good idea for me to have kids, maybe, but let's assume. And they will ask me what I did way back when, and I'll pull out the old copy of whichever record I can find and play that and I'll have to explain it to them with a straight face, all the time saying "you know, kids, it actually sounded *much better live.*"

In October of 1992, Picasso's closed its doors. We regrouped to play within its walls one last time. So Picasso's isn't there any more. I had never been clear on whether we settled up our tab, and now no one knows. The building is a banquet room for Mariah's. I haven't seen it since that last night we played there. I want to remember it like it was. I can still smell it. If you pour a bucket of beer on your car floorboard and shut up the windows for a day, you can smell it too.

Two years later, we got together again, for a show in Bowling Green and one in Nashville. Both sold out. In Bowling Green, I saw young people I'd never met getting passed over each others' shoulders in an eye-level mosh-pit. Yes, slamming had become *moshing.* Kids today, I tell ya. We were meeting the new generation, the ones who have an X stuck on their name without asking for it. They had come to pay tribute, and perhaps we hadn't done much to foster them on a national scale, but it surely did appear that we had spiked the petri dish in our own back yard, in our own image, no small amount. We'd left our mark. Government Cheese was from here. This is where we'd lived and laughed, and this is how we did things. Take a picture here. Take a souvenir

Was it fun? You bet your ass it was fun. I have some good memories of it all, real good ones, but I know I'd have a lot more if I hadn't been such a person of low character as often as I was. A lot of those great moments we had, I look back on and I know what most others didn't at the time — that I was either overdoing some vice, embroiled in the odd peccadillo or just simply not being as good a person as I could have been.

I've come to realize that, in those first couple of years of the band, I was the best person I've ever been.

I never got any sleep. The band sounded like shit and the whole idea of what we were doing was categorically insane, but every day was a step up and there was a purity and innocence to it all. It was a beautiful thing, and I was fiercely involved. I had enthusiasm and I made it contagious. I was the best person I have ever been in my thirty-two pockmarked cheekwipes of the calendar. Then we handed the reins over to Tutt, and for the next five years I was easily the worst person I've ever been.

It's probably true that we would have folded things up soon enough if Tutt hadn't come along to offer his hope and/or hype, and so maybe that justified giving him our band and our dreams. Otherwise, there would have been no MTV, no touring and I might be selling whitewalls in Bowling Green with two kids now, I don't know, but it was the wrong choice for me.

Once it wasn't my dream any more, it didn't mean much, and things just putrefied over time. I know now it's always best to retain proprietorship over your own dream. Even if you drown yourself you'll go down happy, with dignity, as a good person with your own ideas, nobody's puppet. You must always be defiantly free, because then you'll take care of yourself and make better decisions. You'll be more alive.

I sent Ort some of the rough draft of the book, and he corrected me on his waist size in 1986. He wants Government Cheese to reunite and play his wedding. There is no special someone for Ort yet, but I suppose when she does show up, we'll get together and bash through everything one more time.

Ort says we were the best Athens band that never came from there. I'm sure there are plenty of people who would dispute him, but still, hearing him say that is almost reason enough for what we went through, reason enough for writing this book. The best Athens band that never came from there. I like that. Thanks all the same, though, because it's outside Bowling Green, Kentucky, where somebody spray-painted *'Cheese Rules!!'* on an exit sign years ago—some of the nicer graffiti we inspired over time. That was home. And now there's nothing. Not a plaque or a signpost or even a tombstone to throw up on out of respect. There is just a town, and its ghosts.

So whenever you drive through Bowling Green (assuming you ever have such an inclination), take the time to wind your way downtown. Be careful—the guy who designed the street layout was apparently drunk at the time—but as you amble around, taking in that lazy bucolic vibe and driving the wrong way up the one-way streets like all visitors do, think of us. There were good times in that town. There were dreams.

I like to think Government Cheese packed a bunch of dreams in a burlap sack and swung it over our heads. While the bag emptied, we kept swinging, and it got lighter and faster, and we spun until we fell down, all dizzy and spent. Those dreams had to go somewhere. They lie where they fall, spread-eagled, pink and healthy forever.

\* \* \* \*

*Left to right: Me, Chris, Billy, Joe*
*front: Skot*

# afterword

Joe is Joe Elvis on 103 KDF now, the afternoon drive-time guy, flying planes in his spare time. Skot is married and planning an assault on the retail industry. Billy lives in Lexington and recently released a damn good solo record, *Moral Chain of Custody/Recycle Love, Vol. I.* Write him at P.O. Box 8221, Lexington, Kentucky, 40533-8221. Ten bucks for a disc, six for cassette, a dollar per for shippage. I played for two years in a band called the Bis-quits, who made a record for John Prine's Oh Boy label. We had a couple of nice tours, got some good reviews, saw John perform close-up and did a gig with Uma Thurman dancing five feet in front of us—all of which are damn nice things to have happen.

Chris moved out to LA to try the rock scene with Pat. They worked for a house-keeping service, cleaned Gary Coleman's lair once, stole one of his socks and sent it home to the Cheese P.O. Box. A year after going, they were back. Chris now plays in Nashville with the Vegas Cocks, and goes by the name of Viva Las Vegas. Whenever I call him up I inadvertantly ask for Chris and no one knows who I mean. I feel like Marion Cunningham still calling Fonzie Arthur.

Tutt lost his Alabama tunes in '92, when the band sued for back-payment of royalties and, in a series of lawyerly manuevers, took their songs back. He then lost the Dusters when they broke up. Susan is still with him. I see posters for her gigs occasionally, with the little Reptile logo down in the corner.

Beth is the morning anchor on Channel 5 here in Nashville. Skip is in Bowling Green, and so's Ken Smith, Broma, Jeff Sweeney, John Boland and Johnny Thompson, who's group is called Envy Estate now. Ort is in Athens, writing for the *Flagpole*. Ken McMahan recently released his solo debut in France and plays with his group, Slumpy Boy. Jerry Dale McFadden plays keyboards with the Maver-

icks. Chief guitar-techs for Carlene Carter. Byron's an in-demand
bass player. Jonell is one of the top club attractions in Nashville. My
parents are alive and well in Madisonville, assuming that reading the
book didn't kill them. The Kentucky Headhunters and Bill Lloyd
have enjoyed considerable success and influence. Big Dave's in Flor-
ida. Sherlock's in Delaware. Pat's in E-Town. Jack's in Louisville. I
saw Toby a couple of years back in Lexington; we listened to Zappa's
"Rat Tomago" while he read aloud from Kahlil Gibran. It was very
nice. Marc Owens went digital in his basement studio recently. Everyone else is alive and well that I know of.

Jason and the Scorchers reunited for a two week tour in the summer of '93. They'd all cleaned up their acts and bloodstreams independently of each other, and were a bit shocked at the combined
bright-eyed, bushy-tailed shadow they instantly cast on the wall. The
tour became a month and no more, then two months and I swear this
is it, then it went to four months and, whaddya know, Jason and the
original By God Scorchers were recording again. I realized a dream
by jamming onstage with them in Louisville that fall. Their new record, *A Blazing Grace*, is now available on Mammoth Records.

Tom Sturges is now President of Chrysalis Music Group.

R.E.M. are the biggest band in the world.

I married Beth on December 12th, 1992, fifteen years to the day
after seeing Kiss with AC/DC at Freedom Hall in Louisville. That
was the original AC/DC, with Bon Scott singing lead.

I can only assume Muscles is still in Hoboken, taking things one
psychotic day at a time.

\* \* \* \*

# about the author

The author is a 1984 graduate of Western Kentucky University. After college, he spent seven years as the guitarist in Government Cheese, the subject of which is this book. Following that, he spent two years as a member of the Bis-quits, who had a critically-acclaimed release on the Oh Boy label in 1993. He lives with his wife and pets in the wilds of suburban Nashville.

# ORDER FORM

Use this form to order additional copies of
*Cheese Chronicles*
for your friends or family members.

Name: _____

Address: _____

City: _____ St:____ Zip: _____

Daytime phone: (_____)_____

    If gift, message that you would like enclosed: _____

_____

_____

_____

    If gift, ship to:

    Name _____

    Address: _____

    City: _____ St:____ Zip: _____

Method of Payment: *(Make payable to **Eggman Publishing, Inc.**)*

    ❑ Check  ❑ Money Order  ❑ VISA  ❑ MasterCard  ❑ Discover

Card# _____ Exp. _____

Signature: _____
        Required for credit card purchases

| | | | |
|---|---|---|---|
| Quantity: _____ | x | $14.95 = | $_____ |
| Shipping & Handling Quantity: _____ | x | $1.00 = | $_____ |
| | | Sub Total: | $_____ |
| | | TN residents add 8.25% sales tax | $_____ |
| | | Total: | $_____ |

Please return form and payment to:    **Eggman Publishing, Inc.**
                                  **2909 Poston Avenue  Suite 203**
                                  **Nashville, TN 37203**

## FOR FASTER SERVICE CALL 1-800-409-7277

*Thank You!*
*Your order will be shipped within 1-3 weeks from receipt*